THE BEAT
OF A
DIFFERENT DRUMMER

PETER LANG
New York • Washington, D.C./Baltimore • Boston
Bern • Frankfurt am Main • Berlin • Vienna • Paris

THE BEAT
∽ OF A ∽
DIFFERENT DRUMMER

Essays on Educational Renewal in Honor of JOHN I. GOODLAD

Edited by
Kenneth A. Sirotnik and Roger Soder

PETER LANG
New York • Washington, D.C./Baltimore • Boston
Bern • Frankfurt am Main • Berlin • Vienna • Paris

Library of Congress Cataloging-in-Publication Data

The beat of a different drummer: essays on educational renewal
in honor of John I. Goodlad / edited by Kenneth A. Sirotnik and Roger Soder.
p. cm.
Includes bibliographical references and index.
1. Education—Aims and objectives—United States. 2. Educational change—
United States. 3. Curriculum evaluation—United States. 4. Teachers—Training of—
United States. 5. Community and school—United States. 6. Educational equalization—
United States. I. Goodlad, John I. II. Sirotnik, Kenneth A. III. Soder, Roger.
LB7.B396 370'.973—dc21 98-44638
ISBN 0-8204-3797-2 (hardcover)
ISBN 0-8204-4593-2 (paperback)

Die Deutsche Bibliothek-CIP-Einheitsaufnahme

The beat of a different drummer: essays on educational renewal
in honor of John I. Goodlad / ed. by: Kenneth A. Sirotnik and Roger Soder.
−New York; Washington, D.C./Baltimore; Boston; Bern;
Frankfurt am Main; Berlin; Vienna; Paris: Lang.
ISBN 0-8204-3797-2
ISBN 0-8204-4593-2 (paperback)

Cover design by Lisa Dillon

The paper in this book meets the guidelines for permanence and durability
of the Committee on Production Guidelines for Book Longevity
of the Council of Library Resources.

© 1999 Peter Lang Publishing, Inc., New York

Printed in the United States of America

Acknowledgments

There are many people without whose assistance and involvement this book would not have come to pass. The book is a collection of essays, the authors of which are to be thanked for devoting considerable time and energy to the task of drafting, rewriting, and often rewriting once again. It should be noted that each of the essayists told us in one way or another of their pleasure in taking on the task. Many, many others who could not because of limitations of space be included as essayists for the book contributed useful suggestions: we would be looking at a series of books, with many volumes, were we to include all of those who could have added useful commentary and insights. Perhaps others had been thinking along similar lines, but it was Gary D Fenstermacher who first broached the idea of a festschrift and got us moving from the good idea stage to actuality. Joan Waiss competently and quietly put the manuscript into final prepared form, and Paula McMannon demonstrated that no matter how many pairs of eyes peruse a manuscript, another pair—hers—is always useful. It is obvious—but, as Bronislaw Malinowski reminded us, nothing is as difficult to see as the obvious, so we'll make the point anyway—that we all owe much to the person whose work, ideas, and behavior over the last half-century and more we have honored in this volume.

Ken Sirotnik
Roger Soder

Grateful acknowledgment is hereby made to copyright holders for permission to use the following copyrighted material:

Excerpts reprinted with permission from *Access to Knowledge*. Copyright © 1994 College Entrance Examination Board. All rights reserved.

Goodlad, John I., *Educational Renewal: Better Teachers, Better Schools*. San Francisco: Jossey-Bass Inc., copyright © 1994. Reprinted by permission of the publisher. All rights reserved.

Contents

The Editors

Kenneth A. Sirotnik is a professor in the department of Educational Leadership and Policy Studies, the director of the Institute for the Study of Educational Policy, and a senior associate in the Center for Educational Renewal, all in the College of Education at the University of Washington. Prior to this, he was a lecturer and researcher at the UCLA Graduate School of Education and Center for the Study of Evaluation. Sirotnik's areas of teaching, research, and service range widely over many areas: measurement and assessment, statistics, research design, evaluation, teacher education, educational policy, organizational change, and school improvement. Among his many publications are the coauthored book *Understanding Statistics in Education* (1992) and the coedited book *The Moral Dimensions of Teaching* (1990).

Roger Soder is co-director of the Center for Educational Renewal at the University of Washington and vice president of the independent Institute for Educational Inquiry. He is editor of *Democracy, Education, and the Schools* and coeditor (with John I. Goodlad and Kenneth A. Sirotnik) of *The Moral Dimensions of Teaching* and *Places Where Teachers Are Taught*. His articles in professional journals center on education, politics, professionalization, and rhetoric. His research interests continue to focus on the ethics and politics of rhetoric and education and the role of the university in a free society. Prior to joining with Goodlad and Sirotnik in creating the Center for Educational Renewal in 1985, Soder was an administrator in the Cape Flattery School District on the Makah Indian Reservation at Neah Bay, Washington, and education director of the Seattle Urban League.

The Contributors

Edward F. Ahnert is president of the Exxon Education Foundation and manager of contributions for the Exxon Corporation. After teaching English and international politics on the faculty of Tunghai University in Taiwan, he joined the Treasurers Department of Exxon Corporation in New York in 1973 and held various positions in the treasurers and corporate planning functions in New York, Houston, Sydney, and Hong Kong. In 1986, he left Exxon to found two companies in Hong Kong. In 1990, he returned to the United States and to Exxon to head the Exxon Education Foundation, and in 1992 became manager of Exxon's corporate contributions activities.

Robert H. Anderson is president of Pedamorphosis, Inc. He has been a teacher, principal, superintendent of schools, professor of education in the Harvard Graduate School of Education (for nineteen years), and dean of the College of Education at Texas Tech University for ten years prior to retirement. His lifelong interest has been in how schools should be organized and how professionals as well as children should be helped to collaborate with each other.

John M. Bahner retired from his position as president of the Institute for Development of Educational Activities (/I/D/E/A/) in November 1997. He has been a secondary school science teacher, guidance counselor, principal, assistant professor at Harvard University, and associate superintendent of instruction for Dade County (Miami) Florida. He worked for thirty years with the /I/D/E/A/.

Richard W. Clark has been a senior associate at the Center for Educational Renewal at the University of Washington since 1985 and at the Institute for Educational Inquiry from its founding in 1992. He has also served as an independent consultant regarding the simultaneous renewal of schools and the education of educators in more than thirty states. He has written language arts textbooks as well as books, articles, and chapters on a wide range of educational issues. Clark worked in the Bellevue (Washington) Public Schools as a teacher and administrator, completing his last twelve years with that district as deputy superintendent.

Gary D Fenstermacher is professor of education at the University of Michigan, Ann Arbor. His specialty is the philosophy and politics of education, particularly as these pertain to teaching and teacher education. His work has appeared in *Curriculum Inquiry*, *Educational Theory*, *The Review of Research in Education*, *Teachers College Record*, and many other periodicals in education. With John Goodlad, he edited *Individual Differences and the Common Curriculum: Eighty-second Yearbook of the National Society for the Study of Education* (1983), and with Jonas Soltis he authored three editions of *Approaches to Teaching* (1986, 1992, 1998).

Calvin Frazier has been a senior associate at the Center for Educational Renewal at the University of Washington since 1987 and at the Institute for Educational Inquiry from its founding in 1992. He has also been a senior consultant for the Education Commission of the States since 1989. He has held both teaching and administrative positions in K–12 districts and schools, as well as faculty and administrative positions at the university level. He was the Colorado Commissioner of Education for fourteen years until he retired in 1987; president of the Council of Chief State School Officers, 1983–84; and a United States representative at many international education policy meetings.

Allen D. Glenn is dean of the College of Education at the University of Washington. After teaching social studies at the junior high and high school levels, he joined the faculty at the University of Minnesota where he taught social studies education and educational technology courses at the undergraduate and graduate levels; he also served as department chair and associate dean. Glenn has coauthored five textbooks and over forty publications in textbooks and professional journals. He chaired the educational technology advisory panel for the Office of Technology Assessment for the United States Congress.

Paul E. Heckman is an associate professor in the College of Education at the University of Arizona and principal investigator of the Educational and Community Change (ECC) Project. Prior to beginning the ECC Project, Heckman developed school-university partnerships at the University of California at Los Angeles, the University of Southern Maine, and the University of Arizona. His interests continue to be in promoting and understanding the critical dimensions of educational change, especially in economically poor neighborhoods, and relating universities to schools and neighborhoods.

M. Frances Klein is professor emeritus of the University of Southern California where she held the Robert Naslund Endowed Chair in Curriculum Theory. Her extensive publications include books, monographs, encyclopedia articles, and contributions to professional journals. After retirement, she was elected to the Laureate Chapter of Kappa Delta Pi and has continued writing for professional journals on curriculum. She recently received the Distinguished Educator of the Year Award from Pi Lambda Theta.

Martin Lipton taught high school English for thirty-one years. He has taught disaffected students in special, separate school programs as well as college-bound students in wealthy school districts. Coauthor, with Jeannie Oakes, of *Making the Best of Schools (1990)*, *Teaching to Change the World* (1999), and *Becoming Good American Schools: The Struggle for Virtue in School Reform* (forthcoming), Lipton has contributed to numerous articles on educational research, bringing a practitioner's perspective to theory and policy.

Dorothy M. Lloyd is currently dean of the Center for Collaborative Education and Professional Studies at California State University, Monterey Bay. Beginning as a teacher in the Los Angeles city schools, she went on to hold positions that included founding faculty, director of teacher education, and associate dean of the College of Education at California State University, San Marcos; professor at San Francisco State University; eight years as demonstration teacher and team leader in the Laboratory School at the University of California at Los Angeles; and lecturer and researcher in the UCLA Graduate School of Education.

James G. March is the Jack Steele Parker Professor of International Management (emeritus), professor of political science (emeritus), professor of sociology (emeritus), and professor of education at Stanford University. He is also director of the Scandinavian Consortium for Organizational Research at Stanford. March is the father of four children and the grandfather of seven. He has been on the faculties of the Carnegie Institute of Technology (now Carnegie Mellon University), the University of California at Irvine, and Stanford University. He is best known professionally for his work on organizations and decision making.

L. Scott Miller is director of the National Task Force on Minority High Achievement at the College Board. Formerly, he was the senior program officer at the Exxon Education Foundation and senior vice president of the Council for Aid to Education.

Jeannie Oakes is professor of education and assistant dean in the Graduate School of Education and Information Studies at the University of California at Los Angeles (UCLA) where she directs Center X— Where Research and Practice Intersect for Urban School Professionals—home of UCLA's teacher education program. Oakes conducts research that examines inequalities in United States' schools and follows the progress of equity-minded reform. This work is the subject of six books, including *Keeping Track: How Schools Structure Inequality* (1985), and numerous scholarly articles.

Arturo Pacheco is dean and professor of educational leadership at the University of Texas at El Paso. He held prior administrative and faculty positions at Stanford University and the University of California at Santa Cruz. His interests and publications are in philosophy of education, teacher preparation, and educational renewal and change. Coauthor of *Centers of Pedagogy* (1999), Pacheco serves on several state and national boards, including the Texas State Board for Educator Certification.

Janice M. Reeder is an adjunct professor in the Educational Administration Program at the University of Puget Sound in Tacoma, Washington, and codirector of the Northwest Center of the Coalition of Essential Schools. She recently retired after eight years as principal of Gig Harbor High School in Gig Harbor, Washington. Reeder also served as principal of Newport High School in Bellevue, Washington, for eight years.

Seymour B. Sarason was born in Brooklyn, New York, in 1919, went to a local commuter college in Newark, New Jersey, and did graduate work at Clark University. In his forty-five years in Yale University's Department of Psychology, he conducted research in and wrote about mental retardation, clinical psychology, community psychology, social policy, and educational reform. In 1962, he founded and directed Yale's Psycho-Educational Clinic. He has been the recipient of numerous awards, the most recent of which was the Lifetime Career Award for Contribution to Psychology in 1996.

Jianping Shen is an assistant professor of educational leadership at Western Michigan University. His research interests include theory of leadership, policy analysis, research methods, and comparative education. Shen's articles have appeared in professional journals such as the *American Journal of Education, Educational Evaluation and Policy Analysis, Journal of Education Policy*, and the *Journal of Psychology.*

Theodore R. Sizer is founder and chairman of the Coalition of Essential Schools. He is University Professor Emeritus at Brown University where he served as chair of the Education Department from 1984 to1989. Sizer was also professor and dean at the Harvard Graduate School of Education (1964-72) and headmaster of Phillips (Andover) Academy (1972-81). Three of his books, *Horace's Compromise* (1985), *Horace's School* (1992), and *Horace's Hope* (1996), published by Houghton Mifflin, explore the motivation and the ideas of the Essential school reform effort. Sizer currently joins his wife as acting principal of the Francis W. Parker Charter Essential School, one of the first charter schools authorized under the Massachusetts Education Reform Act of 1993.

Wilma F. Smith is a senior associate of the Institute for Educational Inquiry and of the Center for Educational Renewal. A public school educator for thirty-three years, she served in six school districts as teacher, principal, special educator, and area superintendent, ending her public school career as superintendent of the Mercer Island (Washington) School District. For ten years, she taught graduate-level educational leadership courses at the University of Washington and at Western Washington University. She now facilitates all aspects of the Institute's leadership programs, which serve to build cadres of leaders committed to the simultaneous renewal of schools and the education of educators.

Zhixin Su is professor of education and director of the China Institute at California State University, Northridge. Prior to this position, she was a professor at UCLA's Graduate School of Education and Information Studies. She worked as an educational administrator in the Chinese National Ministry of Education before joining the education community in the United States and her position as a research assistant in the Center for Educational Renewal at the University of Washington. Her current teaching and research work covers the fields of teacher education, comparative education, and educational policy studies.

Kenneth A. Tye was an elementary and secondary teacher and administrator in the California public schools and then program officer at the research division of the Institute for Development of Educational Activities (/I/D/E/A/). For nine years he was professor and chair of the Department of Education at Chapman University and is now professor emeritus. Tye has recently completed a book, published by Interdependence Press, that reports on the results of a survey of global education practices in fifty-two countries. He also teaches a course in comparative education and consults on a variety of projects having to do with global education.

Richard C. Williams was a professor of education administration for twenty-four years in the Graduate School of Education at the University of California at Los Angeles, where he also served as assistant dean and as director of the Corinne Seeds University Elementary School. In 1990, he was appointed professor of education in the College of Education at the University of Washington, where he also served as executive director of the Puget Sound Educational Consortium until 1994 and then as director of the Danforth Educational Leadership Program until 1998.

Chapter 1

On Inquiry and Education

Kenneth A. Sirotnik

You'd think there would be no need to be so redundant. What would education be without inquiry, and what would inquiry be if not wholly educative? Yet, it seems that even at the brink of the twenty-first century, we are still caught up in unproductive dualisms—theory versus practice, mind versus hand, thought versus action, and the like. Every year in my thirty years of teaching in higher education, I have challenged one or more students to think more critically about their assumptions when they ask questions like, "That's an interesting philosophical notion, but what about the real world of schools?" I have often challenged faculty colleagues as well on their reasoning behind such comments as "If only school people would read the literature and apply it."

How ironic that inquiry and education are not seen as synonymous activities by many educators. Of course, it's not just educators. Consider the general public. Consider how anti-intellectual, acritical, and instrumental our society seems to have become. I remember when the network news actually resembled more of what you can find now only on public broadcasting stations (which are struggling to maintain their existence). Today, network news is a series of sound bites; if any inquiry is going on, it is more akin to *The National Enquirer*.

We've had nearly two decades of sustained educational reform rhetoric that mostly seeks justification not in what it means to be an educated and caring people in a political democracy, but in what it means to be economically competitive in the nation and the world. We have ample evidence, of course, that this is a shallow ploy by many politicians who use public schools as scapegoats and use illogical arguments as cover-ups for other, more deeply rooted social, political, and economic problems. Now that we appear to be no longer a "nation at risk," now that we can see black in the future of the budget deficit, now that others' economies are in trouble and ours is doing relatively better, where are the voices extolling the virtues of our public schools? We can't have it both ways. Our schools can't be both "the problem" when things seem to be going badly, and still "the problem" when they're going well.

If we were a more thoughtful public, we would recognize the absurdity of economic arguments no matter how things are going. The fact is that public education in this country is and always will be a social experiment, one with extraordinary successes, and one with major problems still needing to be addressed (particularly the education of children from economically poor families and communities). Well, perhaps some do recognize this.[1] But it sure feels like I and my like-minded colleagues, past, present, and no doubt future, are in the minority.

For example, it's rather demoralizing to find out from public opinion polls (whether done well or not) that we professors are "out of touch" with the general public, that the general public wants more practical, basic skills teaching and learning, while professors are more attuned to idealistic notions of critical thinking and problem solving.[2] Aside from the silly stereotypes and misperceptions this kind of survey and these false dichotomies generate, I'm still in the dark as to what the implications ought to be. Are they supposed to be somehow self-evident, e.g., "professors" need to accommodate the "public will"? I'm reminded of professors in China who—had the surveys been commissioned—would have been found to be out of touch with the Cultural Revolution. We know what the implications were for them. Actually, I need not travel that far. I'm reminded of 1950s McCarthyism and the Canwell hearings right here in Seattle, and the professors at the University of Washington who suddenly found themselves out of touch and out of a job.

The right, responsibility, and freedom to inquire, to think critically, to see this as fundamental to the concept of an educated person and becoming such seem to be obvious features—indeed, prerequisites—for a functioning and always-struggling democratic society. I'm reminded now of two other "out-of-touch" professors, both Johns. Both have cared very deeply about democracy and education and the fundamental roles of thoughtfulness and experience in ongoing, reciprocal relationship.

Toward the end of his life, however, Dewey was deeply discouraged. Notwithstanding seven decades of published work with recurrent themes arguing against "either-or" thinking and the separation of intellect from education and the test of experience, Dewey found himself in the early fifties lamenting those very practices. His ideas about progressive education, for example, were still misunderstood by many; demonized by conservative ideologues on the one hand and trivialized by "progressive" hucksters on the other. His last published statement (perhaps the briefest and most lucid) about his core educational ideas appears the year of his death in an introduction to a book by Elsie Clapp on progressive schools. He tells us for the last time that

> For the creation of a democratic society we need an educational system where the process of moral-intellectual development is in practice as well as in theory a cooperative transaction of inquiry engaged in by free, independent human beings who treat ideas and the heritage of the past as means and methods for the further enrichment of life, quantitatively and qualitatively, who use the good attained for the discovery and establishment of something better.[3]

He ends this statement still hopeful about the "practical demonstrations of the good that has been attained . . . and of the better that is to come."[4]

Although he has well over a decade to go until age 93, John Goodlad also remains optimistic—perhaps as much as he remains "out of touch" with those who would have education reduced to a collection of facts and basic skills in a pedagogical environment that minimizes critically analyzing and constructively engaging ideas in and of the world. In some five decades of published work, Goodlad has honored and extended significantly many of Dewey's core ideas and commitments to democracy in studies of curriculum, schooling, educational change, school-community relationships, teacher education, and working connections between P-12 schools and institutions of higher education. He has explored many of these ideas in an increasingly pluralistic and contentious society, in a society with a rapidly growing gulf between rich and poor, and in a society where it is less than fashionable to speak of moral and ethical dimensions in public education in other than relativistic terms.

Goodlad, of course, is not a philosopher, at least not in the way philosophers are apt to define themselves. But much of his writing is philosophical. In fact, I would venture to say that Goodlad has "out-Deweyed" Dewey in at least one key respect: He has engaged the world of experience continuously and in big ways with powerful ideas, testing and retesting them in both large-scale research projects and large-scale field initiatives. And he has done this with enduring commitments to inquiry and education and the idea that there cannot be one without the other.

Those who have had the good fortune to work with John Goodlad have profited from this commitment. In the typical environment of large-scale research and the hustle for funding and unrealistic time frames, one is often forced into the rather ironic position of "more thinking about doing" than "doing more thinking." Not so on Goodlad's major projects. It was always clear that there was room (or that room would be made) for important tangential inquiries. Moreover, there was always a healthy dialectic pervading the research environment; no decisions were ever made that could not be unmade, and often "for two cents," as he put it, Goodlad himself would argue the other side.

A major "tangential inquiry" for me occurred after completing the Study of Schooling and analyzing more data than I thought I'd ever want to see again. I had lingering concerns about what had been accomplished. To be sure, we had pulled off a study that many thought couldn't be done, and we had much to say to those concerned about public education and the future of public schooling in this country. But what of the 38 schools and over 1,000 classrooms we had studied in depth? Were the data of any use to them? They were useful to us; surely they would enlighten the people and organizations to whom the data belonged. So we decided to give the data back. We devoted considerable time and resources to developing computerized feedback packages containing what we felt were some of the more interesting slices of data at both the school level and at the level of each of the classes observed. We returned in teams to each and every school in the study, delivered these packages, and presented key results at staff meetings.

Teachers are wonderful human beings. By and large, they are extraordinarily gracious and tolerant. They let us do this to them, they were pleasant enough, they asked a few questions, and then went on with their day as we did with ours—on to the next school and the next presentation. Teachers didn't ask questions like: "So what?" "What do we do with all this information?" "Who said we wanted it in the first place?" "What makes you so presumptuous to think that you know what the important data are for our school?" "This information may have been useful to you for research purposes, but what makes you think it would be useful for us?"

These, in fact, were the questions I had for myself by the time I finished this little road show. I had these questions for John as well. We talked. And even though we were on to a new field-based initiative to experiment with the idea of a school-university partnership, I was encouraged and supported to continue to think about what we were calling, for a lack of better terminology, "contextual appraisal." Essentially, I was convinced that information of the type we collected in the Study of Schooling—and other types of information as well—could, and in fact should, be of use to practicing educators in the context of their work. But I needed to develop the rationale for this idea. Little did I know at the time what a career-changing adventure this would be, one that would transform a relatively satisfied statistician-psychometrician into a continually frustrated, quasi-epistemologist/organizational theorist/critical pragmatist. Little did John know that I and my colleagues would find conceptual comfort in radical (at least for the late 1970s and very early 1980s) literatures like critical theory (e.g., Jurgen Habermas) and liberatory pedagogy (e.g., Paulo Freire) and extend these to praxis in schools.[5]

Coming out of a Deweyan tradition, Goodlad is not now, nor has he ever been, a "neo-marxist/critical theorist." Nor has he had much sympathy for recent deconstructionist and postmodern developments. But he has been consistently concerned with matters of fair play, of equity, of social justice in the treatment of all children and in ensuring their access to excellent public education. Consequently, he had no trouble relating to what my colleagues and I were producing under the auspices of the larger projects he directed. In fact, over the years as our colleagueship and friendship have grown, he has continued to encourage me to bring these critical perspectives to bear on many of the central ideas that have always informed his work and that still inform our work together.

Thinking critically, I suppose, will always put one out of touch with whatever is being popularized. The trick is to maintain a healthy skepticism and a constructively critical attitude while avoiding the abyss of pessimism and cynicism. Recently, I asked John how in the world he has stayed optimistic in the face of so many pendulum swings, educational fads, and a half-century of often unheeded lessons for more successful and enduring educational change. He smiled and said it wasn't easy, but the alternative was no more appealing than that of growing old. This optimism has rubbed off on many who have had the good fortune to work with John, including those who have contributed chapters to this volume.

This has not been an easy volume to edit. In many ways, it resembles Goodlad's corpus of work, which does not lend itself easily either to chronology or taxonomy. This is a measure, I think, of the depth and breadth of his contributions and the thematic tapestry of the whole. In the field of education, people often find comfort in discipline-based homes for their work. Goodlad, however, is more of a nomad in this regard.

I suppose if asked, he would turn to his graduate experience and mentor Ralph Tyler, and proudly state his field to be curriculum inquiry. But it is much more than that. Using Goodlad's two most favorite curriculum concepts—organizing elements and centers—we can get a handle on how to characterize his work and why it is difficult to pigeonhole. The organizing elements or themes are many and interactive, but I will suggest five big ones for purposes of synthesis: (1) the form and function of schooling, including curriculum writ large (e.g., teaching, learning, assessment, etc.) and how the whole is organized and for what purposes; (2) the dynamics of school improvement and educational change, including emphases on schools as well as their community and policy contexts; (3) the preparation of educators and the form and function of university/college units responsible for this critical activity; (4) the ecology of critical connections among educational providers, including partnerships between schools, colleges/universities, and communities; and (5) the moral commitments to equity and excellence in education as foundational building blocks for a healthy, democratic society.

Although emphasis varies, aspects of each of these organizing elements can be found throughout the chronology of Goodlad's activities and writings. If a single phrase were needed for purposes of summary, this work could be described as inquiry into *educational renewal* (versus reform). *Reform* is about whatever is politically fashionable, pendulum-like in popularity, usually underfunded, lacking in professional development, and short-lived. *Renewal* is about the process of individual and organizational change, about nurturing the spiritual, affective, and intellectual connections in the lives of educators working together to understand and improve their practice. Renewal is not about a point in time; it is about all points in time—it is about continuous, critical inquiry in action related to any innovations (including current practices) that might improve education.

The activities and projects marking Goodlad's career in studying and promoting educational renewal can be thought of as the organizing centers or places and occasions where the five big ideas noted above are played with, developed, tested, revised, and played with again. Our colleague Jianping Shen has organized a selected sample of Goodlad's scholarship and provided readers with an annotated bibliography (see the appendix to this book). Just a cursory review of this bibliography will reveal the thematic consistency of Goodlad's work. From his earliest teaching experiences in a K-8, one-room schoolhouse and encountering the demoralized and perpetually held-back student, Ernie, Goodlad began formulating the big ideas that would turn out to be seminal for most of his subsequent work. Images of Monet's haystacks come to mind, a series of interpretive work that changes with the seasons but stays grounded in fundamental commitments to substance and belief.

We have tried to organize what follows in much the same way, admittedly with much less artistic talent than Monet's, and with much less control over the paintbrush. The contributions of John's friends and colleagues vary considerably in style and substance, but all are central to one or more organizing elements and centers of his work. We have decided, therefore, to order the authors' contributions by looking chronologically (with some artistic license) at the major activities that Goodlad organized to pursue a lifelong inquiry into educational renewal. These occur in roughly five overlapping clusters.

Late 1930s to Late 1950s

On the heels of his teaching experiences in public schools and administrative duties in a Canadian school for delinquent boys, Goodlad's early work builds on his dissertation study ("Some Effects of Promotion and Nonpromotion Upon the Social and Personal Adjustment of Children") and activities and projects while at Emory University and the University of Chicago. Although some fifty years of work remained to flesh out the details, it is easy to see how these early experiences were formative, how powerful questions and ideas might emerge regarding purposes of public education and schooling, equity and access to knowledge, curricular and structural innovation, dynamics of organizational change, and ecological connections between school, community, and university.

The Nongraded Elementary School (coauthored with Robert Anderson) was perhaps the most significant contribution to come out of this period of work. In the next chapter, Bob Anderson reflects not only on this contribution and its current status—still an innovative idea—but also on his colleagueship with John during their graduate school days at the University of Chicago and then again in Florida on the Englewood Project. In chapter 3, Frances Klein and John Bahner recall the history of this project and show clearly how cutting-edge ideas, even by today's standards, worked in an elementary school with good leadership, necessary resources, supportive community, and a thoughtful, hard-working group of skilled educators.

Early 1960s to Early 1970s

During his early years at the University of California at Los Angeles (UCLA), Goodlad and his colleagues delved ever more deeply into curriculum, early and elementary schooling, global education, and the dynamics of educational change—a broad array of inquiries and activities that would lay the groundwork for major research projects and networking efforts to follow.

Early activities formed around the lab school at UCLA—the University Elementary School (UES)—where Goodlad had the opportunity to bring together many of the ideas already formulated from previous research and experience. In chapter 4, Dorothy Lloyd recalls the energy and excitement of these early years at the UES, draws out lessons from those experiences, notes their enduring relevance, and shares with us recent applications to teacher education in a new university setting where she has had the unique opportunity to build a program from scratch.

For Goodlad, curriculum has always included but has been much greater than subject matter alone, embracing not only teaching, learning, and assessment, but the purposes and functions of public schooling and the multiple constituencies and levels at which such judgments are made. Consequently, early inquiries were also launched into what was, in fact, going on in schools as well as what *ought* to go on and how the whole could be conceptualized.

Goodlad has never shied away from "ought" questions, and a central belief that has informed his conceptions of education and schooling pertains to what it means to be an educated person in a democracy and in an increasingly interconnected, global community. *Toward a Mankind School: An Adventure in Humanistic Education* was the first major work to come out of these early explorations. Ken Tye, a coauthor of *Toward a Mankind School*, reviews this seminal work in chapter 5 and brings us up-to-date on what has become a world-wide social movement promoting global education.

While pursuing these and other inquiries, Goodlad and his colleagues created the League of Cooperating Schools. This turned out to be a particularly productive, multiyear, action research project that networked principals and their school faculties while focusing on the Study of Educational Change and School Improvement. Although the importance of leadership, collaboration, and the school as the unit of change were themes in Goodlad's research from the start, it is in this project that these ideas are studied in systematic and critical ways. A wealth of publications by Goodlad and his colleagues emerged, including Goodlad's *The Dynamics of Educational Change*. Dick Williams, one of the researchers on this study, reminds us in chapter 6 of the enduring lessons learned in this project—lessons that appear in need of relearning even as we enter a new millennium.

This last statement has a familiar, Sarasonian ring to it; indeed, Seymour Sarason's work, perhaps more than that of any other contemporary writer, has complemented and informed Goodlad's ideas and the research of Goodlad and his colleagues. In chapter 7, Sarason shares his typically candid insights into the continual problem of educational change, this time focusing on schools and schooling as part of the problem. (Readers familiar with Sarason's work know that no major players get off the hook, be they politicians, policymakers, professors and schools of education, educational leaders, school boards, or even the schools and teachers themselves.)

Mid 1970s to Early 1980s

The latter half of Goodlad's years at UCLA marks the third stage. Based on the above inquiries into schooling, particularly in view of what was found—and *not* found—behind the classroom door in a sample of elementary schools, a more ambitious, in-depth research project, A Study of Schooling, was launched by Goodlad in 1976 and resulted in his widely acclaimed *A Place Called School* and a number of other important books by his colleagues.

Were it not for publisher delays, *A Place Called School* would have appeared closer to 1982 than to 1984, its actual year of publication. Sometimes the gods are with you. In the intervening period, the report *A Nation at Risk* pounced on the American public, and likely would have put a serious dent in the impact of *A Place Called School*.

Instead, the book served as a serious counterpoint to the same-old same-old arguments in *A Nation at Risk*. In chapter 8, friend and colleague Ted Sizer shares an insightful comparative analysis of these two documents and risks a recent, historical look at the last several decades of educational reform.

Sizer also reflects on the popularity of the "do better and more" rhetoric of the *A Nation at Risk* report, in contrast to the unheeded call for deeper renewal and more penetrating inquiry in *A Place Called School*. Underneath it all, however, there are dedicated, hardworking, and thoughtful educators laboring behind the scenes who are, indeed, paying attention. Jan Reeder is one of them, and in chapter 9, she shares her views as a veteran educator and former high school principal, strongly influenced by Goodlad's (and Sizer's) work.

The data collected in A Study of Schooling provided Goodlad and his colleagues with a gold mine of information for exploring issues of equity and access to knowledge—or, as it turned out, issues of inequity and restricted access to knowledge, mainly for children of color and/or poverty in the schools studied. Jeannie Oakes's book *Keeping Track* was an important outcome of these analyses; in chapter 10, she and Marty Lipton bring us up-to-date on these perennial concerns and remind us of how, notwithstanding all the important research that can be done, treating children fairly and educating all of them well is fundamentally a moral matter.

Issues of equity and access to knowledge are not only problems unique to the vast racial, ethnic, and economic diversity of the United States. Other countries have their share of diversity and concomitant educational issues as well. A Study of Schooling, like much of Goodlad's other work, as well as his leadership of the Graduate School of Education at UCLA, attracted the attention of the international community. Of particular note was China's invitation to him and several other educational scholars to visit in 1981. The interpreter assigned to him on that trip was Zhixin Su, who would later come to study in the United States with Goodlad at the University of Washington and work with us on the Study of the Education of Educators. In chapter 11, Su provides an interesting comparative account of Goodlad's historical visit to China with a similar visit made by John Dewey some six decades earlier. The primary focus of both educators was on open inquiry, fairness, and the opportunity for all students to have the best possible educational experiences.

Toward the end of A Study of Schooling, Goodlad initiated the Laboratory in School and Community Education (LSCE) and the development of a major school-university partnership. These activities emerged naturally out of the recommendations in *A Place Called School* and laid the groundwork for a premise that would guide all future work—the simultaneous renewal of schools and the education of educators. This notion was embedded in an even more comprehensive idea of an educational ecology that connected meaningfully all the educative places (e.g., family, community organizations, schools, colleges, and universities) where students could learn and garner resources for doing it. Paul Heckman was intimately involved in A Study of Schooling and directed the LSCE. For the past half decade or more, he has tried to bring all of these ideas together in an ambitious project of school-community change, and he shares that experience with us in chapter 12.

Mid 1980s to Early 1990s

Upon moving to the University of Washington, Goodlad and his colleagues created the Center for Educational Renewal in the College of Education, as the home for yet one more ambitious, national research project—the Study of the Education of Educators. Together with the earlier Study of Schooling, this project completed necessary empirical work to better understand the connections between improving both the schools and the places and programs preparing teachers for the schools—what has come to be termed, for shorthand purposes, "simultaneous renewal."

Central to this work, and perhaps its greatest contribution, is the moral foundation upon which it is situated. We have not been reluctant to articulate positions on what *ought* to matter when it comes to the purposes of public education in our democracy and the moral dimensions inherent in the relationship between those who teach and the students and institutions entrusted to their care.[6] Gary Fenstermacher's thinking on these matters has always influenced this work, and in chapter 13, he offers yet another angle on how we might construct these moral dimensions and make sure that they are not relegated only to what happens behind the classroom door.

Overlapping substantially with the Study of the Education of Educators, and anticipating the next major initiative, the National Network for Educational Renewal (NNER) was launched. This network of school-university partnerships coalesced around the simultaneous renewal proposition and the idea of mutual partnership beyond the typical *noblesse oblige* variety.

Part of these early efforts with the NNER consisted of getting clearer conceptually about what school-university partnerships could be and how they played out differently in different community contexts and types of higher education institutions.[7] Dick Clark and Wilma Smith were involved early on in these efforts, and they continue to reflect on these matters. With the recommendations in Goodlad's *Teachers for Our Nation's Schools* (and later in *Educational Renewal: Better Teachers, Better Schools*), things got more complicated with the notions of "centers of pedagogy" and "partner schools." Combined with the notion of "school-university partnerships," these three importantly connected concepts can be confusing, and Clark and Smith sort things out for us in chapter 14.

Mid 1990s and Beyond

Once the Study of the Education of Educators was put to rest, Goodlad's attention turned with increased vigor to simultaneous renewal and the NNER. A difficult part of the renewal agenda at most of the institutions was, not surprisingly, the focus on and commitment to the renewal of teacher education and dealing seriously and programmatically with the implications of the ideas in the nineteen postulates that guided and were reinforced by the Study. "Ed Schools" seem to have an easier time thinking about and getting involved in K-12 school change activities than in activities that directly focus on changing their own organization. It was time to fish or cut bait. Following a process of reviewing partnership commitments and ongoing activities, a few institutions dropped out of the NNER and, following an application and review process, new ones were invited to join.

Fortunately, our own College of Education at the University of Washington was among the survivors. In fact, we were already heavily involved in substantial reconstruction of both elementary and secondary teacher education programs in ways that were aligned (deliberately or otherwise) with many (not all) of the postulates. This is not easy stuff in a major research university given to the usual tensions between research agendas, graduate studies, professional studies, service to the schools, and the demands of a fairly traditional promotion and tenure system. Nor is it easy to be a dean in the middle of all this, advocating for fundamental changes, as Allen Glenn tells us in chapter 15. But his story is positive and instructive; it suggests that appropriate counterweights can be struck among the perennial tensions in the university and that multiple agendas can actually complement one another in productive ways.

Interestingly and, perhaps, arguably, the "mid 1990s and beyond" has been Goodlad's most activist stage—activist in the sense of directly organizing and supporting some thirty-three colleges and universities and over 400 partner schools to engage the hard ideas spelled out in his book *Educational Renewal: Better Teachers, Better Schools*. Activism is about inquiry—it is an *educative* act. Consequently, considerable support was garnered for what has become known as the Leadership Program, a very successful, cohort-based program that brings educators to Seattle from the various NNER sites around the country for four intensive, week-long inquiry and study sessions over the course of a calendar year. Educators from both the K-12 schools and the colleges and universities ("ed school" and arts and sciences faculty) come together to reflect on core ideas, and most importantly, on what it might take for them, as educational leaders, to work with others back home in significant renewal efforts.

The most central ideas informing these leadership institutes revolve around the moral dimensions of teaching and the importance of finding common ground (the *unum*) in our wonderful, pluralistic, struggling, democratic society. This is the continuing challenge of our political system, as pointed out by Arturo Pacheco in chapter 16. Pacheco was a member of the first leadership cohort and, as dean of a college of education in an urban setting, knows first-hand how important and difficult it is to bring multiple voices to the table to engage the human conversation toward finding that common ground.

Goodlad's activism has always walked the fine line between becoming more heavily engaged in large-scale advocacy in the policy arena, e.g., fronting big commission reports and the like, and *scaling down* by working with others in relatively few (but challenging and representative) places to further develop and refine ideas in the context of practice. Although there is much merit in action on both sides of this line, Goodlad has, by and large, chosen to walk the side of the latter. This has frustrated, at times, friend and colleague and former Colorado commissioner of education, Cal Frazier, who shares with us in chapter 17 how profoundly Goodlad's influence is felt nonetheless in state and federal policy domains.

Research and activism do not come cheaply, and much time and effort has been expended on grant getting. In fact, this current period is marked by Goodlad's return to substantial fund raising to support the initiatives and activities in the NNER member settings that relate directly to the ideas that continue to inform the work of the Center for Educational Renewal (and Goodlad's nonprofit organization, the Institute for Educational Inquiry).

Goodlad has likely set the standard for what it means to work with multiple, philanthropic foundations toward sustained funding of major research studies and complex educational renewal initiatives. Many foundations have played key roles over the years; these are foundations whose leadership had the wisdom to recognize the importance of investing over the long haul. The Exxon Education Foundation (EEF), for example, has made a substantial investment in the work of the Center for Educational Renewal since its inception in 1985 (including a planning grant in 1984). This support reflects a sixteen-year commitment through the start of the next millennium; it made possible both the Study of the Education of Educators and the core support necessary to sustain the NNER. In chapter 18, Scott Miller, former EEF program officer, and Ed Ahnert, current EEF president, reflect on the importance of substantial and long-term private grantmaking to the success of major educational renewal efforts.

Raising money is one thing, staying the course with respect to a core set of ideas and principles is quite another. It's nice when these two things come together. One of my favorite "out of touch" educators (I hope he would think of himself as such) is the organizational theorist Jim March. Anyone who would advocate a "technology of foolishness" as an evaluation and decision-making metaphor for the educational research community, who would suggest that sometimes you have to "be willing to forego some truth in order to achieve some justice," would find a kindred spirit in John Goodlad (and vice versa).[8] One of Goodlad's most enduring educational themes throughout his research and scholarship—funded or not—is countering the ever-popular, instrumentalist-type justifications for what matters in education and schooling. In chapter 19, March honors Goodlad with an essay on this issue, but also on an even more central theme—the importance of knowing oneself and staying the course.

In the final analysis, what March is talking about is *character*. And in chapter 20, Roger Soder picks up on this and several other key themes throughout this book, such as the problem of educational change, the optimism shared by those such as Goodlad who stay with it, and the principled nature of the work that ought to characterize such optimism.

* * * * *

I hope it is apparent that in this *festschrift* honoring John Goodlad's work, we are honoring inquiry itself and the moral obligation to inquire and think critically, an obligation that we all have as educators by the very nature of what education ought to be.

As critically inquiring educators, we can wear the label of "being out of touch" with pride. I don't think you can be making significant contributions to a field like education if everyone always seems to agree with you. Goodlad, of course, has never been in danger of mainstream appeal. There are, in fact, positive ways to talk about being intellectually creative and countervailing to whatever happens to be educationally in vogue. In summarizing the lessons learned from the Study of Educational Change and School Improvement, Goodlad told us that

> *there must be a compelling, different drummer whose drumbeat somehow is picked up by the school's antenna.* The sounds must be intriguing, challenging, countervailing, perhaps disturbing, but most of all they must be difficult to ignore.[9]

He went on to add that "*not only must the alternative drummer be perceived as salient, there must be a perception, also, of longevity. A temporary, waxing and waning drumbeat will not suffice.*"[10] Finally, he noted that

> It is my belief that a drummer with an intriguing idea will be more compelling than a drummer with a process. . . . But just an idea is not sufficient. There must be a vehicle and an infrastructure to carry the idea, plant it and, subsequently, nourish it.[11]

As I now look back on my long association with John and read these words of his in the context of his sustained and thematic scholarship, they seem more like autobiography. John Goodlad has been and continues to be that alternative drummer, and he continues to live up to his own prescriptions for educational change. May we all be so fortunate—here's to the joy of drumming and the challenge of "being out of touch."

Notes

1   A sensible discussion of this matter can be found in Henry M. Levin, "Educational Performance Standards and the Economy," *Educational Researcher* 27 (May 1998): 4–10.

2   Ann Bradley, "Professors' Attitudes Out of Sync, Study Finds," *Education Week*, 29 October 1997, 3.

3   John Dewey, "Introduction," in Elsie Ripley Clapp, *The Use of Resources in Education* (New York: Harper & Bros., 1952), xi.

4   Dewey, "Introduction," 134.

5   See, for example, Kenneth A. Sirotnik and Jeannie Oakes, "Critical Inquiry for School Renewal: Liberating Theory and Practice," in Kenneth A. Sirotnik and Jeannie Oakes, eds., *Critical Perspectives on the Organization and Improvement of Schooling* (Boston: Kluwer-Nijhoff, 1986); Kenneth A. Sirotnik and Jeannie Oakes, "Evaluation as Critical Inquiry: School Improvement as a Case in Point," in Kenneth A. Sirotnik, ed., *Evaluation and Social Justice*, New Directions in Program Evaluation, No. 45 (San Francisco: Jossey-Bass, 1990); and Kenneth A. Sirotnik, "Critical Inquiry: A Paradigm for Praxis," in Edmond C. Short, ed., *Forms of Curriculum Inquiry: Guidelines for the Conduct of Educational Research* (New York: SUNY Press, 1991).

6   John I. Goodlad, Roger Soder, and Kenneth A. Sirotnik, eds., *The Moral Dimensions of Teaching* (San Francisco: Jossey-Bass, 1990).

7   Kenneth A. Sirotnik and John I. Goodlad, eds., *School-University Partnerships in Action: Concepts, Cases, and Concerns* (New York: Teachers College Press, 1988).

8   See James G. March, "Model Bias in Social Action," *Review of Educational Research* 42 (1972): 413–29.

9   John I. Goodlad, *The Dynamics of Educational Change* (New York: McGraw-Hill, 1975), 178.

10 Goodlad, *Dynamics*, 178.

11 Goodlad, *Dynamics*, 178.

Chapter 2

Invigorating Elementary Schooling: Savoring a Long-term Partnership

Robert H. Anderson

Honoring as eminent and deserving a person as John Inkster Goodlad, especially in a significant way, is in fact a difficult task. Aware that other authors will be celebrating their relationship with John and/or his almost-unmatched contributions to the field of education, one seeks to identify either some less known aspects of his career or some particularly spectacular dimensions of his work that might balance out the Goodlad story or at least clarify its significance in some interesting way. Since my relationship with John spans more than a half-century, and since our collaborations have focused primarily on the structure and organization of elementary schools, I have opted to provide some observations about early elementary school improvement efforts along with a mixture of personal reminiscences and comments on some things that have been happening since what now seem somewhat like "pioneering" days.

I first came to know and to share professional experiences and insights with John in the early months of 1946. He and I were among the students who enjoyed the rich environment of the University of Chicago back in those exciting post-war days. The great majority of the Ph.D.-bound students with whom we associated, many of whom became famous in their subsequent careers, had been freshly discharged from the military. In fact, for the first several months, many of us came to class still wearing our uniforms, or pieces thereof, while re-orienting to the civilian world and gradually getting a civilian wardrobe together. In my own case, for many months I wore my blue and khaki naval uniforms stripped of their military stripes and buttons, and I sought to appear as a full-fledged civilian, albeit somewhat conservatively attired. Some of us came to the University with families, having begun to produce progeny during the war years, and of course, some of the older students who had not been in the services had more mature families.

The University was a great and exciting place, with a distinguished faculty and an atmosphere that challenged us all to perform at a high level. Within the student group—many of whom were supported by the GI Bill and all solemnly aware of the challenging future for which everyone was preparing—there was a remarkably cohesive spirit and a pervasive seriousness of purpose. It may, in fact, have been a kind of "Golden Period" for doctoral study, and most of us realized, or at least in retrospect it seems reasonable to claim, that somehow we were a special group of people assembled at a unique time, in a very special place, under the guidance of a very special faculty, and likely to have eventful and productive careers if we fared well in such an environment.

Not incidentally, Ralph Tyler was chairman of the Department of Education in those years, and even before we became adequately aware of his already-distinguished history, we were conscious of his unique influence upon our programs. I wish I could dredge up the class list for Tyler's course in curriculum, the one for which his syllabus later became almost a bible for curriculum students everywhere; I suspect that at least half of our fellow students later became well-respected scholars. I also remember another Tyler course, which he team taught with Lawrence Kimpton (later the University president) and Cyril Houle, where again the students enrolled were mostly future "stars."

One reason for the above reminiscences, which may seem immodestly oriented toward the important future work that was germinating within and among us at the time, is that John Goodlad was already perceived in those days as a "major player," and within a group of very promising peers, he was particularly visible and respected. Professor Virgil Herrick, representing elementary education in particular, immediately identified John as a promising disciple and set him up along with two other students to work with him. After more than a half-century, not all of the details remain in focus, but I certainly do remember the respect that I and many others had for John, and I know that I gravitated toward him not only because of his likable way of being, but also because of the keenness of his intellect and his extraordinary verbal skills.

That we played a little golf together, that we both perceived ourselves as excellent softball pitchers, that we shared such a strong interest in elementary education, and that by happy circumstance both his doctoral dissertation and my experiences with nongradedness in a superintendency formed a substantive as well as an intellectual bond between us rounds out the early part of my story.

There is one event that comes to mind with respect to the University of Chicago period. It speaks to a problem that has long existed, and unfortunately still exists, concerning the fact that under typical circumstances so much of the great talent within the teaching profession often goes unrecognized and untapped. This event happened while both of us were still students, although our dissertation activities were already under way. We were involved in a rather large and ambitious cooperative study in which university personnel (under Professor Herrick's direction) spent more than a year in a partnership with educators from the elementary school district in nearby LaGrange, Illinois. I don't remember what my role was in the project, but I do recall most vividly a big year-end report meeting that brought all of the university people and the LaGrange staff together in a large auditorium. The main business of the agenda called for reporters from each of eight joint study groups to make progress reports to the assembled audience.

John and I were near the front, and we watched Professor Herrick announce, almost in a military mode, that each of the group reporters would be given exactly three minutes to make his/her report. No more than three minutes, under any circumstances! Well, when the time came for an eighth-grade shop teacher, Mr. Hansen, to report for his group, he walked up front, faced Dr. Herrick and his watch-holding timekeeper and, while pointing his finger at the timekeeper, announced emphatically that he wanted to say something personal first, and he didn't want his personal statement to be counted as part of his three minutes.

Dr. Herrick, perceived by all of us students as a kind of General Patton "tough guy," seemed almost ready to explode when faced by Hansen's ultimatum, but fortunately he kept his silence and Mr. Hansen proceeded. "All I want to say," the mild-mannered little shop teacher continued, "is that I have been in this school district for thirty-eight years, and I have just realized that this is the first time that I have been invited to say something to all of my colleagues that is important to me. I am grateful for this opportunity, and I want to express my gratitude to Professor Herrick and the others who have made this opportunity possible." Pointing again to the timekeeper, he then smiled and said "now, young lady, you may start counting my three minutes!"

I don't know if John was able to see the expression on Herrick's face, but I was. The stern professor was almost dumbstruck, and I think there was a tear in his eye. For all of us, it was a moment to remember. In fact, I have often cited the Hansen episode as an example of the great reservoir of talent and feeling that exists within our huge profession, whose members, alas, are usually hidden, to use John's apt phrase, "behind the classroom door."

Post-Chicago Connections

While I was completing work on my dissertation, which incidentally included Mr. Hansen and about thirty other LaGrange teachers, I served for two years as a principal in nearby River Forest, Illinois. The general focus of my study was upon staff development, and LaGrange was obviously my experimental location. At the same time, John was busy working on his own study, the focus of which was on the reporting of pupil progress to parents. We both received our degrees in 1949, and John went to Emory University while I accepted a superintendency in a venturesome new community known as Park Forest, in southern Cook County. Happily, the newly formed Park Forest School Board had come almost immediately to the conclusion that they wanted to have an ungraded primary program, which then became a source of national interest, and it was a lucky stroke for both me and Goodlad that the Board invited me to develop such a program.

Fast forward to 1954, when after five years of successful and nationally visible experience developing the nongraded program in Park Forest, I went to Harvard University. By that time, both John and I had already published a bunch of articles both together and separately, his having to do primarily with reporting to parents and mine talking about nongradedness as an organizational reality. During those years, John and I had been attending several annual professional meetings together, sometimes as roommates, and during one of our conversations, John suggested that we ought to package our several articles together in order to create a book. Quick and simple, it was implied!

Well, two things happened. We did use our various articles as skeletal material for a book, and although hardly any of the original paragraphs remained intact and/or unamplified, eventually we had put a book together with which we were both reasonably satisfied. Next, however, we discovered that although we were convinced that we had produced a worthwhile book, it proved to be almost nonmarketable. In fact, it took John (who served as the project manager, and therefore, the negotiator with publishers) about two years to persuade one of them, Harcourt Brace, to give us a contract.

Paul Brandwein, a distinguished educator who was then serving as a consultant to Harcourt Brace, saw merit in the idea of publishing something "different and offbeat" (which I remember as his exact words), and he managed to push our contract through the system. In retrospect, it seems odd that Brandwein did not expect the book to be financially successful, but he saw its publication as potentially worthwhile, primarily because it might add a bit of interest and even novelty to the company's publications list.

No doubt, the strong success of the book came to the company as a great surprise.[1] And the rest is history: the 1963 edition of this book was eventually translated into four languages, it sold enough copies so that John and I shared some very nice royalties (mine were enough to put one of my sons through Dartmouth!), it stimulated a great deal of interest in school reorganization around the country, and it became a kind of standard reference within the field of school reform.

The 1959 edition was only a couple of years old, however, when we recognized that two major changes would have to be made. In an appendix, we had listed about fifty schools or school districts that allegedly (and I use that word advisedly) had exemplary or pilot nongraded programs. It was not very long before we learned that at least half of them were not very authentic examples, and soon we were hoping that a second edition could be scheduled with the appendix no longer included.

Also, following the time during which we wrote the first edition, two things happened that would forever change the way we and others define the optimal organization pattern. One was the burgeoning of multiage (or, often, multigrade) class arrangements. The other was the rapid spread of team teaching. Both of these arrangements had, and continue to have, tremendous implications for the cause of nongradedness. Fortunately, again it seems because of Paul Brandwein's clear vision, Harcourt Brace was willing to have us make some minor changes in the 1959 text so that multiage grouping and teaming could be brought into stronger focus.

An interesting aspect of book production, by happy circumstance, made it possible for us to produce a slightly revised edition without too much disturbance to the basic page structure of the book. In those days, the printing was done from expensive copper plates, and by careful re-editing (and the counting of words and lines) we improved the book's contents by adding a small amount of material about multiaging and teaming without costing the publisher a total re-engraving. The minimally revised edition, therefore, appeared in both hardcover and paperback in 1963.

In the two decades that followed, the organizational structures within elementary schools underwent slow but steady changes. Some of these changes had important implications for personnel utilization and school design, and perhaps in small part, our volumes contributed to the restructuring and redesign that became widespread. Too, communities all over the country were expanding because of the population boom that began after World War II and that continued over a long stretch of time. This resulted in an incessant need for additional school space, and with the three quintessential structural features that we had identified (nongradedness, multiage pupil grouping, and team teaching) gaining in importance at least at the advocacy level, that space began to be used in different ways.[2] American (and, in fact, international) schooling found itself breaking away from the pattern that was enshrined in the traditional egg-crate architectural style and embodied in the self-contained, age-graded classroom.

A fundamental, even revolutionary, redefinition of the teacher's role was stimulated by proposals for teachers to work cooperatively rather than in isolation, in an environment (both administrative and psychological) provocative of both individual and collective achievements. Perhaps less fundamental from a conceptual perspective because of centuries of growing insight into human development, but nonetheless revolutionary in practice, was the philosophical abandonment of literal gradedness with its strangulating dependence on sequenced textbooks and graded curriculum guides.

Neither university-based teacher education programs nor the textbook publishers (who, as noted, were threatened by the less structured alternatives offered within nongradedness) responded very enthusiastically to mounting evidence of the preference for nongraded and teamtaught programs. Even governmental agencies and school boards tended to resist calls for changes that might "rock the boat" in unwelcome ways. To this can be added the general discomfort that was felt by parents and teachers alike when confronted by seemingly experimental deviations from familiar arrangements.

For a period of at least twenty years following the appearance of *The Nongraded Elementary School*, sentiments and practices within the profession remained ambivalent with respect to advocated structural and practical alternatives. It is encouraging to note, however, that although the oppression of habit has been and remains powerful, emotional and intellectual support for traditional arrangements have significantly eroded. One looks in vain, for example, for statements in the educational literature to the effect that graded structure is indeed to be valued, or that the isolation of teachers from each other is productive of superior services to children, or (especially) that children of the same annual-chronological age are best served when they are not connected regularly with other age groups. I frequently think back to the days in the late 1950s when linking the three organizational concepts together was regarded as unusual if not actually heretical.

This brings us back to the story about the Goodlad-Anderson publications and their influence. It was disappointing when we learned that Harcourt, despite having made significant profits on the two editions of our earlier books, had resisted pressure from the field in the early 1980s to update the book. Not only had the publisher apparently lost interest in doing so, but it seems at least possible that the textbook division of the company, which right from the beginning was less than happy about Harcourt's apparent advocacy (via our book) of arrangements unfriendly to the use of graded textbooks, played some role in discouraging the company's further pursuit of nongradedness. However, Harcourt graciously let us turn over the updating project along with publication rights to Teachers College Press, which in 1986 offered to publish a revised edition. John and I came up with a plan—approved by Teachers College Press—for updating the material by simply providing an introductory dialogue, after which the 1963 Harcourt Brace version was reprinted. The Teachers College edition appeared in 1987, and even ten years later that book still enjoys at least small sales.

Let me reiterate that in all of this activity John was the leader and prime mover of our writing team.

Another Co-Involvement: The Englewood Project

While Goodlad was still at Emory University in Atlanta and I was at Harvard, I became involved in a consultant role with an exciting project in what was then a kind of sleepy and undeveloped place in the southern part of Sarasota County, Florida. William H. Vanderbilt, his wife Anne, and in a small way, his brother Alfred G. Vanderbilt, had become residents of Englewood, near their large experimental cattle ranch designed to produce Santa Gertrudis cattle. Because of their elementary-aged son, William Jr., they became eager to help the public school that he would attend in Englewood to be improved. The Vanderbilts gave a substantial grant to the county school district in support of a school-improvement project in Englewood. In 1954-55, however, they had become disappointed in the project's progress, and they telephoned Harvard University to ask for someone to come down and offer some assistance. The dean of the Graduate School of Education asked me to take on the assignment, and so I spent some time helping to reorganize the Englewood Project. This provided an extraordinary opportunity in which John and I were again coinvolved.

One of the first moves that I made, after suggesting some significant personnel changes, was to propose that John, who was geographically much closer to Englewood than I was in Boston, be invited to become the new director of the project. Soon Goodlad found himself making regular visits to Florida as the guiding spirit of the project; and as his extensive publications about the Englewood Project attest, a great many important lessons for American school reform grew out of John's significant and creative work there.

Since Goodlad has himself written extensively on the Englewood Project, interested readers can turn to his reports for the more complete story. (Also, see chapter 3 in this volume.) One cannot read that story without getting a clear sense of how skillfully Goodlad guided that project. In fact, the ever-growing literature about school change in the 1990s, decades later than Goodlad's writing, probably has very little additional to say about important principles and practices that should be honored and followed. One can only admire the clairvoyance and the passion with which Goodlad made good things happen, even way back then.

An End-of-Century Assessment

John Goodlad's impact upon public education, here and abroad, has been so broad-gauged and so deep that even in a volume such as this it is not possible to take its complete measure or even to describe it sufficiently. Furthermore, throughout his career Goodlad's *modus operandi* has been one that regularly connects him with colleagues and provides wonderful opportunities for other persons to share with him in both the creation and the fulfillment of important mechanisms and ideas. He is a partner, a colleague, a collaborator, and a sharer, which not only enriches the collaborators but also widens his own range of understanding and productivity. Although there are some "lone wolves" within our profession, Goodlad is surely not one of them.

It is also true that, while a recognized and admired leader, Goodlad has many peers (in the democratic sense of the term) who have plowed some of the same scholarly fields and struggled with some of the same puzzles or challenges. The second half of the twentieth century has been a tumultuous time not only in world affairs generally but also, and very decidedly, in the field of education. The significant contributions of many other respected scholars and school leaders who have played important roles in the ever-changing educational scene should not be overlooked as we salute the great things that their admired colleague has accomplished. So, as I proceed to review a few concepts and practices (or at least dreams of practice) that may at this moment be of prime importance, let us all remember that Goodlad's voice, though loud and clear, has always been part of a much larger chorus.

One enormous gain for all of us has been the inspired awareness that intellectual talent and promise are, in fact, universal as well as multifaceted, and that the human capacity for greatness is not the exclusive property of any one segment or group within the world. While opportunity to develop that greatness still remains unavailable to many if not most, the prejudices and suppositions that have subjugated and frustrated so many humans are now at least being challenged, and there is a growing realization that, as Benjamin Bloom[3] and Jerome Bruner[4] and hosts of others have made abundantly clear, under favoring circumstances virtually 100 percent of our children can achieve significant success within educational programs and as members of the adult world.

Guided by the seminal work of Howard Gardner[5] and his associates, among many others, we also have come to understand that "favoring circumstances" must include learning opportunities that enable children/youths to exploit and develop a variety of "intelligences" and "predispositions" in addition to the two (verbal and mathematical) on which curricula, measurement, and advancement decisions have traditionally been based. Guided also by a more positive view of the human spirit and the human capacity for goodness, we are coming to more accepting interpretations of worthiness (and even entitlement) than once prevailed.

Some of the educational habits and practices that over the years grew out of an uncomplimentary view of human nature and potential are, alas, still in full view. Some of those practices began during times when schooling itself was neither universal nor esteemed, a situation that also applied to medical and other "professional" training. Because teachers came to be the only "professional" workers whose preparation and working conditions were subject to public taxation policies, their progress toward a truly professional status has lagged far behind that of medics, lawyers, engineers, and others whose value has been determined largely by the marketplace.

At the risk of oversimplification, it seems possible to note that once an economical system had been devised for preparing and supervising teachers (especially at the elementary level), and once a presumably efficient system had been developed for packaging children and their instructional programs into a sequential, graded structure, it became very difficult for more flexible and more child-respecting systems to take their places. Remembering Washington Irving's story about Rip Van Winkle, it seems quite probable that had Rip fallen asleep after visiting local public schools around 1925 and come back to life about fifty years later, he might have found very few differences in schools to scratch his head about (except perhaps for the presence of electronic equipment). He would have found teachers working alone, each in a graded classroom with children born mostly in the same year, textbooks dominating the shelves, the program closely sequenced, and bells ringing.[6]

Although many politicians and bureaucrats have yet to abandon some of the attitudes and values implicit in the old arrangements, it is, nevertheless, possible to argue that schooling is moving (albeit too slowly) in a bright new direction. More and more, schools are becoming places where there is self-initiated and teacher-facilitated learning, rather than didactic, authoritarian, text-and-test-directed instruction. More and more, children and youths are cooperating, rather than competing, with each other during much of the day. More and more, the pupil mix is intentionally heterogeneous, with respect to both presumed or assumed talent and to age or experience. More and more, teachers, instead of working alone, are intimately connected with each other and are providing the school program as a joint effort. More and more, the artificiality and disconnectedness that derives from a compartmentalized and overloaded curriculum is giving way to interdisciplinary, thematic, and coordinated studies, most of which are closely related to problems of immediate importance to children and youths. Less and less is the school day divided into time blocks, within each of which is manifested the tyranny of the textbook with its arbitrary and inflexible sequences and its ponderous redundancy. And, thanks in large part to the pioneering work of such trailblazers as Henry Levin and his colleagues at Stanford, there is less and less of the watered-down, repetitive, and unchallenging instruction that used to be provided to learners identified as "behind" the others for some uncomplimentary reason. Again, these are only early trends, not yet major changes in American schooling.

There is also the new technology that must be taken into account, and it is in fact very exciting to contemplate how schooling will change over the next decade or so as computers evolve into powerful instructional and learning aids. One wonders just how radically the school itself might change both as an institution and as the official site for what we now call learning.

One thing that does seem certain is that the fundamental values to which John Goodlad is committed, along with the positive influence that his writings and work have had on the schooling enterprise, will be mentioned long after he has, as pledged, gone fishing.[7]

Notes

1   John I. Goodlad and Robert H. Anderson, *The Nongraded Elementary School* (New York: Harcourt, Brace & World, 1959, revised edition 1963; New York: Teachers College Press, revised and reissued edition, 1987).

2   Robert H. Anderson, "The Organization and Administration of Team Teaching," in Judson T. Shaplin and Henry F. Olds Jr., eds., *Team Teaching* (New York: Harper & Row, 1964), 170-215; and "Public Relations," in Judson T. Shaplin and Henry F. Olds Jr., eds., *Team Teaching* (New York: Harper & Row, 1964), 241–69.

3   Benjamin S. Bloom, *All Our Children Learning: A Primer for Parents, Teachers, and Other Educators* (New York: McGraw-Hill, 1981).

4   Jerome Bruner, *Toward a Theory of Instruction* (Cambridge: Belknap Press of Harvard University, 1966).

5   Howard Gardner, *Frames of Mind* (New York: Basic Books, 1983).

6   See Kenneth A. Sirotnik, "What You See Is What You Get: Consistency, Persistency, and Mediocrity in Classrooms," *Harvard Educational Review* 53 (February 1983): 16–31.

7   John I. Goodlad, *In Praise of Education* (New York: Teachers College Press, 1997), 155.

Chapter 3

Curriculum Change in Concert: The Englewood School Project

M. Frances Klein and John M. Bahner

Englewood, Florida, during the 1950s and early 1960s, was a most unlikely place for school renewal to transpire, especially renewal that was to have profound consequences upon the future of students, teachers, and administrators who worked there. Englewood is a small, semitropical community that lies directly on the coastline of southwestern Florida. Because of its geographical location eight miles from the nearest highway, no one passes through the community by chance. A traveler must deliberately turn toward Englewood and, in the 1950s, use one of the desolate washboard roads that for years had been paved solely with the promises of the county commissioners.

During the prosperous 1920s, the approximately 1,500 people who had discovered this restful haven had grandiose ideas of developing Englewood into a residential metropolis to equal Tampa or even Miami. Although embryonic in stage, these ideas began to take the form of reality. Big business tycoons and well-known personalities, as well as the so-called middle class populace, bought property and began building homes. But the stock market crash was even more disastrous to Englewood than it was to the nation. People could no longer afford their second home in Florida, and the population dwindled almost to the point where it resembled a "ghost town" of the West. This sudden collapse of the town seemed to create a defeatist attitude among those who remained—an attitude that was to linger for more than two decades.

During the next twenty-five years, the community drowsed along, its existence enlivened by nothing more dramatic than an occasional rattlesnake bite, a small town scandal, or the visit of some famous personage who found a seasonal retreat and wonderful fishing. The population was composed primarily of retired folks and families of commercial fishermen, who barely eked out a living.

The general apathy of many people in this section of the country permeated all aspects of life. "Live and let live" was the motto. This was reinforced by the fact that the line dividing Sarasota and Charlotte counties bisected the Englewood community. It was the most remote area of both counties, had relatively few voters, and therefore was seldom on the minds of government and school officials. Few persons were concerned about schools, and they had even less to do with the school district personnel in the two county seats. In both counties, officials in the courthouses were unconcerned about what happened in Englewood, and this was reflected strongly in the school. Physical facilities were deplorable. Only emergency maintenance was done, and this was performed mostly by parents who volunteered their services and sometimes even donated the materials. Educational supplies and equipment were almost nonexistent. A complete turnover of the teaching staff was usually an annual occurrence. In short, throughout this time, Englewood was in the educational doldrums.

In the beginning of the 1950s, small changes in the community began to occur. The population was beginning to expand; there were almost a hundred pupils in the sixth-grade elementary school. (Secondary pupils were transported to a six-year secondary school eleven miles to the north.) People who left the circus and carnival circuits came to the community and worked as building tradesmen who were now replacing commercial fishermen as the second-largest group of persons living in Englewood. (Retired folks, some of whom were just winter visitors with large homes fronting on the beach, remained the largest category within the population.)

In the spring of 1953, the school received a grant to supplement regular tax funds. The Vanderbilt family had large land holdings in the area, a portion of which they were turning into a real estate development. They recognized that a strong school serving the area would be a major attraction for people with enough money to buy expensive land and build costly homes. Moreover, there were Vanderbilt children of elementary school age for whom this local school, in their minds at least, was totally inadequate. Thus, they also had personal reasons for creating a much-improved school.

The Vanderbilt grant was renewed annually for eight years. These monies could be spent on anything educational except capital improvements, which they believed should remain the responsibility of the two counties. With a large portion of the grant, salary supplements were offered to teachers and the principal, which attracted educators who otherwise would not have considered living in such an isolated area. The Vanderbilts also insisted that a nonresident director of the school be hired to work intensively with the faculty and turn a very mediocre (or worse) school into an exemplary one.

At the beginning of the third year, John Goodlad was selected as the director of the project. Little had been done regarding comprehensive school improvement, and bringing about change in the prevailing conditions seemed improbable. He immediately hired a new principal, and the task to which these two gave the highest priority was the improvement of school-community relationships. Next in priority was purchasing much-needed instructional supplies and equipment. After two years, the principal left to pursue a doctorate with Goodlad at the University of Chicago.

When Goodlad hired John Bahner as principal in the summer of 1957, only one teacher was a carryover from previous years. Frances Klein, who had been hired a year before Goodlad arrived, took a year's leave of absence to obtain a master's degree. She returned in Bahner's second year (Goodlad's fourth) and joined with other members of the faculty in their effort to create the best elementary school they could envision.

During the years we spent in the Englewood School Project, the faculty learned to work together under the guidance of John Goodlad to reconsider every aspect of schooling. Nothing was accepted as a given. As we now reflect on our experiences there, we identify several areas that illustrate the content and processes Goodlad used to foster change. Even though we left Englewood in the early 1960s (Klein to the University of California at Los Angeles to work on a doctorate with Goodlad; Bahner to become an assistant professor at Harvard's Graduate School of Education), Goodlad's ideas and style of working with educators continued to be fundamental to our study and professional work. We identify five of them for further discussion in this chapter.

Creative Curriculum Development
for a Variety of School Purposes

Of all our efforts at school improvement, the most time was consumed by curriculum development. Originally, the faculty believed curriculum matters should be our only major thrust. In less than three months into the 1958–59 school year, we realized curriculum change as we envisioned it could not take place or be maintained unless it was considered in concert with almost all other aspects of schooling.

Language arts was the first area of concern, and Goodlad identified a consultant who was willing to come to the school four times during the year for three days on each visit. Prior to his first trip, we decided we wanted help in four traditional aspects of language arts (basic reading skills, vocabulary enrichment, expressing ideas clearly, and creative expression) and three nontraditional aspects (organizing data and ideas, critical thinking, and defending and supporting ideas).

A curriculum envisioned and articulated by Goodlad has never centered on the selection of better texts or other materials. Nor did he advocate the creation of lists of behavioral objectives based on a state or district framework. In faculty meetings, he led us in discussions of the importance of teacher-planned curricula in keeping with state and district guidelines, but keyed directly to the needs and interests of students working in various sized groups. Teachers had a great many individual meetings with Goodlad and other consultants in planning and implementing their own curricula, which also were designed to reflect consistency with the overall school attempts at improvement.

As a beginning teacher, Klein remembers the excitement of planning her own curricula and then drawing on the large collection of learning materials (including many different sets of basal texts as well as supplemental material) to implement it. The Englewood School curriculum was never perceived as a given emanating from a higher source to be implemented in some rigorous way by every teacher at a predetermined grade level. Curriculum development was a creative activity designed to appeal to the students' interests and help them grow in a variety of ways.

The major thrust of the curriculum dimension was on intellectual development that emphasized thinking rather than factual accretions. An illustration of this is noted in a letter from Goodlad to Bahner following a visit to the school:

> I am impressed with the extent to which teachers are moving from "what" questions to "why" questions. There seems to be a decided emphasis on thinking through and thinking about problems rather than memorizing facts for their own sake. This is to the good and we want to continue to develop this as much as possible. For instance, in one classroom the assignment on the chalkboard was to write a story imagining that there was no force of gravity. What would happen as a result? This is a much more significant question than simply, "What is the force of gravity?"

Concept formation and generalizations were the bases of our academic planning in every field of instruction. Traditional subject areas were usually integrated into units of study with an overall theme lasting three to six weeks. Content-specific skills (e.g., creative writing, map reading, library research) were taught in ad hoc groups as needed throughout the unit of study. The arts were correlated with the ongoing unit of instruction of the classroom so that the students had a holistic approach in their education.

Coupled with this emphasis was a strong thrust in every classroom to help students develop self-esteem. Every person associated with the school believed deeply in the inherent worth and dignity of each individual student and did everything possible, inside and outside the classroom, to help each student feel positively about himself or herself. Some of our students came from very poor families and lacked what some of the other students considered to be the basics of life. We worked long and hard to make all students feel intellectually competent at their own level of performance in every learning task.

There were the usual chicken-and-egg discussions about what comes first. Do we have specific activities to develop self-confidence so that they will then perform better socially and academically? Or, do we ensure academic success and increasing academic achievement so that they will enhance their self-esteem? True to our mindset of providing individualized education, we faculty members realized there was a time and place when each approach was the appropriate one to use. All of us believed that if students lacked self-esteem, their learning in all aspects of school would be handicapped. We remember this curriculum emphasis as being one in which we took a great deal of satisfaction as our hard work paid off in innumerable ways for the students.

Other aspects of student development were also highlighted. Strong programs in physical education were developed to help foster physical growth and development. A variety of activities characterized the program, which was guided by a teacher with considerable expertise in the area. Intra-school teams and contests were sometimes formed for the fun and excitement of competing against friends and other age groups. One of the most popular activities was the annual softball game in which faculty members played against the students. Friendly competition was in evidence with good sportsmanship always being emphasized.

When it became evident that a number of our students came from homes where they did not receive an adequate breakfast, a program (relatively rare in the 1950s) was begun in which a hot breakfast was served to any student who needed it. Food service personnel were viewed as contributors to the education of our students. Time in the cafeteria, whether at breakfast or lunch, was also considered a time for learning.

Social interaction in any part of the school and classroom environment was viewed as an opportunity to foster positive social growth and respect for each other. Any time students and teachers gathered was considered to be a learning opportunity—bus and playground duty, movement of students on campus, interactions with all teachers, trips to the office or central library, as well as student interaction within classrooms. Each teacher accepted responsibility for all students wherever they were on school property. The success of these attempts was undoubtedly linked to the amount of social interaction among the teachers and principal themselves. We were comfortable with each other as persons as well as teachers. Also, a key factor was the respect and support all teachers perceived they had from the principal. From these efforts to help students grow socially came a view of discipline throughout the school as guiding students in their normal growth rather than being a system of rewards and punishments to control their behavior.

Individualized Education

In his earliest years in education, John Goodlad found himself in the equivalent of a one-room country schoolhouse. The students had an age span of six to seven years and a wide range of abilities and learning styles. There was practically no parental involvement. Goodlad had only himself to teach all subject areas. He often referred to this experience as a way to get the Englewood faculty to understand the changes in schooling he was advocating. Just as he had done in his early teaching assignment, he helped us bring about change by having us challenge the status quo, keeping the proven and true, but devising replacements for those processes and procedures based primarily on tradition or administrative expediency.

Another technique he used to define needed changes was to have us think of our most able student and the student who had the most difficulty in school. We then brainstormed ideal learning conditions for each. The results demonstrated the need for change because the ideal for these two students differed from each other significantly; moreover, each ideal was quite different than traditional schooling.

The exercise was motivational and also began the process of developing constructive alternatives to the status quo. Goodlad had completed the first step of change—getting participants to generate their own answers to the question "Why change?"

With only two students to consider as a starting point, each teacher was able to devise a language arts learning environment that was highly individualized. When we intertwined our thinking with that of our colleagues, both the definitions of ideal and the means of providing ideal conditions were more creative. We were eager to try out our ideas knowing that our colleagues would be doing likewise. Two more factors of the change process are illustrated by this: (1) change is more creative when there is interaction among participants, and (2) change is more likely to occur when teachers know that their colleagues are also sincere about changing.

Goodlad stressed the position that individualizing education is an infinitely complex matter. It is not a set of mandates and expectations created outside the school. It is having the school staff create personal plans for individual students while considering all the factors that comprise the educational environment. Typically, student activities are prescribed by an existing curriculum after grouping and other conditions of instruction have been determined—fitting the individual into the school. Ideally, individualizing reverses that process by identifying what a student should be learning next and then determining the learning activities and enabling conditions best suited for that student to be successful—fitting the school to the individual.

This concern for the individual and the quality of the education he or she was receiving was reflected in all classrooms throughout the school. As Goodlad worked with us—individually, in small groups, and as a total faculty—he would raise questions that reflected his continuing concern for each student in the classroom. How the student was progressing in skills and knowledge identified by some commercial publisher was only a small part of those discussions. Most of the conversations were devoted to the interests and needs of each individual student in our classes and how we were able to meet them. He had us think and make recommendations about what else we needed in the form of educational materials or consultant services to help us do a better job.

Bahner attempted to provide strong daily leadership and, influenced by Goodlad, prepared faculty meeting agendas to encourage teacher interaction because of a strong belief that coworkers were the single best source of help. Several faculty meetings were spent on how the following factors could be used to individualize learning for a given student.

Pre-learning Evaluation:

In regard to a given learning objective, how do you get data to determine . . .

> Where is the student now?
> How did he/she get there?
> What is the most appropriate next step?

Grouping:

> Under what conditions do you work with two or more groups simultaneously?
> When should groups be homogeneous on some factor? Heterogeneous?
> What other criteria do you consider for determining group membership?
> How do you manage to keep two or more groups going?

Time:

> Under what conditions do you vary time allocations for different students?
> How do you keep things flowing smoothly when time is varied?

Teaching and Learning Styles:

> How many different teaching styles should one teacher use?
> What criteria do you use to determine which style to use?
> How many different learning styles should a given student exhibit?
> What criteria should be considered in determining which should be used?

Using the ideas we gained from our colleagues at these meetings, we not only continued the highly individualized program for the two students representing the extremes of our classrooms, but we increased the degree of individualization for others as well. As a staff, we were successful with our individualized programs for a few students all of the time, and with all the students some of the time. We were not successful with all the students all of the time—nor were we expected to be.

We were realistic; we all recognized that we were striving for an ideal that might never be achieved, yet we were dedicated to the goal of doing the best for all the students. Given the diversity of students in the community, that was a significant challenge.

A Team Approach to Educational Leadership

Although each teacher was expected to (and did) put in very long hours in developing the educational program for his or her classroom, we knew all teachers were considered an integral part of the leadership for the school. While ultimate responsibility for leadership was gradually passed from Goodlad to Bahner, each teacher was valued as a part of the collective team that was working to make Englewood School the best we could imagine.

Goodlad realized that neither he personally nor the position of director was a fixture in the long-range scheme of things at Englewood School. Therefore, as Bahner became more adept in formulating and understanding the collaboratively developed vision of the future, Goodlad took on the title and role of consultant. Similarly, we realized the power of looking inward to our basic thoughts and sideways to our colleagues, rather than always looking to the hierarchy for answers. Each of us was expected to make contributions in planning and implementing the total effort. This team attitude created more work for us in the form of meetings, extended planning time into late night hours, as well as frequent meetings with small groups of teachers and as a total faculty. Much attention was paid to communicating with parents and interested citizens in the community. Descriptions of the Englewood School Project appeared in the professional literature causing additional time to be consumed in meeting with educators in the school district and from throughout the state and nation as the project became recognized for the work we were doing.

All of these aspects of school improvement took considerable time and effort beyond what some faculties expend but well within what any faculty should devote to the task of being a successful, highly professional group of educators offering an exemplary educational program to all their students. The Englewood faculty met the time demands fully knowing that we had set for ourselves a challenging goal, yet one toward which we were making significant progress.

No one person was considered to be more important than another. Each had a critical role to play, and if that did not occur, the whole school felt the impact. This included the school secretary, custodian, bus drivers, and lunchroom workers.

A significant factor in helping teachers overcome limitations stemming from their own inadequacies was the policy used in selecting new teachers. Englewood School was a small school thirty miles from the school district's central office and eleven miles from the nearest elementary school. In 1958–59, there were no itinerant teacher specialists. Music, art, physical education, library, and guidance all had to be provided by classroom teachers on the Englewood School staff. To help reach our goal of providing the best possible education for each student, it was considered very important to have a variety of skills and backgrounds represented within the building faculty. School staffing was guided by this desire. With the lack of specialists, classroom teachers with varying talents and interests accepted as part of their job responsibility the obligation to assist other teachers as they worked to provide appropriate learning experiences for their students.

Goodlad was a source of significant ideas about school improvement and, along with two long-term consultants, spent many hours discussing the implications of new concepts for classroom practice, materials acquisition, communication with parents and interested others, school organization, and providing professional resources upon request. It must be emphasized, however, that the team concept regarding school leadership provided overall policies, and each teacher (or later, each team of teachers) made classroom decisions independently. Each classroom (or team) program did not rely upon the work of any other classroom (or team) or upon administrative needs for scheduling of time and resources. Any scheduling beyond the individual classroom (or team) occurred only as necessary to make the resources of the school available to all in an equitable manner.

Perhaps another significant factor in maintaining the commitment of the faculty to the demanding challenges we set for ourselves was the informal times spent together beyond the school. Although social events among the faculty and with the community occurred only three or four times a year, usually in conjunction with a visit from consultants, they were a carefully planned part of our life outside the school and did much to contribute to the cohesiveness and commitment of the faculty.

School as the Unit of Change

When striving to bring about change, individual classroom teachers, or even a group of two to six teachers working closely together, are destined to "wither on the vine" within several years if their ideas are not picked up by other members of the school staff. For this reason, Goodlad has a strong bias that the school is the unit of change. Teachers need the support and encouragement from the entire staff if change is to be successful and enduring. There must be a united effort by all staff members to define the conditions of good schooling if they are to provide adequate, compelling arguments when informing the school community, which consists of parents, central office staff, and school board members.

This is not to say that the school superintendent and central office staff are unimportant. The superintendent surely should set an expectation that all schools must improve and that they have a professional obligation to be better this year than they were last year. Neither superintendents nor their staff members should prescribe the specifics of such improvements, however. The varying talents and interests of teachers and the differing nature of students at each school justify having the school as the unit of change wherein it defines that change. The central office should help motivate, provide support in the forms of money and ideas, and help explain to the school board, the media, and other community members just what is transpiring in each of the schools.

The emphasis of the Englewood School Project was consistently upon *school* improvement. It was not focused upon teacher development or improvement of student test scores as the exclusive measurement of success. The school was considered an integral whole with the principal and teachers being key players within it. Individual teacher development was not neglected; rather, it was encouraged whenever it contributed to the development of the school as a whole. Plans for improvement were therefore integrated into a single focus rather than existing as a group of individual, possibly unrelated, courses of action. Two examples are illustrative.

Nongrading

Much of our collective effort revolved around how the school was organized. In addition to the major focus upon the classroom learning programs, it was recognized that the organization of the school was an important factor related to the success of the overall program. We did not look to outside models of how schools might be organized. With the leadership of Goodlad and Bahner, we began to conceptualize a unique form of school organization. This topic was an ongoing opportunity for change throughout the life of the Englewood School Project.

A multiage, team-teaching approach evolved over approximately three years of deliberative inquiry. We began slowly and implemented decisions only as we understood where we were going and how those decisions influenced the school and our classrooms. Since this concept of school organization affects all other dimensions of schooling, including the curriculum, placement of students, and allocations of teachers, these decisions were not taken lightly.

We began slowly by encouraging teachers who were comfortable with the idea of combining two grades into one classroom. Not all classrooms exemplified this organizational plan during the first three years of initiating multiaging. Originally, we decided it was not appropriate to include the kindergarten in this organizational scheme. During the life of the project, however, all classrooms, including kindergarten, became multiaged. We began to realize that our ultimate goal was to become a nongraded elementary school. This was achieved organizationally and "grade level" was excluded from our vocabulary. Nongraded also means that classroom teachers have a mindset that what is taught at any given moment is based on an assessment of the individual student, not on a predetermined curriculum with a grade-level designation. We attained this goal in many respects, and it continued to be a goal toward which we strived rather than one which we achieved to perfection.

Team Teaching

Along with our emphasis on multiaging, we began to explore teaching teams as a way to augment our program. Goodlad helped the Englewood staff realize that the most powerful of in-service training technique is having teachers interact with each other, preferably in teams working with the same group of students. We had almost complete responsibility for planning, scheduling, implementing, and reporting progress. Deliberating and making decisions about the education of our students gave us the opportunity to confront the important educational issues and to enhance our thinking. At the operational level, working as a team increased our repertoire of teaching techniques and increased the range of experiences we could offer our students.

As with our exploration of multiaging, we implemented the concept of teaming only as individual teachers felt ready and comfortable to combine their class with that of one or two other teachers. This meant not only comfort with the instructional approach of another teacher, but also a comfortable personal relationship that would facilitate the very close working arrangements required by teaming.

The growth of the community necessitated the building of more classrooms on the school site. We worked with the architect to design a building specifically to house teaching teams. Instead of fixed walls between every classroom, collapsible "accordion" walls were used to enhance the instructional program for the combined classes and especially to allow more flexibility in grouping students. When two (or three) teachers decided to begin teaming, the combined groups of students were always considered as one organizational unit with two (or three) teachers. Many hours were spent determining how to plan together, how to coordinate in the classroom, and how to evaluate and report student progress. Much thought was given to how each team and the entire school would assess the extent to which we were doing better than when we had been in self-contained classrooms.

Undoubtedly, a very important factor in the success of our changes in school organization was the decision that a given teacher would pursue any change only as he or she was ready. No change was made because of the beliefs of any consultant or because of administrative needs or edicts. No consultants came to Englewood School to implement a predetermined program. No consultant was coercive or controlling. As modeled by Goodlad, consultants relied on the power of their ideas to influence the faculty. At the same time, consultants encouraged those with whom they worked to challenge those ideas with the expectation that fuller understanding and modifications of their ideas would result.

Our staff made changes only as we explored ideas and alternatives until we were convinced that a new way of organizing the school or the curriculum would facilitate the stated goal of providing the best possible educational program for every student. To make these changes, sometimes very daunting ones compared to traditional school practices, much support was needed by each of us from many sources: other staff members, consultants, students, parents, and other community members, as well as the professional lore to which we were exposed.

It was never expected that we would achieve a lasting form of school organization. Each year we were encouraged to think about and improve upon what we did during the past year. Many of our teachers liked to move from one age group to another from year to year. Sometimes new hires fit into the existing organizational structure and sometimes we would change the structure to fit the new teacher. Shifts in the student population and student achievement highly influenced the organizational structure. School organization was viewed as a dynamic factor in the education of children that should be characterized by continuous improvement just as the educational program of each classroom or team was expected to improve over time.

Change has seldom been attained and maintained by either legislation or administrative edict. Lasting change depends on the evolution of a superior set of techniques, processes, structures, and rewards within the persons who must create and sustain the change. Goodlad did not expect perfection in a short time. In our minds, change should be a matter of continuous improvement, a matter of striving constantly toward the ideal with the realization that one will never fully achieve perfection—in part because of our individual limitations and in part because our understanding of the ideal keeps evolving to a higher level.

Education as a Moral and Ethical Enterprise

The importance of education to the individual and to society was an underlying value in all our planning and work in the school and in the community. We constantly examined how the practices and values of the school and classroom affected the student, his or her family, and the community at large. "Is it good for our students?" became the ultimate test of whether a decision was an appropriate one. A part of many faculty discussions and team meetings centered on the moral issues of educational practice, such as tracking, other types of homogeneous grouping, and the relative values of following directions versus encouraging nonconformity propelled by self-direction and self-motivation. We took time in faculty meetings and other conversations to talk about moral matters. We considered why students and teachers did what they did and what else they might have done to improve the situation. Such discussions were encouraged in the classroom, too. Small- and total-group discussions included moral issues that confronted our daily lives as teachers and students and that affected the standards we set for human behavior. The principal, the teachers, and all other adults working at the school in any capacity were expected to be strong role models of ethical and moral living in all aspects of their lives.

Neither the school nor the individual classrooms had written lists of rules. There was a common expectation among adults and students alike to respect the rights and property of others. If this tenet appeared to be violated, any teacher might speak to any student at any time to reflect on the situation and have the student commit to more acceptable behavior in the future. We did not interject ourselves into the situation as judge, jury, and executioner. The emphasis was on helping the student to analyze what transpired and to define remedies. It was important to us that we not deny students learning opportunities that could stand them in good stead later. They learned how to resolve problems resulting from poor interpersonal relationships in school and did not have to wait until they were in the outside world. They realized that they must assume responsibility, not rely on others to solve their problems.

The Enduring Power of What Transpired

The portrayal of our work in the Englewood School Project may sound as though it was recalled through rose-colored glasses and selective memory as the years have gone by. Perhaps we are somewhat guilty of that failing. We do know, however, that our work of forty years ago, guided by ideas and processes of John Goodlad, had a major impact on most of the faculty members. For example, of the twelve faculty members on the staff during the 1958–59 school year, six went on to receive doctorates—four of whom later taught in higher education, and another five had or received master's degrees and became principals or supervisors. We do not believe this was due to happenstance. It was due partially to the fact that superior educators were hired for the Project, and even more due to the quality of experiences and the patterns of educational thought in which we engaged throughout our lives at the Englewood School.

John Goodlad made an impact not only on the staff members of the Englewood School Project, but through them he touched the lives of far more. Eleven of the twelve faculty members (the twelfth retired shortly thereafter) moved into new career positions where they, in turn, influenced literally thousands of educators throughout the country. He was the inspiration that enabled us to realize the tremendous professional satisfaction one gets from dealing with important educational issues and doing the best that one can for learners.

We are not sure that we could have articulated the above generalizations as so integral a part of our work during the period we were immersed in the day-to-day decisions of school living. As we reflected on our work in those days, we had no difficulty in recognizing how essential a part of our work they were then and how they continued to influence us even after we left Englewood School. We both had direct relationships with John for many years after the Project. Each of us believes that the principles he modeled for us in the Englewood School Project are a fundamental part of his belief system and continue to characterize his work as a dynamic change agent. They also continue to be a significant part of ours.

Chapter 4

Preparing Exemplary Teachers for the Twenty-first Century: Challenges and Opportunities to Use What We Know

Dorothy M. Lloyd

"Future educators must be prepared with the expectations, knowledge, and skills to participate effectively in the renewing process."

Educational Renewal: Better Teachers, Better Schools
–John Goodlad[1]

Introduction

American education continues to face difficult challenges in meeting the changing learning needs of school-age children and youths—challenges that are the result of constant economic, sociological, cultural, and technological changes taking place in our society. Educational reform initiatives have abounded during the 1980s and 1990s in an attempt to meet these changing learning needs. Many of these efforts have noted that, to continue to flourish as a nation, America must attend immediately to the changing learning needs of a growing, and increasingly more diverse, school-age population, as well as to consistently declining student achievement.[2]

Although some educational change initiatives have brought about improvement in schools and the learning outcomes of students, it is far from enough. Great numbers of students still lack the opportunity to acquire the knowledge, skills, abilities, and values that will allow them to become successful and contributing members of an information-age society.[3] Why is this the case? A great part of the answer, I believe, rests on the fact that school reform initiatives of the past two decades have directed little attention to teachers and to their preparation. Reform has focused mainly on setting higher and more rigorous standards, establishing what curriculum should be offered, and developing alternative approaches to student assessment, school restructuring, and uses of emerging technologies.

Given the relative lack of attention to the preparation of teachers and to their ongoing professional development, the education of teachers (and, thus, their students) has not kept pace with the rapid technological, cultural, and economic changes occurring in American society. Statistics on teachers who are entering teaching reveal that a large percentage of the roughly 200,000 annual inductees into the profession (a number that will increase dramatically over the next five years) are not prepared for teaching in today's society. They do not meet entry-level expectations—that is, they do not possess the content knowledge and the skills required for making appropriate curricular and instructional decisions that are supported by research and theory; they do not possess the values, beliefs, and qualities conducive to fostering student motivation and learning; and they understand neither the schools as they are nor the alternatives that would effect the changes required for transformation.[4]

Good Teachers, Good Schools:
The University Elementary School Experience

The decade of the 1990s has brought a full realization that the education of teachers and that of their students are connected and that "No school can be better than its teachers."[5] To my knowledge, the ongoing work of John Goodlad and his colleagues represents the only major renewal efforts based explicitly on the intersection of improving both the K–12 schools and the colleges and universities preparing teachers for them.

> We are not likely to have good schools without a continuing supply of excellent teachers. Nor are we likely to have excellent teachers unless they are immersed in exemplary schools for significant portions of their induction into teaching. . . . There must be a continuous process of educational renewal . . . the simultaneous renewal of schooling and the education of educators.[6]

What do we know about teachers, particularly good teachers? What do we know about their development into exemplary teachers? What do we know about their impact on their students' learning, their classrooms, and their schools?

We know that the teacher is the most important single factor in the classroom that affects students' cognitive learning outcomes as well as their attitudes toward learning, self, and others. It is the teacher who establishes the culture of the classroom environment by maintaining high expectations for student learning and by modeling responsibility, inquisitiveness, character, caring, creativity, reflection, and excitement for learning. When teachers who possess these capabilities and skills, and who are also well grounded in their subject matter, work in collaboration with others in the school (teachers, principals, parents, university faculty, and other community members) in an inquiry and problem-solving mode, the school can become a "center of change."[7]

An exemplary case in point was UES (University Elementary School, now the Corrine A. Seeds University Elementary School) at the University of California at Los Angeles. John Goodlad served as director of this laboratory school while dean of the Graduate School of Education. As I reflect on my experiences at UES, we teachers saw ourselves not only as teachers but equally as learners, change agents, and stewards of our school. We initiated and facilitated many classroom and school changes, and our students exhibited high levels of interest and achievement. In our role as demonstration teachers for university courses, we were often asked to provide a self-analysis of what we were doing and why we were doing it. Sharing and discussing these analyses with prospective teachers, university faculty, and other educators enabled us to identify and track common elements of instructional decision making.

Our reflections about our instructional decisions, teaching, students, and the curricula led to deeper levels of inquiry, often developing into a teacher-driven, action research project or a university, faculty-assisted research study on a particular aspect of our work with students (e.g., grouping students for instruction, increasing reading comprehension of eight- to ten-year-olds, moving to more learner- and learning-centered activities, and establishing the criteria and benefits of independent work and learning activities for students and teacher). Study results led to changes in our own teaching methods and strategies, and this process was modeled for preservice teachers. Changes in the organization of school also occurred. For example, the school changed to nongraded, team-taught, multiage classrooms with differentiated staffing, and time was secured and sustained for instructional and curriculum planning.

The excitement surrounding collaborative inquiry and reflection on teaching and learning was contagious and renewing. In effect, we experienced ongoing professional development in elementary school curriculum and instructional decision making. We shared, discussed, and disseminated our learning through presentations, publications, and other creative work. This was in keeping with the described role and functions established for UES in 1963 to "be a center of inquiry through experimentation and research into basic and applied knowledge in education and related fields . . . with important supporting functions of demonstration, observation, and participation involved in the preparation of professional persons."[8]

UES, like other good schools then and now, served as a demonstration, training, and professional development site. UCLA's teacher preparation program used the school for weekly classroom demonstrations and for field experiences that included classroom observation and participation. Cohorts of teacher preparation students acquired the greater portion of their preparation in the Lab School, which included a year-long student teaching internship. These teacher candidates were full participants in all the work experiences and activities of the school. They practiced instructional decision making and reflection on their own and in collaboration with those of us who served as their supervising teachers. With guidance and practice, they became reflective practitioners and, increasingly, better curriculum and instructional decision makers. They were sought after by school districts throughout the state. Follow-up discussions with school and district administrators revealed these beginning classroom teachers to be highly successful and effective first-year teachers.

Many of the school districts that hired the teacher education graduates also participated in UES-UCLA public school partnerships, as well as in the UES-UCLA summer workshops and training programs for educators. Primarily, it was UES faculty and administrators who conducted these workshops for the large numbers of educators who attended. The workshop topics ranged from the nongraded school and team teaching to teacher effectiveness and the appraisal of teachers and their teaching. Some public school educators received professional development leaves from their districts to spend up to a year as a working member of a UES teacher team. Upon return to their own school or school district, they applied their learning to their day-to-day work in the classroom or in administration.

Much of the work in which the Lab School and its teachers were engaged from 1965 to 1985 resulted in the establishment of several university-school partnerships; for example, the League of Cooperating Schools, established in 1967, comprised of UCLA education faculty, UES faculty, and twenty public schools became known as the Study of Educational Change and School Improvement (SECSI). Another, Project Linkage (1971–74), a research project in teacher education linking the California State Department of Education, UES, and an inner-city Los Angeles elementary school, focused on the preparation of teachers and the professional development of classroom teachers in the "real world" of teaching and schools.

These two school-university partnerships and their aligned studies were followed by the Laboratory in School and Community Education (1982–85), a partnership between UCLA and several southern California school districts, county offices of education, and community colleges. The activities and endeavors of UES and its university-school partnerships provided continuous professional development for both UES and public school educators and contributed significantly to the ongoing, national, school-change efforts. They provided up-to-date data about schools, schooling, and the change process. Based on these studies, many recommendations were made that identified the role and functions of university-school partnerships in the restructuring and renewal of schools.

Lessons Learned from Experiences and Work at UES

A number of highly interrelated lessons were learned from the experience and work at UES that are as relevant today as they were then for preparing exemplary teachers.

1. *Exemplary teachers are learners.* They learn from their own experience and from the experience and insights of other teachers in the group or school. Their learning is ongoing, self-motivated, and collaborative.

2. *Exemplary teachers create learning-centered environments that foster the development of themselves and their students.* The classrooms of exemplary teachers foster and facilitate student learning and the development of qualities and values that are critical to students becoming productive, contributing, lifelong learners. In creating a learning-centered environment, these teachers become models of the expectations they hold for their students. They model reflection, inquisitiveness, creativity, caring, and responsibility. Their classrooms also provide an environment where prospective teachers can observe these qualities and behaviors and their impact on students.

3. *Exemplary teachers are catalysts for change.* They initiate change based on their reflections and inquiry surrounding their work and actively investigate such questions as "Why are the students not learning this skill, this content, or this concept?" "What is interfering?" "What might facilitate learning?" "How can we work better together to solve common problems?"

4. *The presence of certain conditions in schools fosters development of the qualities and values exhibited by exemplary teachers.* Three primary conditions at UES promoted and fostered the qualities and values exhibited by exemplary teachers and by those preparing to teach. There were multiple opportunities to engage in ongoing dialogue about learning and teaching: with teaching-level teams, in weekly faculty meetings, with teachers and principals in the K–12 schools, in focused workshops with K–12 educators, and with university faculty and others in the state and national arenas. There also was the opportunity to move from reflection to focused inquiry. Finally, there was a school culture that encouraged awareness and recognition that reflection about work can contribute to a teacher's understanding of learners, learning, and teaching.

5. *School and university settings in which teachers are prepared should be inquiry-centered.* In an inquiry-centered school, prospective teachers will learn to draw on knowledge about their own and others' teaching in deciding what and how to teach. They will observe and practice inquiry that leads to increased effectiveness. The teacher education program, therefore, will be inquiry-centered, focusing on how teachers learn to think and act upon their own reflections, how they learn their craft, and what other sources of knowledge can contribute to their learning.

6. *School-university partnerships promote simultaneous and ongoing renewal of schools, schooling, and the teacher preparation programs.* These partnerships enrich the dialogue around issues of schools, learners, and learning; they put theory into practice. They ensure relevance and provide the opportunity for documenting the continuous renewal of both schools and teacher preparation.

The Preparation of Exemplary Teachers

Much can be gleaned from the experiences and work at the UCLA Laboratory School and its university-school partnerships. It is not surprising that midway during his tenure as director of UES, Goodlad anticipated most (if not all) of the basic concepts grounding today's creative efforts to improve education. He told us then as he tells us now "that nothing short of a simultaneous reconstruction of preservice teacher education, in-service teacher education, and schooling itself will suffice if the change process is to be adequate."[9]

The flaws that plagued many teacher education programs and that worried Goodlad when he wrote that statement continue today: fragmentation and disconnectedness of coursework and practice teaching; teaching methods that do not reflect active hands-on learning; superficial curriculum that does not equip candidates to handle the real problems of practice; inadequate and unsupervised school-based experiences; university faculty inexperienced in schools; poor quality of many teacher candidates; and inadequate time provided to prospective teachers to learn what they need to know.[10]

To date, the changes in teacher preparation have been small, limited to simply tinkering with some program elements or components. The main changes have been to schedule field experience in schools earlier, prior to the entry of prospective teacher candidates into a teacher preparation program, and to rearrange or add content to some courses. The real challenges, those that would make a significant difference in how well teachers entering the profession are prepared, remain challenges in many settings.

Goodlad's major Study of the Education of Educators in the late 1980s proposed and investigated nineteen "postulates" for renewing teacher education.[11] These were not proposals for tinkering around the edges; they represented fundamental calls for change. Others have since made similar calls for change, and now there seems to be some consensus on many common elements.[12] Based on my review of current work, fourteen elements can be identified consistently as needing to be operative if teacher preparation programs are to meet the challenges of preparing exemplary beginning teachers.

1. *Clear Goals* stated as outcomes, giving direction to curricular and instructional decisions and experiences.
2. *Program Coherence* connecting various components of the program to ensure programmatic integrity and continuity.
3. *Relevance* to the situations that are likely to be confronted by future teachers.
4. *Pedagogical Content Knowledge* that provides candidates with an array of teaching strategies and the theory

underlying each, which are connected to the disciplines and ways of knowing.

5. *Field Experiences* throughout the program linked to courses and seminars.
6. *Selection of Professional Development Schools and Master Teachers* based on a set of criteria agreed on by both university and public school educators.
7. *Reflection and Inquiry* that are central to the program and are developed throughout.
8. *Cohort Groups* that stay together throughout the program, thereby providing formal and informal interactions and support among the teacher preparation students.
9. *Collaboration* with K–16 schools, community organizations, and appropriate community agencies.
10. *Candidate Recruitment, Selection, and Retention* based on criteria that align with criteria of teaching excellence in a diverse society.
11. *An All-University Responsibility* for teacher education, operative at the institutional level.
12. *Technology* used as a tool to facilitate, strengthen, and enrich various aspects of the program.
13. *Alternative Pathways* that maintain quality and integrity for nontraditional students.
14. *Assessment and Evaluation* that are systematic and ongoing for all components of the program and its graduates.

Addressing each element fully, drawing from current knowledge and "best practices," would eliminate most of the decades-old challenges and flaws found in most teacher preparation programs. In other words, the gap between what has existed in large numbers of teacher education programs and what should exist would narrow greatly.

Teacher Education at California State University, Monterey Bay: A Case in Point

In 1995, California State University, Monterey Bay (CSUMB), California's newest university, joined the ranks of the more than 1,300 United States institutions that prepare teachers. CSUMB is committed to outcome-based education and to the development of innovative, high-quality, learner-centered, interdisciplinary, diversity-oriented programs. These programs are relevant to both present and future and are based on current knowledge and research. The Center for Collaborative Education and Professional Studies has taken on the University's commitment as a challenge and as an opportunity to collaborate with the discipline-based institutes across the campus and with the K–16 schools in the tri-county region to bring the preparation of teachers into the twenty-first century.

As a new university, without any history, and without any preexisting conditions, we have grasped this opportunity to "rethink" the preparation of teachers. We have asked ourselves, in concert with our K–12 partners (educators from throughout our service region), what we can do to close the gap between what is and what ought to be. We have made significant progress in addressing all fourteen elements noted above.

For example, the program goals have given direction to the curriculum and sequence of the program, recruitment of faculty, and evaluation. The program is designed to develop effective professional classroom teachers who (1) are knowledgeable about theory and its application in classrooms; (2) have acquired knowledge and skills for teaching in an ever-changing multicultural, technological society; (3) are skilled curricular and instructional decision makers; (4) are reflective about their work; and (5) view their role to be teacher, learner, leader, and change agent. From these five overall goals of the program, a number of specific learning outcomes have been derived that address the question: "What should our graduates know, believe, be able to do, and value?" These goals are aligned with the California and National Standards for the Teaching Profession.

Based on these goals, we developed a field-based multiple subject (elementary) credential program. This fifth-year program prepares teachers to teach in crosscultural, linguistically diverse classrooms. Students enter the program via several routes and places in the approximately five-year sequence: (1) at the beginning of the fifth year with a bachelor of arts or bachelor of science degree from an accredited institution of higher education; (2) after approximately two years of undergraduate work at CSUMB or as a transfer student from a two-year community college; or (3) after approximately four years of study at CSUMB through the Liberal Studies Bachelor of Arts Degree program, the preprofessional portion of the teacher preparation program.

The Liberal Studies Bachelor of Arts Degree program is an outcome-based, interdisciplinary, service-learning, diversity-oriented major that integrates the sciences, arts, and humanities. Ninety percent of its students plan to become teachers. The program major emphasizes breadth across a variety of disciplines and requires a concentration in at least one academic discipline. It is based on the concept that a well-educated person is an informed and reflective person who is also bilingual, cross-culturally and technologically competent, and in possession of expert work skills, ethical principles, and social responsibility. It is further driven by the goal to provide the subject matter foundation for the preparation of teachers for quality instruction in schools. Five broad competency areas define and undergird the major (see Figure 1).

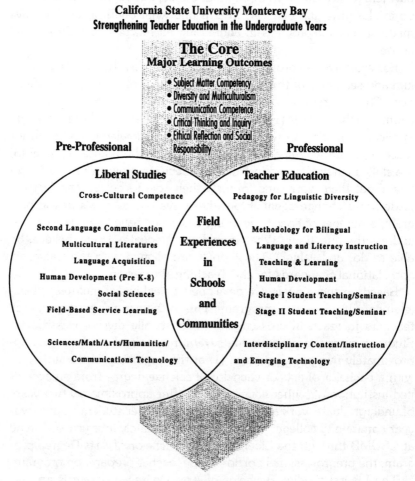

California State University Monterey Bay
Strengthening Teacher Education in the Undergraduate Years

The Core
Major Learning Outcomes

- Subject Matter Competency
- Diversity and Multiculturalism
- Communication Competence
- Critical Thinking and Inquiry
- Ethical Reflection and Social Responsibility

Pre-Professional   **Professional**

Liberal Studies   **Teacher Education**

Cross-Cultural Competence   Pedagogy for Linguistic Diversity

Second Language Communication   Methodology for Bilingual

Multicultural Literatures   Language and Literacy Instruction

Language Acquisition   Teaching & Learning

Human Development (Pre K-8)   Human Development

Social Sciences   Stage I Student Teaching/Seminar

Field-Based Service Learning   Stage II Student Teaching/Seminar

Field Experiences in Schools and Communities

Sciences/Math/Arts/Humanities/   Interdisciplinary Content/Instruction

Communications Technology   and Emerging Technology

Figure 1

1. *Diversity and Multiculturalism* (pluralism, globalism, second-language competency, cross-cultural literacy knowledge)
2. *Communication Competency* (written, oral, visual, numeracy)
3. *Critical Thinking and Inquiry*
4. *Ethical Reflection and Social Responsibility*
5. *Subject Matter Competency* (natural, social and technological sciences, humanities, human development)

This field-based teacher preparation program curriculum, which is built on the well-defined and strong interdisciplinary foundations begun in the undergraduate liberal studies program, is being continuously updated and improved to provide a fully integrated program that engages the student from the freshman through the fifth year, or from community college through the fifth year.

At CSUMB, teacher preparation is an *all*-university responsibility. To date, there has been strong administrative and campus-wide support. A CSUMB steering council for teacher preparation has been established that is comprised of the academic leadership: the vice president and associate vice presidents for academic affairs, the academic deans, the directors of discipline institutes, and the directors of teacher education and liberal studies. This group meets regularly and has oversight for strengthening teacher education at the undergraduate level. Liaisons from each of the content disciplines who work with the liberal studies faculty comprise a subcommittee of the council. This subcommittee addresses the challenge of subject matter competence. Since the liberal studies program's connection to all disciplines (science, math, art, humanities) is critical, the subcommittee ensures that the effort to strengthen, evaluate, and continuously renew the program components are concentrated and coordinated. In addition, their work ensures congruence between the learning experiences offered in their respective areas and the assessment criteria, documentation, and standards being collaboratively designed. The collaboration is both valuable and necessary in maintaining a strong outcome-based, integrated liberal studies major that is seamless from the liberal studies program, on through the completion of the professional curriculum in the teacher preparation program.

Reflection and inquiry are core elements of the program; therefore, the assessment and evaluation, formative and summative, include these components. The assessment takes various forms, including documentation of learning outcomes while prospective teachers are in the program, at the conclusion of the program and as CSUMB graduates begin their teaching careers in schools in the University's service areas.

Conclusion

The major hope in preparing exemplary teachers for the twenty-first century lies in designing innovative, high-quality programs that are based on relevant research and best practices. Program graduates must possess the knowledge and exhibit the qualities cited in this chapter; that is, they must be able to "combine various bodies of knowledge into applications that meet changing or unique circumstances," and exhibit behavior that is "characterized by a drive to know why things are as they are and driven by passion to know more in order to improve existing conditions."[13] Building alliances with schools and communities, and institutionalizing teacher preparation as an *all*–university responsibility, will create the necessary collective momentum for preparing exemplary teachers for the twenty-first century.

Goodlad has recently reminded us that

> there is now sufficient unrest and uncertainty both within and beyond the institutional setting to facilitate the easy entry of countervailing ideas likely to be rejected out of hand during more settled times. It is an opportune time for deans and chairs of [schools, colleges, or departments of education] and directors of centers of pedagogy to lead. But I must remind them of John Steinbeck's admonition in *East of Eden*: Take a long look at your destination and then concentrate on your feet, lest ye stumble.[14]

John and I, each in our own way, have been trekking along the rather treacherous road to better teacher education for almost thirty years since our work together at UES. Finally, we seem to be in a more positive era with respect to receptivity for fundamental change. Although a "stumble" or two is inevitable, we are forging ahead with an innovative program at our institution. Time will tell. . . .

Notes

1 John I. Goodlad, *Educational Renewal: Better Teachers, Better Schools* (San Francisco: Jossey-Bass, 1994), 197.

2 National Commission on Excellence in Education, *A Nation at Risk* (Washington, D.C.: National Commission of Excellence in Education, 1983); John I. Goodlad, *A Place Called School* (New York: McGraw-Hill, 1984); Carnegie Forum on Education and the Economy, *A Nation Prepared: Teachers for the 21st Century* (Washington, D.C.: Carnegie Forum on Education and the Economy, 1986); Holmes Group, *Tomorrow's Teachers: A Report of the Holmes Group* (East Lansing, Mich.: Holmes Group, 1986); John I. Goodlad, *Teachers for Our Nation's Schools* (San Francisco: Jossey-Bass, 1990); Goodlad, *Educational Renewal: Better Teachers, Better Schools*; and Leonard Kaplan, and Roy A. Edelfelt, eds., *Teachers for the New Millennium: Aligning Teacher Development, National Goals, and High Standards for All Students* (Thousand Oaks, Calif.: Corwin, 1996).

3 Linda Darling-Hammond and Velma M. Cobb, "The Changing Context of Teacher Education," in Frank B. Murray, ed., *The Teacher Educator's Handbook: Building a Knowledge Base for the Preparation of Teachers* (San Francisco: Jossey-Bass, 1996), 14–53.

4 Goodlad, *Teachers for Our Nation's Schools*, 230–34; Goodlad, *Educational Renewal: Better Teachers, Better Schools*; National Commission on Teaching & America's Future, *What Matters Most: Teaching for America's Future* (New York: National Commission on Teaching & America's Future, 1996); and Thomas Barone, David Berliner, Jay Blanchard, Ursula Casanova, and Thomas McGowan, "A Future for Teacher Education: Developing a Strong Sense of Professionalism," in John Sikula, ed., *Handbook of Research on Teacher Education* (New York: Macmillan, 1996), 1106–10.

5 Goodlad, *Educational Renewal*; Martin Haberman, "Selecting 'Star' Teachers for Children and Youth in Urban Poverty," *Phi Delta Kappan* 76 (June 1995): 777.

6 Goodlad, *Educational Renewal*, 1–2.

7 Kenneth A. Sirotnik, "The School as the Center of Change," in Thomas J. Sergiovanni and John H. Moore, *Schooling for Tomorrow: Directing Reforms to Issues That Count* (Boston: Allyn and Bacon, 1989), 89–113.

8 John I. Goodlad, "Research and Development at University Elementary School September 1960–January 1963," *A Report of the Director* (University of California at Los Angeles Library, 1963): 1.

9 John I. Goodlad, "The Reconstruction of Teacher Education," 72 *Teachers College Record* (September 1970): 61–62.

10   National Commission on Teaching & America's Future, *What Matters Most,*
      31–34; Barone, Berliner, Blanchard, Casanova, and McGowan, "A Future for
      Teacher Education," 110–25; Sharon P. Robinson, "Building a Strong Foun-
      dation: The Importance of Knowledge and High Standard in Improving Teacher
      Education," in Kaplan and Edelfelt, eds., *Teachers for the New Millennium,*
      187–88; and Mary H. Futrell, "The Courage to Change," in Kaplan and
      Edelfelt, eds., Teachers for the New Millennium, 10–11.

11   Goodlad, *Teachers for Our Nation's Schools.*

12   Carnegie Forum on Education and the Economy, *A Nation Prepared;* Na-
      tional Commission on Teaching & America's Future, *What Matters Most;*
      Charles W. Case, Judith E. Lanier, and Cecil G. Miskel, "The Holmes Group
      Report: Impetus for Gaining Professional Status for Teachers," *Journal of
      Teacher Education* 37 (1986): 36–43; Michael D. Andrew, "What Matters
      Most for Teacher Education," *Journal of Teacher Education* 48 (May–June
      1997): 167–70.

13   See Case, Lanier, and Miskel, "The Holmes Group Report," 42.

14   Goodlad, *Educational Renewal,* 156.

Chapter 5

Global Education at the
Beginning of the Twenty-first Century

Kenneth A. Tye

The Reality of Today's World

Since the sixteenth century, and speeding up at an exponential rate
after World War II (and despite the Cold War), there has been an
inexorable movement toward regional and international cooperation
and the integration of ecological, economic, political, technological,
and even cultural systems of the world. Collaboration through such
agreements as the European Union (EU), the Asian Free Trade Agreement (AFTA), and the North American Free Trade Agreement (NAFTA),
as well as broader international cooperation represented by the General Agreement on Tariffs and Trade (GATT), demonstrates the movement toward economic integration. The trend is supported politically
and culturally by such regional arrangements as the Organization of
African Unity (OAU), the Organization of American States (OAS), the
Association of Southeast Asian Nations (ASEAN), and the Conference on Security and Cooperation in Europe (CSCE), as well as by the
convening of international conferences on specific topics such as banking, population, environment, hunger, human rights, the status of
women, and weapons control.

Arjun Appadurai suggests that there are global cultural flows that
move in irregular ways and that are helping to create an integrated
global society.[1] First, there are what he calls *ethnoscapes,* which are
the various flows of people: tourists, refugees, immigrants, and guest
workers. Second, there are *technoscapes,* which are the machinery
and plant flows of multinational and national corporations and government agencies. Third are the *finanscapes,* which are produced by

rapid flows of money in the currency markets and stock exchanges. Fourth are the *mediascapes,* the images and information produced and disseminated by newspapers, magazines, television, film, and electronic networks. Finally, there are *ideoscapes,* linked to flows of images that are associated with state or counterstate movement ideologies, and which are comprised of elements of the Western Enlightenment worldview: democracy, freedom, separation of church and state, welfare, human rights, and so forth.

There is little doubt about the move toward globalism and a more integrated, interdependent world. That is not to say, however, that there is no longer a good deal of nationalism in the world. The resistance in several European countries to the Maastricht Agreement is a case in point. Probably the most obvious examples of nationalism are to be found in the dissolution of Communist hegemony in the former Soviet Union, as well as in Yugoslavia and Czechoslovakia, which has resulted in the formation of numerous smaller political entities based upon historic ethnic, religious, and/or nationalistic groupings. While one might draw the conclusion that these events represent a reversal of the trend toward cooperation and unification, that is not really true. The breakup of the Soviet empire is more or less anomalous in terms of world trends. For example, the extensive migration of peoples experienced in other parts of the world in the recent past never occurred on any large scale in this part of the world. Only recently has this begun to happen, as many Russians attempt to find their way to what they see as the "motherland" from those new countries that formerly were dominated by Russia in the Soviet Union. Czechoslovakia and Yugoslavia also were unique, being formed after World War I by the victorious Allies without adequate recognition of the fact that historically unlike, and even hostile ethnic or religious groups, were thrown together to form nation-states.

It is in some of the less-developed countries that there is suppression of ethnic and religious minorities in the name of nationhood. Most of these nations were colonized by the various European powers. When they received independence after World War II, they found themselves with arbitrary geographic boundaries drawn by their former colonizers without consideration for tribal, ethnic, or religious groupings. Leaders in the newly independent countries have urged loyalty to the nation as a virtue and have seen nationalism as a liberating and modernizing concept.

Some scholars feel that the growth of nation-states has been, in itself, simply one historical step toward globalization.[2] Others suggest that the move away from the nation-state will result in a world divided into several regions, each with its own cultural, ethnic, or religious identity and each competing economically and politically with the others.[3] It may well be that the world will pass through some kind of regionalization phase in the relatively short term. However, it is likely that what eventually will emerge is what Carlos Fuentes describes as a new form of world federalism wherein there is a strong central government that itself is controlled by checks and balances, separation of powers, and diffusion of decision-making authority to more local entities.[4] Not only will the people of the planet live in a more integrated and interdependent world according to this scenario, but they also will be part of vital and important local and regional units and identities.

Educating for This Reality

The pressing question, then, is: "Given the realities of today's world, what should schools be doing to prepare students to live worthwhile, productive lives?" In seeking a tentative answer to this question, it seems appropriate to turn to the emerging worldwide social movement known as "global education."

Principles Established by the Idea of Mankind

Early in my career, I was a social studies teacher. Then, in the late 1960s, I was introduced to global education in an in-depth manner while I was a member of the staff of the Research Division of the Institute for Development of Educational Activities (/I/D/E/A/), funded by the Charles F. Kettering Foundation and directed by John Goodlad.

In the 1960s, Goodlad began to work with the Council for the Study of Mankind. These scholars met periodically to explore the concept of mankind and to address such questions as "How can we solve current world problems not in the interest of any nation or group of nations but in the interest of mankind?"[5]

As one outgrowth of such discussions, Goodlad brought together a small group of staff members at /I/D/E/A/ who began to address the question of what the mankind idea meant for schooling, or, put another way, what would constitute a "mankind school." Ultimately, an implementation experiment was conducted at the University Elementary School (UES), the Laboratory School of the Graduate School of Education at the University of California at Los Angeles where Goodlad also was dean.

Mankind schooling, not unlike other global education efforts in the world, is based upon Enlightenment principles. Thus, education is thought of as a process that focuses on "an effort to promote maximum self-fulfillment." However, in a time when humankind is searching for a balance between the rights of the individual and a concern for the common good, such fulfillment is not enough by itself. It must be accompanied by "a transcendence of self, an identification with others."[6]

To be sure, as Klaus Schleicher says, "schools need to be concerned with fostering self-identity as well as interactions in cultural terms in order to root children in time and space." This leads to reflective thinking about loyalties to various social groups—for example, family, neighborhood, ethnic group, and nation. Such reflective thinking is important "for moral responsibility, democratic behavior, and conflict resolution and involves development of the abilities of social communication and political participation."[7]

It is through the attainment of healthy self-awareness and fulfillment that a person becomes able to transcend self. This is a complex process that is not fully understood. However, learning theory does give us insights into how cognitive and moral development grows and deepens over time, and such insights can give guidance to those who plan learning experiences for students.

In addition to the qualities of self-awareness and transcendence, the emerging era of global interdependence calls for behaviors guided by rationality, tempered with a recognition that there are no simple, permanent answers to complex problems. Rationality, according to Goodlad, is dependent upon a relationship among understanding, commitment, and action.

> The rational man not only is committed to the rich fruits of inquiry but also is prepared to act and, indeed, acts upon insight rendered compelling by commitment. He knows, as perhaps the most vital ingredient of his rationality, that only through action following understanding and commitment does man forge the links in the chains of his own humanity and of mankind's immortality. He senses his place in time and space and his individual responsibility to that place, time, and space.[8]

It is these three tenets of the mankind idea (self-fulfillment, transcendence, and rationality), then, that are the cornerstones of the worldwide social movement known as global education, which, in turn, is a response to the growing integration and interdependence of the systems of the world.

Global Education and Nationalism

There is a fairly rich body of writing and comment about the global education movement. Much of it has to do with the rationale for its inclusion in the curriculum. Such statements point to the changes taking place in the various world systems. Unfortunately, many advocates of global education end up justifying it on nationalistic grounds. That is, they urge educators to provide a global education to students so that the nation can stay economically competitive in the world. In the United States, this view of the field is presented partly to co-opt the vocal nationalists who see un-American or secular-humanist "plots" in any works that attempt to shed light upon the prevailing mythology of national superiority. In the main, however, this nationalistic justification of global education is a result of the tremendous power of the enculturation process. Goodlad described this power a number of years ago, as follows:

> We are brought up in partisan identifications and thought patterns. Encouraged to think primarily as Americans or Chinese, Christians or Jews, Buddhists or Muslims, communists or capitalists, black or brown or white or yellow, we interpret the beliefs and aspirations of other people in the light of our indoctrination. Each of us is tied to long-established values, loyalties, traditions, languages, and relationships. To expect people to loosen these ties sufficiently to make room for the awareness of mankind and to recognize the mankind imperative is expecting a great deal.[9]

We are beyond having to prove that the world has become interdependent and integrated. Neither is it necessary to continue to talk about global education *within any national context*. The dialogue needs to be raised to the international level, and it should focus on how best to help students gain the skills, abilities, and knowledge that will lead to self-fulfillment, transcendence, and rationality.

Beginning an International Dialogue about Global Education

The Questionnaire

As a means of examining and encouraging dialogue about what the schools of the world are doing and what they should be doing to provide the kind of education being discussed here, a survey of global education practices worldwide was initiated in 1992.[10]

A brief questionnaire was developed that asked about such things as definitions, goals, content, teaching methods, teacher preparation, decision making, and barriers. Ministry of education people in a number of countries were contacted and asked to respond. In addition, a number of global educators in the United States were asked to identify potential respondents from around the world. Finally, selected members of the International Association for Intercultural Education (IAIE) were sent questionnaires. This was a long, difficult process, often involving much follow-up. By the middle of 1996, after efforts had been made to collect data in more than one hundred countries, responses had been received from fifty-two countries, which literally were from every region of the world.

There are limitations to these data. They were gathered over several years and changes could have occurred in countries from which early responses were received. Second, there was only one respondent per country, and even though each was thought to be fairly knowledgeable, no one could be expected to know about all global education activities in his or her country. Third, not every country was represented by the data collection. In fact, and despite a good deal of effort, responses were not received from some important nations, for example, France and the People's Republic of China. Despite the fact that the questionnaire was in English, Spanish, and French, it is possible that it was found by some to be unclear or hard to understand. Finally, there is evidence to suggest that global education is sometimes viewed as a political matter. For example, it is clear that some people in less-developed countries see the movement as a western one, part of the old hegemony, not appropriate to them because they are more interested in nation building or some alternative view—e.g., Islamic values. Such a perspective would more than likely cause a potential respondent to dispose of the questionnaire rather than complete it.

The Definition of Global Education
At the beginning of the questionnaire, respondents were asked about the following definition:

> Global education involves learning about those problems and issues which cut across national boundaries and about the interconnectedness of systems— cultural, ecological, economic, political, and technological. . . . Global education also involves learning to understand and appreciate our neighbors with different cultural backgrounds from ours; to see the world through the eyes and minds of others; and to realize that other people of the world need and want much the same things.[11]

It seems from the responses to this question that "global education" is not a widely used term in much of the world, but that (1) the concept is widely understood, (2) elements of the definition are common to educational systems in many nations, and (3) there are global education movements in a number of countries. Fourteen respondents said that the definition does not fit the philosophy of education in their countries. The importance of nation building, regionalism, or religion was given as the reason. Responses from twenty-four countries indicated that, while the term is not commonly used, the definition is generally acceptable, and there are some elements to be found in the curricula of their schools. The remaining fourteen respondents stated that the definition is appropriate and global education is a factor in schooling; and there is official government support in Canada, Korea, and several states in the United States.

The Content of Global Education
Respondents were asked to identify the global issues that are emphasized in their global studies programs. The issue most often identified was the environment (38 responses), followed by development (31),* intercultural relations (27), peace (18), technology (18), and human rights. (14)**

It appears that much of what is focused on in global studies in any given nation is dependent upon local circumstance. Intercultural education is a good example. Respondents from several western European countries with significant guest-worker populations identified it as important: Austria, Denmark, Germany, Italy, Luxembourg, the Netherlands, and Sweden. Several African respondents chose intercultural relations because of tribal or racial tensions: Kenya, Malawi, Sierra Leone, and South Africa. Eastern Europeans in countries with significant minority populations also said it was essential: Latvia, Poland, Romania, and Russia. The Vietnamese respondent noted that his country has fifty-three minority groups. Bolivia, Mexico, and Nica-

---

* Development usually refers to economic development; at times it includes both political science and economics content, e.g., concern for the disparities between more-developed and less-developed nations. Likewise, population studies, health and AIDS studies, and even world trade can be viewed as development issues.
** This includes human rights, social justice, and democracy studies, as well as studies of racism and sexism.

ragua are concerned about the long-overdue integration of their Indian populations. Australia, England, Israel, and the United States have significant numbers of immigrants. Spain has separatist movements in its Basque regions and in Catalonia.

Respondents indicated that the social studies at the primary level and the various social sciences at the secondary level (history, geography, civics) were usually where global content was taught. Also mentioned frequently were foreign language, literature, and the various sciences for environmental studies (biology and chemistry).

The "expanding community" as an organizing principle for primary level social studies is popular throughout the world. That is, in the earliest grades, students focus upon studies of self, family, and the community. Gradually, their visions are (supposedly) expanded through studies of the state, nation, region, and world. A good summary statement came from Russia:

> Global education problems can be discussed at any level and practically at any lesson in the form appropriate to the age group in science, arts, languages, history, and geography.

Most of the responses to questions about content were normative in the sense that they spoke of the formal curriculum, that which appears in various national or state frameworks or guidelines. To see how much actually appears in the instructional curriculum, that with which the teachers in various countries actually engage their students, would require a different kind of study, one in which classroom observations are used.[12]

So far, what has been described is the "infusion" of global content into existing courses. On the other hand, there are those who advocate separate global education curricula, and they usually suggest that this be done through interdisciplinary planning and teaching. In Denmark, for example, several subjects are involved in secondary level ecology units on topics such as pollution and world population. Although the national curriculum developed during the Thatcher years in England supposedly did away with interdisciplinary units in favor of subject-based studies, they still persist in some schools and, in fact, it was reported that the topic or theme approach is still favored in most primary schools.[13] Nineteen other respondents indicated that there was at least some project teaching or cross-subject teaching in global education in their countries. Also, something called "civic education" is beginning to emerge. This was described in some depth by the

Polish respondent and is part of a worldwide "democracy" movement in education that is interdisciplinary and focuses upon a number of global education issues.

In a survey conducted in Korea, a large number of teachers rejected the notion that global education is "a matter for the social studies." They felt it was best carried out by both infusing global aspects into the entire curriculum and developing interdisciplinary curriculum modules.[14]

Such responses to questions about content bring to mind Goodlad's urging of schools to reconsider the old idea of a core curriculum. Rather than dividing schooling into typical subject areas, he suggests the development of organizing centers for learning that cut across subject matter and focus on the world's systems and "the tools for inquiring into and conversing about them."[15]

Teaching Methods in Global Education

About half the responses reported what might be called "traditional" methods of teaching, ranging from *very* traditional (lectures, readings, questions to answer, tests) to more modern (current events, debates, field trips, camping, lab work, films, pen pals, speakers, cultural festivals).

Several respondents, describing more "progressive" teaching methods, indicated that "process approaches," "active learning strategies," "inquiry," and "discovery" were employed in their countries in the classrooms where global education was part of the curriculum. One famous program, *Columbus in the World*, was initially developed at the Mershon Center at Ohio State University and replicated throughout the United States and the world.[16] Students conduct a thorough investigation of the ways various sectors of their own community (for example, banking, medicine, religion, labor, real estate, research, education, agriculture, sports, media, business) are linked to the rest of the world.

Other examples of active learning include (1) a Danish program wherein primary school children track the use of various kinds of energy in their own homes or the amounts of trash accumulated in their neighborhoods; (2) an Israeli secondary school program where students do community service work in culturally diverse communities; (3) a German project in which secondary school students "adopt" and provide needed resources to a sister school in a less-developed country; and (4) extracurricular activities sponsored by UNESCO clubs in Romania and Korea.

A number of travel programs, mostly for senior secondary pupils and teachers, are described by respondents. For example, in both Swaziland and Denmark, senior secondary students travel to neighboring countries, and the South Asian Association of Regional Countries sponsors exchange programs for students in Pakistan, Bangladesh, India, Sri Lanka, and Bhutan. The American Field Service has sponsored exchanges for United States students for many years.

Finally, as the world moves into the global age, there is a growing use of technology in schools. Through e-mail, classrooms around the world are now connected to each other. Exchanges of information range from simple pen pal type activities to learning of foreign languages to large-scale projects that cause students to gather and exchange data about such things as their respective cultures, histories, and economic and political structures.

Teacher Education and Global Education

The overall impression gained from the responses to the question "How are teachers in your country trained to teach global issues?" is that there are only a small number of programs in the world, particularly at the preservice level, directed specifically to developing global education teachers. The respondent from England clearly states the case as follows:

> In general, teachers are inadequately prepared for global education. Only a few teacher training courses have programs in teaching about global issues; learning style theories and their implications are not widely understood and teachers are not usually trained in a wide range of methods.

Some respondents stated that global education is dealt with, at least in part, within the various "traditional" courses. For example, the New Zealand response was

> Global education is not explicit in curricula of teachers' colleges, but it does arise in the context of other curriculum areas (e.g., geography, biology, economics at the secondary level and integrated studies and social studies at the primary level).

There were a variety of special courses having to do with global education topics that were identified as being part of preservice teacher education programs in Australia, India, Israel, Mexico, Spain, and Sweden. In 1990, the Mershon Center published a report of a study of teacher education programs in the United States that include a global perspective.[17] The study identified thirty-two programs that fit its criteria, as well as a number of other programs that offered some courses with global education content.

There appears to be a good deal of in-service teacher education devoted to global education throughout the world, and it takes many forms. A variety of pedagogical institutes, some located at universities and others at government regional centers, provide workshops on many topics, including global education topics such as peace education, environmental studies, development, and intercultural relations. These workshops deal with both content and pedagogy. In some countries, the ministry of education provides such workshops, and in the Czech Republic, the Free University is involved.

Perhaps the most interesting models are those found in Canada, the United Kingdom, and the United States because they represent various kinds of institutional collaboration. For example, many of the provincial teachers' associations, funded by the Canadian Agency for International Development and supported by various universities and a special International Institute for Global Education at the University of Toronto, provide in-service education. In the United Kingdom, there are a few university-based global education centers that work closely with local education agencies.

In the United States, there have been a variety of collaborations involving two or more agencies, including universities, state government, nongovernmental organizations, school districts, or schools. One such collaboration, for example, involved the Center for Human Interdependence at Chapman University in southern California in a collaboration with eleven elementary and secondary schools in seven local school districts. The four-year project included the infusion of global education into the existing curricula and involved the study of a site-based strategy of school improvement.[18]

At this point, it is important to note that the Associated Schools Project has grown from thirty-three schools in fifteen member nations in 1953 to over thirteen hundred schools in approximately seventy-five countries today. This UNESCO project is devoted to encouraging schools and teacher training institutions to organize special programs designed to increase knowledge of world problems and international cooperation with special emphasis upon peace, human rights, the environment, and intercultural education. While the project is careful to insist that schools work within their own national structures and guidelines, it does have the effect of creating international dialogue and agreement about what global education is and how it should be implemented.[19] The strength of this model is its focus upon the single school as the unit of improvement. The weakness is that, as a unit of the United Nations, UNESCO has a policy of not interfering with national values and priorities. Thus, the problem of nationalism and its effect upon education is probably not dealt with adequately.

Summary and Conclusions

There is a major paradigm shift under way in the world today: globalization. In many countries, some policymakers and educators alike recognize this fact and are acting accordingly to promote global education. Unfortunately, far too many are not.

Data were collected from knowledgeable individuals in fifty-two countries as a means of providing a basis for international dialogue about what global education is and how it should be implemented in the schools of the world.

In terms of curriculum considerations, the data suggest that the issues of environment, development, intercultural relations, peace, technology, and human rights are currently seen as the most important content of global education. The infusion of global content into existing courses and separate courses with global content are currently the main ways global education is included in the curriculum. However, the use of themes, curriculum integration, and interdisciplinary teaching is seen as the most desirable means of organizing a core curriculum for global education.

From the responses to the question about teaching in global education, it is apparent that most teachers in the world use traditional methods. This includes lectures, practice exercises, audio-visuals, field trips, laboratory work, and guest speakers. Some responses, focusing on more progressive teaching methods, indicate that process approaches, active learning strategies, and inquiry and discovery lessons are employed in classrooms where global education programs are found. Several concrete examples, including *Columbus in the World*, travel programs, and the use of technology are cited.

There are only a handful of preservice teacher education programs that have a global education focus or component. However, there are a variety of interesting institutional collaborations in the world involving schools, universities, and other educational agencies that provide in-service global education programs.

Despite the various limitations of the study, the data do lead to some clear conclusions. Most important, there is a growing awareness of the need to prepare students, wherever they live, for a more interdependent and integrated world. Further, there is evidence to suggest that there are a growing number of programs dedicated to accomplishing this task through improved curriculum and the development of modern teaching methods and the training of teachers in the use of both of these.

Second, it seems obvious that there should be much more international dialogue and research about global education, what it means and how it can be implemented. The conversation should involve scholars, policymakers, and educators. The data from the study discussed in this article are designed to serve such a dialogue. They also point to a number of areas in need of further research. For example, examining actual classroom practice (instructional curriculum) in various settings should allow for the generation of hypotheses, subsequently to be tested, about what teaching methods best serve the goals of global education at the various levels of schooling.

Third, the implementation of global education programs can serve as a valid strategy for the general improvement of schooling worldwide. Researchers and scholars who have concerned themselves with questions of school change have identified a number of elements necessary to school improvement that are found within global education programs.[20] The need to bring a global perspective to teacher education is one. Curriculum integration and progressive teaching methods focusing upon inquiry are two others. Having the single school as the focus for improvement, as in the Associated Schools Project, while more subtle, also is a significant element. And, as the data from this study suggest, there is great potential in the formation of collaborations between schools, universities, and other educational and resource agencies for the training of teachers.

Finally, those who come to work in global education should understand that it is not simply a movement dedicated to advancing the economic advantage of a particular society. Rather, it is about educating people to understand the interconnectedness of the various systems of the world and about promoting the ability of people to understand each other. In the final analysis, it is the three underlying principles of the idea of mankind that can guide the global education movement: education for self-fulfillment, self-transcendence, and rationality, including action on behalf of humankind itself.

Notes

1   Arjun Appadurai, "Disjuncture and Difference in the Global Cultural Economy,"
     in Mike Featherston, ed., *Global Culture: Nationalism, Globalization and
     Modernity* (Newbury Park, Calif.: Sage Publications, 1990), 26.

2   See, for example, Roland Robertson, "Globalization, Politics and Religion,"
     in James A. Beckford and Thomas Luckmann, eds., *The Changing Face of
     Religion* (London: Sage Publications, 1989); and Kenichi Ohmae, *The End
     of the Nation State* (New York: Free Press, 1996).

3   See, for example, Samuel P. Huntington, "The Clash of Civilizations," *For-
     eign Affairs* 72 (Summer 1993): 22–49; Brian Beedham, "Islam and the West:
     The Next War, They Say," *Economist*, 6 August 1994, 3-6; and Mahathir
     Mohamad and Shintaro Ishihara, "Will East Beat West?" *World Press Review*
     42 (December 1995): 6–11.

4   Carlos Fuentes, "The Federalist Way," in Nathan P. Gardels, ed., *At Century's
     End: Great Minds Reflect on Our Times* (La Jolla, Calif.: ALTI Publishing,
     1995), 296–99.

5   Gerhard Hirschfeld, *An Essay on Mankind* (New York: Philosophical Library,
     Inc., 1957), v.

6   John I. Goodlad, M. Frances Klein, Jerrold M. Novotney, Kenneth A. Tye,
     and Associates, *Toward a Mankind School: An Adventure in Humanistic
     Education* (New York: McGraw-Hill, 1974), 8.

7   Klaus Schleicher, ed., *Nationalism in Education* (Frankfurt am Main: Peter
     Lang, 1993), 27.

8   John I. Goodlad, *Some Propositions in Search of Schools* (Washington, D.C.:
     National Education Association, 1962), 8.

9   John I. Goodlad, M. Frances Klein, Jerrold M. Novotney, Kenneth A. Tye,
     and Associates, *Toward a Mankind School,* 3.

10   A full report of the survey results will be published in Kenneth A. Tye, *Global
     Education: A Worldwide Movement* (Orange, Calif.: Interdependence Press,
     in press).

11   Kenneth A. Tye, ed., *Global Education: From Thought to Action* (Alexan-
     dria, Va.: Association for Supervision and Curriculum Development, 1991), 5.

12   For a discussion of such methodology and its results, see the following de-
     scriptions of A Study of Schooling conducted in the United States in the late
     1970s: John I. Goodlad, *A Place Called School* (New York: McGraw-Hill,
     1984) and Phillip Giesen and Kenneth A. Sirotnik, "The Methodology of
     Classroom Observation in a Study of Schooling," Technical Report No. 5 (Los

Angeles: The Laboratory of School and Community Education, University of California at Los Angeles, 1979).

13   The first white paper issued by the new Labour Government is *Excellence in Schools* (London: Department of Education and Employment, July 1997). While it is preoccupied with raising standards, it does mention the importance of international understanding.

14   Heather Kim, "Global Understanding and Global Education in Korea," *Global Connection* 5 (Spring 1997): 8–12.

15   John I. Goodlad, "A New Look at an Old Idea: Core Curriculum," in Willard Kniep, ed., *Next Steps in Global Education: A Handbook for Curriculum Development* (New York: American Forum for Global Education, 1987), 15–24.

16   Mershon Center, *Columbus in the World: The World in Columbus* (Columbus, Ohio: Mershon Center, Ohio State University, 1976).

17   See, for example, Merry M. Merryfield, Elaine Jarchow, and Sarah Pickert, eds. *Preparing Teachers to Teach Global Perspectives: A Handbook for Teacher Educators* (Thousand Oaks, Calif.: Corwin Press, 1997); and Merry M. Merryfield, ed., "Teacher Education in Global Perspectives," *Theory into Practice* 32 (Winter 1993).

18   See, for example, Kenneth A. Tye, ed., *Global Education: School Based Strategies* (Orange, Calif.: Interdependence Press, 1991); and Barbara B. Tye and Kenneth A. Tye, *Global Education: A Study of School Change* (Albany: State University of New York Press, 1992). For a good general discussion of collaboration, see Jan Tucker, "Global Education Partnerships between Schools and Universities," in Kenneth A. Tye, ed., *Global Education: From Thought to Action,* 109–24.

19   Associated Schools Project, *International Understanding at School,* 1994–95, (Paris: Bulletin of the United Nations Educational, Social, and Cultural Organization, 65/66).

20   There are a number of publications to cite. Among the most relevant are Robert Freeman, ed., *Promising Practices in Global Education: A Handbook with Case Studies* (New York: National Council on Foreign Language and International Studies, 1986); John I. Goodlad, "The Learner at the World's Center," *Social Education* 50 (October 1986): 424–36; Willard Kniep, "Global Education as School Reform," *Educational Leadership* 47 (September 1989): 43–45; Torsten Husén, *Education and the Global Concern* (Oxford: Pergamon Press, 1990); Barbara B. Tye and Kenneth A. Tye, *Global Education: A Study of School Change;* and Kenneth A. Tye, *Global Education: A Worldwide Movement.*

Chapter 6

K-12 Educational Change: Building Responsive Schools

Richard C. Williams

Since *A Nation at Risk* was published in 1983, numerous groups have been advocating ways in which America's schools could be reformed and improved. The solutions suggested range across a wide spectrum. Some reformers, for example, urge vouchers and charter schools to enlist market forces to overcome what they view as the bureaucratic inertia that stifles significant change and reform. Others feel the system is basically sound but could be vastly improved by developing, adopting, and implementing high standards, new curricula, and accountability systems.

One group, which includes prominent educational researchers and reformers who have designed and implemented change in some of America's most troubled and challenged schools, insists that the key to lasting and significant change rests with mobilizing and empowering the local school. Their research and experience tells them that schools will not change or implement innovations unless the principals and teachers who work there and the schools' parents feel ownership for the proposed changes. This ownership is accomplished by having those who will be impacted by the change engage in discussions that identify the school's needs, consider possible solutions to address the identified needs, and participate in decisions about the changes that will be made. School community members are assumed to be interested in and capable of engaging in these procedures. However, often they will need individuals or groups external to the school to raise concerns, provide guidance in group processes, help identify possible innovations that will address identified problems, and provide peer support.

These general themes might be summarized in the following quotations:

> The single school with its principal, teachers, pupils, parents, and community links is the key unit for educational change. . . . The school is a social system with regularized ways of behaving by those who inhabit it: certain expected activities, patterns of rewards, and the like. . . . No matter what the approach to change, it must reckon ultimately with the functioning reality of this social system. . . . The school itself is an agent for change, potentially or actually.[1]

> The major mechanism for encouraging and supporting change [is] the peer-school network.[2]

> External change agents, instead of trying to insert something into the school's culture, first should be trying to help that culture develop an awareness of and a responsiveness to itself. [3]

These quotations were not written in the 1990s by such noted reformers as James Comer or Henry Levin or Deborah Meier or Ted Sizer. I suspect, however, that these school reformers would find these ideas compatible with their thinking about improving schools. The quotations were published in 1975 by John Goodlad in *The Dynamics of Educational Change: Toward Responsive Schools*. The book served as the culminating volume in a series of publications based on a five-year Study of Educational Change and School Improvement (SECSI) that began in 1967. Goodlad also described in *Dynamics* how his experiences as a teacher, consultant, researcher, and director of the University Elementary School (UES) at the University of California at Los Angeles had helped shape his thinking about the change process.

In this essay I want to acquaint, or reacquaint, readers with the pioneering and unique work on educational change carried out by Goodlad and his colleagues over twenty years ago. For reasons that are described later in this essay, this research and the publications from it have virtually disappeared from the memories of current reformers. One is hard-pressed today to find references to the study and its findings. Yet, Goodlad's insights into the change process that stretch back forty years, and the unique research that he and his colleagues began thirty years ago, anticipated the work of many of today's prominent educational reformers.

My association with John and this work goes back many years. I first began working with him in 1967 when I served as his assistant dean in UCLA's Graduate School of Education. In 1969, I joined a team of researchers John had gathered to conduct research on the change process in education in what was known as the League of Cooperating Schools. In 1972, while on sabbatical, I worked in Oslo, Norway, on an educational change project called IMTEC, which was associated with the Organization for Economic Cooperation and Development (OECD). John served on IMTEC's board, and I continued to be associated with his work on the change process.

In this essay I will revisit Goodlad's central ideas about the change process as described in *Dynamics* and consider how relevant those ideas are today, twenty years later. First I will describe the context within which Goodlad was writing in 1975, that is, the assumptions then held about what needed to be done to improve the educational system and the dominant educational reform strategies that were driving educational reform efforts. Then I will briefly discuss Goodlad's experiences and research activities prior to the League of Cooperating Schools project that had influenced his thinking about the change process. Next I will briefly describe the SECSI research project conducted with the League of Cooperating Schools. I will then describe selected themes elaborated in *Dynamics* and indicate how they differed from the dominant thinking in 1975. Finally, I will look at current educational reform efforts in light of Goodlad's theses about the change process and comment on the degree to which current thinking about the change process is consistent with the ideas he had elaborated over twenty years ago.

Context

Peter Shrag has aptly described the public's continuing preoccupation with returning to some idealized golden age in education, "an era when school maintained rigorous academic standards, when all children learned, when few dropped out and most graduated on time."[4] Clearly the decades preceding the publication of *Dynamics* would not fit that description. In the 1950s and 1960s, criticism of public schools packed the pages of popular and professional books and journals. The debate was spurred in part by *Sputnik* and by the real or imagined damage wrought by "progressivism." Some critics focused on the shortcomings of life-adjustment education, others on what they considered wrongheaded instructional methodologies. A major unifying theme of many critics was that the education of our children and youths had been taken over by the "'interlocking directorate' of professors of education, the school administrators they trained and the state departments of education that required their courses for teacher certification."[5] If this group of self-serving educationists could be eradicated, they argued, our schools could "regain the healthy glow associated with the cultivation of the intellect."[6] Critics issued a "call to arms" to transfer the control of teacher education to respected academics and to recruit into our nation's classrooms a group of more intellectually capable teachers who were thoroughly grounded in their chosen academic fields.

The federal government, partly in response to these criticisms, but also spurred on by policymakers who saw the schools as major instruments for correcting racial, social, and economic injustice, funded and managed a large number of national educational reform efforts.[7] Some of the more significant are as follows.

1. Beginning in the late 1950s, the National Science Foundation initiated curriculum development efforts in science, math, and social studies that included both developing materials and training teachers to use them. In 1965, the federal government initiated Title III, and later Title IVc, of the Elementary and Secondary Education Act. This legislation funded classroom teachers to develop instructional processes and materials that would be field tested, evaluated, and disseminated to classrooms everywhere.
2. In the late 1960s, Project Follow Through tested several models that had been developed in "lab schools" and elsewhere for educating disadvantaged children in kindergarten through third grade.
3. In the early 1970s, the Office of Economic Opportunity initiated a performance contracting program that encouraged independent, profit-making companies to establish inner-city schools on the assumption that their fresh thinking and management skills would succeed where the public schools had not.

What is noteworthy about these school change efforts is that they were based largely on the assumption that the solution to school improvement must come from outside public schools and classrooms—in university academic departments, with policymakers, and in the private sector. The exceptions were Title III and IVc, which utilized classroom teachers to develop new educational practices and materials.

But even that approach assumed that the ideas of a relatively few innovative teachers would be disseminated to their less innovative and motivated colleagues.

Accompanying the growth of new products and processes was a growing need for implementation strategies. Little attention had been given to this topic since Mort and Cornell's education diffusion studies in the 1940s.[8] The dominant educational change model in the 1950s and 1960s was the Research Development and Diffusion model (RD&D). The basic RD&D strategy was to identify a problem; provide funding to research and development centers to develop appropriate materials, programs, or processes; and evaluate and disseminate the results to "targets," that is, awaiting schools. This strategy was consistent with the prevailing assumption that those who had the expertise and who recognized the need for improvement resided outside the educational system.

The RD&D strategy had a long history of success in other sectors. In agriculture, for example, the work of university schools of agriculture, field agents, and demonstration projects had revolutionized farming practices in the United States. Similarly, the RD&D strategy had proven to be a powerful approach to developing new business products and military weapons systems. If this strategy had worked so effectively in those sectors, surely it would work to develop and implement needed changes in our schools.

Other change strategies were also attracting attention, such as the training and use of "change agents" who would enter schools and districts and help them with the implementation process, and the use of Organizational Development (OD) specialists who would serve as catalysts to help empower school staffs. However, the dominant change approach was the RD&D strategy.

Experiences and Research that Influenced Goodlad's Ideas about the Change Process

During the 1950s and 1960s, when the RD&D strategy was dominant, John was formulating a fundamentally different approach to educational renewal and change. I will briefly describe four activities and experiences that influenced his thinking.

The first was an invitation for John to work as a consultant with the Englewood School in Sarasota County, Florida. Isolated on a vast stretch of sandy beach, Englewood Elementary School was clearly in trouble. Tensions between the community and the school and within the school staff ran high, the school was experiencing unprecedented growth, and the district lacked confidence in the school principal and staff. An independent consultant previously hired by the superintendent had recommended that the district replace the principal and most of the teachers.

Goodlad's approach was decidedly different. He began by scheduling a series of regular meetings with the members of staff and community to explore the school's problems and to devise solutions. This was not an easy process, given the level of distrust and the history of failure. Through these regular meetings with members of the staff and community and the initiation of social events, tensions began to diminish. Study teams were established to explore ideas and to make recommendations to the staff. Goodlad and the school staff began to forge solutions to the problems it was facing, including the development of a sophisticated, multiaged, team-teaching structure and an ongoing process for examining the school's program and development. The school was transformed and soon became recognized for its innovative program. (See chapter 2 for more details.)

The second influential event occurred when Goodlad was appointed in 1960 as a professor in UCLA's Graduate School of Education and as the director of UCLA's University Elementary School (UES). On the surface, UES would seem to be quite the opposite from the Englewood School. Widely known in the 1930s and 1940s for its progressive program and innovation, UES was by any measure a success story. However, UES had suffered neglect since the school's noted principal, Corinne A. Seeds, had retired in 1957. By 1960, the UES school staff and parents, as with the Englewood School, had divided into factions that were warring over the school's direction and program. Prior to his appointment as UES director, Goodlad and Robert Anderson had published *The Nongraded Elementary School*.[9] Many at UES assumed that Goodlad would revitalize the school by implementing the nongraded model for which he was well known. His approach, however, was quite different. As with the Englewood School, he included parents in discussions with the staff about the school's problems and ways in which to meet its challenges. His goal was to develop "a common body of understandings and the realization that there existed a staff responsibility to come up with better ways of arranging and conducting the school environment for living and learning."[10]

Madeline Hunter was hired as the school's principal and, under Goodlad's direction, the school underwent significant renewal and change. As the school's innovative program became publicized, visitors poured in to see its accomplishments. Goodlad was dismayed to observe that the visitors focused on the details of the school's program and, in his opinion, missed the importance of the change process the school had utilized. Many visitors went away impressed with UES's program but convinced that it could "never be done in our school." To Goodlad, the essential meaning of the Englewood and UES experiences was that the power for schools to renew and change essentially resided within the school itself. If the principal, staff, and community members were brought together to discuss problems, identify possible solutions, decide on a course of action, and implement the decisions, renewal and change could occur. This approach to educational change took time and was never easy, but he considered it the most effective way to realize meaningful and lasting change.

Goodlad's views on the importance of building the capacity of schools to change was reinforced through his work with James B. Conant on the study of the education of teachers. During many visits to schools across the country, Goodlad observed that many of the highly publicized school reforms that were reported to be implemented in our schools were, in fact, seldom found in the classrooms he visited. In order to examine this observation more systematically, he and several colleagues visited classrooms in sixty-seven schools across the country to see if the various instructional methods, pedagogical techniques, and RD&D-generated instructional materials were being commonly utilized in America's classrooms.[11] These visits confirmed Goodlad's earlier observations:

> Practice did not nearly match the rhetoric for change. . . . What bothered us most was the apparent absence of processes by means of which the schools and the people in them might have some reasonable prospect for self-renewal.[12]

Based on his experiences and research, Goodlad initiated the Study of Educational Change and School Improvement (SECSI) under the auspices of the Kettering Foundation's /I/D/E/A/ and in cooperation with UCLA's Graduate School of Education. This was a unique project. Unlike other research studies then under way, the SECSI study was a cooperative venture involving a SECSI research team and a network of eighteen elementary schools. The study's purpose was not to investigate what happened to schools that were trying to implement externally driven educational change; it was, instead, the central hypothesis, as stated in the introduction to this chapter:

that the single school with its principal, teachers, pupils, parents, and community links is the key unit for educational change. . . . The school is a social system with regularized ways of behaving by those who inhabit it: certain expected activities, patterns of rewards, and the like. . . . No matter what the approach to change, it must reckon ultimately with the functioning reality of this social system. . . . The school itself is an agent for change, potentially or actually.[13]

The League of Cooperating Schools was a network of elementary schools, one each from eighteen school districts in southern California. The schools, located in rural, suburban, and urban districts, were considered typical schools with typical principals. This was not a league of "super schools." The districts agreed to relax many district policies and practices governing the instructional program, curriculum, and the teachers' roles. Each school was to begin a process to identify problems, agree on ways to address those problems, select and implement the solutions, and evaluate the outcomes.

Assisting the schools in this process was the SECSI staff, which consisted of experienced educational practitioners, UCLA faculty and graduate students, support staff, and external consultants. SECSI provided a supporting "hub" that worked with the schools, assisted them in the change process, conducted research, and disseminated the results. Goodlad was the SECSI director and continued his role as the dean of UCLA's Graduate School of Education and the director of UES.

The League and the SECSI study represented a unique approach to studying the change process in schools. Rather than study, after the fact, what happened to schools that had attempted to implement change, this study investigated what happens when schools attempt change with the necessary resources and support.

Establishing and maintaining the League of Cooperating Schools was not easy, and several problems surfaced. One major problem was to resolve the tension between allowing each school to develop its own reform plan versus having most or all of the League schools adopt a particular plan or approach. This tension surfaced in the League schools and districts and within the SECSI staff itself.

Contributing to the tension was Goodlad's celebrity. His writings on curriculum and nongraded schools were widely known, and many school leaders assumed that the League would make them beneficiaries of Goodlad's expertise. In addition, the SECSI staff members' skills were well known and many school staffs assumed they would be available as consultants.

Some on the SECSI staff, while agreeing with the League goal to help schools engage in the change process, were tempted to implement particular programs they valued when they observed the schools struggling to find answers to their problems. However, this was not the League's purpose nor the SECSI staff's responsibility. As Goodlad described it:

> The League was created both to provide the necessary stimulus and to enable us to observe processes of initiating and developing changes. But the major mechanism for encouraging and supporting change was to be the peer-school network [emphasis added].[14]

The debate over purpose and role continued over half of the project's life. Some schools and districts expected that a specific innovation would be provided to them, and some SECSI staff continued to urge the more direct consulting role for themselves. After careful consideration, Goodlad insisted that the original League model would prevail. Several SECSI staff members left for opportunities elsewhere; however, all of the League schools remained.

The results of the League and the SECSI study have been described in great detail by Bentzen, and I will note only a few observations.[15] The impact of the League model on schools varied considerably. Some schools became models of how a school-centered change process could work. Others changed, but to a lesser degree. Some were beginning to change when the League ended. A powerful peer network developed. Many teachers became deeply involved in the change process and emerged as school leaders, and many of the principals successfully adopted a leadership style that embraced parent and staff participation in the change process.

The SECSI staff described the school inquiry process that emerged from the study as Dialogue, Decision making, Action, and Evaluation (DDAE). Goodlad described the importance of DDAE as follows:

> We feel that one of the essential components of any comprehensive strategy of change in school settings is total group and small group DDAE, guided by criteria such as those developed in the League. . . . External change agents, instead of trying to insert something into the school's culture, first should be trying to help that culture develop an awareness of and a responsiveness to itself. Something akin to DDAE as an ongoing regularity is essential.[16]

Goodlad referred to this approach as a "responsive" model of change. Based on the experience with the League, he proposed several postulates pertaining to school improvement that can be summarized as follows:

The single school is the optimal unit for educational change. An essential element in school-based change is the use of an effective problem-solving process, such as DDAE. Schools engaged in school-based change need a hub—a district, consortium of districts, or intermediate unit to assist them in establishing and maintaining the DDAE process and in identifying programs, materials, and processes that might help them address school-specific problems. There must be a "compelling, different drummer whose drumbeat somehow is picked up by the school's antenna" and that drummer must be there for several years. While the principal must play a key leadership role, ultimately teachers are a powerful leadership resource if opportunities are provided for them to break out of their isolated classrooms. If the school is going to deviate from established norms, it will need a supportive peer reference group and a communication network with the larger system, such as the school district.

This school-centered approach to educational change was almost the reverse of the RD&D strategy, with its reliance on outside agencies to develop materials and processes that would be given trials, evaluated, and disseminated to "target" schools. Responsive schools might need the materials, processes, and programs developed by outside agencies, but decisions about the need for and use of these externally developed materials and processes must rest with the school staffs.

Another theme that appeared in *Dynamics* is also important to mention. Drawing on conceptions from sociology, anthropology, political science, history, and economics, Goodlad urged reformers to view schools as part of an ecological system.

In this conception, there is nobody on the outside trying to do something to someone on the inside. All are part of the same systemic whole or ecosystem. Every person and every thing has consequences for all other persons and things. Nothing is inconsequential. Individuality and uniqueness exist but function and are understood in relation to the whole and to other parts of the whole. [17]

The traditional, linear view of schooling seeks to make the school more productive, almost at any cost—the measure of effectiveness being certain effects produced in the pupil products. Failure to produce calls for more of something—money, time, materials—or some manipulations in classroom management or pedagogy. Usually, the proposed solution deals with a limited set of variables assumed to be modifiable. The results have been disappointing and we have become disillusioned with our schools. [18]

Viewing the school as embedded in an ecological system exposes the limits of summarizing a school's quality or effectiveness in single measures, such as test scores or attendance rates. The students' performance or behavior is in part a function of the school's program and curriculum, but it is also influenced by many interacting external influences, such as television, poverty, gangs, and dysfunctional families. The individual school is itself an ecological system with many internal parts interacting with each other in complex ways. To view the school as a static entity and expect that it will respond in predictable ways to external influences is folly indeed. Because schools differ in the ways external and internal influences affect their performance, individual schools vary in the kinds of challenges they face in addressing the needs of their students—this argues for school principals, staffs, and community having greater authority over identifying school problems and developing and implementing the kinds of programs most suited for their school.

The Impact of Goodlad's Book

Several scholars and organizations were studying the change process in schools and educational systems at the same time Goodlad was conducting his work.[19] Two publications were of particular significance. In 1967, Robert Schaefer published *The School as a Center of Inquiry*. Schaefer's ideas were quite similar to Goodlad's. He urged schools to become places where teachers could engage in rigorous inquiry about their work so that they could become more skilled at their profession, experience personal fulfillment, and allow students to "observe adults honestly wrestling with intellectual problems."[20]

Arguably, the most influential work published during that time was the several volumes reporting the RAND Corporation's studies, entitled *Federal Programs Supporting Educational Change*.[21] This large-scale project examined the impact of several federally funded development activities on local practice, with a view to identifying those factors that most influenced adoption in the schools. Unlike the SECSI study, the RAND studies examined what happened in the schools after they had been engaged in the adoption process for several years. Of interest was their conclusion, which paralleled the findings of the SECSI study and Goodlad's earlier formulations, that

federal policies exercised limited leverage on the course of innovations because they did not critically influence those factors most responsible for effective implementation—the motivations of actors within the institutional setting and the locally designed implementation strategies.[22]

Many of these publications came to conclusions similar to Goodlad's—schools are complex social and ecological systems; lasting change and innovation will not occur in schools unless those who will be most impacted by the changes are actively engaged in an ongoing inquiry about the challenges facing the school. Changes introduced into a school, regardless of their origin, must be seen as valuable by those who will be implementing them. Schools are not passive "targets" to be improved by external experts or policymakers but are powerful agents of change themselves.

What was unique about the SECSI study was that it did not stop with those conclusions, important as they were. It recognized that some schools exhibited those qualities but most did not, and it recognized that there were regularities in the schooling system making it unlikely that "responsive" schools would naturally emerge. Through its close work with and observations of the school's struggles to change, Goodlad and his colleagues developed the DDAE technique, which gave schools a way to approach the challenge of becoming "responsive" schools.

As best I can tell, Goodlad's book did not get very much attention when it was published. One is hard-pressed to find any reviews of the book in major journals at the time. It is rare that the *Dynamics* book or any of the SECSI volumes are referenced today in publications about the school reform or the change process. Goodlad personally disseminated his view of the change process through articles and talks, but the *Dynamics* book and the SECSI project are, today, quite invisible.

There are probably several reasons for this. The research was conducted only in elementary schools in southern California, and some readers may have felt that the research had limited impact in other parts of the country. Others may have concluded that research from comparatively smaller elementary schools might have very limited application in secondary schools—especially, large urban high schools. Also, many of the SECSI project's assumptions, foci, and findings ran quite counter to the prevailing views of how schools should be changed. The RAND Study, on the other hand, examined the change process of familiar federal programs. Published at about the same time as the SECSI project, the RAND Study received widespread and much-deserved attention and simply overshadowed the SECSI project.

Looking Back

The educational change strategies being employed in the 1990s differ somewhat from the strategies in use twenty years ago, but they have a familiar ring. The change agent model has vanished but some districts and schools, especially districts, seek to change by hiring a charismatic leader. However, because the conditions that have created the districts' difficulties have not changed—for example, poverty, reduced financial resources, unemployment, and oppressive bureaucracies—such leaders can usually make only marginal changes. The luster of their promised reformation begins to fade, the district loses enthusiasm for the leader, and it begins looking around for the next great leader. The pattern has been repeated again and again.

The RD&D strategy has not disappeared. One example of its current use is the "standards movement," now flourishing in many states. The elements of this strategy are familiar: external groups establish a set of standards, develop curricula in several subjects, develop tests or evaluative tools, establish accountability systems, and expect results. Some important improvements have been made in applying this strategy to the standards movement. Some states have included educators in developing the standards and curricular materials rather than relying exclusively on academics and other researchers; some states have provided schools with funds to enable them to prepare their staffs for the coming changes; many states have recognized that large-scale change is a slow process and have extended the time frame for full implementation; and some states have adopted multiple evaluation measures.

However, some of the essential elements of the RD&D model remain: the school is a target in need of change; expertise for identifying the school's needs rests outside the school; and some of its proponents, especially some politicians, view school principals and teachers as static forces to be energized through the use of punitive accountability systems.

While there are many desirable elements in the standards approach, it remains to be seen if it will be as fully implemented as its advocates expect. The major challenge will be to see if sufficient resources and time are allocated to schools to maximize their response to the proposed changes. Unless schools have ownership for the standards movement and the capacity to implement its provisions, it too will likely fall short of its advocates' lofty aspirations.

Recognizing the need to develop and utilize the schools' responsive capacity to implement change is advocated today by many leading school reformers. I will mention only a few of the more prominent ones.

> Michael Fullan, in his definitive book on educational change, concludes that countless efforts at change are failing because they do not impact the culture of the school and the profession of teaching. Thus the workplace itself is the key. . . . The only solution is that the whole school—all individuals—must get into the change business. . . . [We need] critical masses of highly engaged individuals working on the creation of conditions for continuous renewal, while being shaped by these very conditions as the latter evolves.[23]

Sergiovanni, drawing upon Selznick's notion of organizations as communities and the need to change schools by developing them into communities, states:

> Communities are organized around relationships and ideas. They create social structures that bond people together in a oneness, and that bind them to a set of shared values and ideas.[24]

> We need to start . . . by building up the capacity of people to become self-managing, and by helping people to connect to shared values and ideas. This approach emphasizes the development of *shared followership* in the school—a followership that includes principals, teachers, parents, and students.[25]

Elmore and McLaughlin, in summarizing what they have learned from their review of the change process, state:

> The RAND Corporation study of federal change agent programs found a high correlation between the persistence of developmental activities and locally initiated problem-solving, adaptation, staff involvement, and administrative support. . . . Most adults act on solutions crafted from their own experience and practical judgment, informed by what they can learn from others whose judgments they trust. If they have no investment in the change, then their willingness to make it work is limited. People develop an investment in change by applying their own skills.[26]

As indicated in the introduction, four of America's best-known and more successful school improvement projects—Comer's School Development Program, Levin's Accelerated Schools, Meier's Central Park East Schools, and Sizer's Coalition of Essential Schools—are similar to Goodlad's notions of responsive schools.[27] These four projects strive to develop the capacity of the administrators, teachers, staff, parents, and students to engage in inquiry about the challenges they face, to forge solutions to those challenges, and to explicate a process for addressing those needs. They trust the intelligence and competency of those in the school community. They provide a "hub" or central resource that the schools can draw upon as they forge their own solutions to the unique challenges they face. They recognize the painstakingly difficult and time-consuming process in which they are engaged.

Personal Reflections

My involvement in John's work on the change process, which began in the 1960s, came full circle in the late 1980s. During the many years he served as the dean of the Graduate School of Education, he had remained as director of the University Elementary School (since renamed the Corinne A. Seeds University Elementary School). John's deanship and scholarly activities placed heavy demands on his time, and the UES principal, Madeline Hunter, increasingly influenced the school's direction and program. During those years, Madeline had developed and implemented her program of clinical instruction at UES. Through her writing and speaking, Madeline disseminated her work throughout the nation. UES soon became widely known as a demonstration school for her method, and literally thousands of visitors came to the school each year for presentations and demonstrations.

In the early 1980s, Madeline Hunter retired and John returned his attention to UES. John felt that it was important to change the direction of the school. While Madeline had brought great renown to the school, the school had to move on to new challenges and research that would be compatible with the expectations of a research university. John, once again, began the dialogue necessary to bring about change, and new staff were appointed to replace those who left. That change process was under way when he accepted an offer to move to the University of Washington to engage in his current work on teacher education and school reform.

Upon John's departure, I was appointed the UES director. I inherited a school that was embroiled in the controversies that inevitably surface when a school is in the middle of the change process. The faculty had considerable doubt about my qualifications to be their director—and rightly so. The last time I had actually worked in an elementary school was when I was a sixth-grade student! But I had long admired UES and its contributions, and I was pleased to have the opportunity to work with the staff to see if we could solve the controversies that gripped the school and then move forward.

We went through some turbulent times—numerous staff members resigned and those who remained divided into opposing factions. The school's program and curriculum lacked definition. Morale was very low. We found our way out of the situation by using the change processes that John had so effectively advocated. For six months, during my second year as director, we engaged in an extensive dialogue about the school's direction. Eventually, we reached consensus on what we wanted to do and the structure and processes we would use to govern our efforts. We examined and implemented ideas and programs from external sources that would help us solve the problems we had identified, and we evaluated our progress and made adjustments when necessary.[28]

Implementing all these changes was a long and difficult process, but the results were quite remarkable. The staff invested considerable creativity and energy in our efforts, and as we focused our attention on the challenges we faced, the internal divisions began to disappear. We reconnected our ties with the Graduate School of Education and began several research studies and development projects. The school was healthy once again. I personally experienced the satisfaction of seeing what can happen when a school staff is empowered to identify its problems, select and implement processes and programs to address those problems, and evaluate the results. Through this personal experience, I came to appreciate the power of John's ideas and to understand both conceptually and experientially why some of America's most successful contemporary reformers so strongly advocated the importance of focusing on the local school as a center of change.

Conclusion

Deborah Meier recently asked when will we be able to establish policies that will encourage the widespread development of "schools that have been successful with students who would otherwise count among society's failures."[29] Describing such schools as small, self-governing schools of choice, she emphasizes that

> every school must have the power and responsibility to select and design its own particulars and thus to surround all young people with powerful

adults who are in a position to act on their behalf in open and publicly responsible ways. . . . Such schools could be encouraged to flourish if we built our system *for them,* not them for our system.[30]

We have learned a great deal over the years about what is needed to ensure that schools become powerful agencies for their students' education. When will we realize, however, that the most promising school improvement plans will make little progress unless the schools are empowered to take ownership for those ideas and are provided the resources to do so? When will we finally come to realize the power of the ideas Deborah Meier and other contemporary reformers are advocating? When will we finally respond to those same ideas that John Goodlad has been advocating for more than forty years? When indeed!

Notes

1   John I. Goodlad, *The Dynamics of Educational Change: Toward Responsive Schools* (New York: McGraw-Hill, 1975), 81.

2   Goodlad, *Dynamics*, 115.

3   Goodlad, *Dynamics*, 177.

4   Peter Schrag, "The Near-Myth of Our Failing Schools," *Atlantic Monthly* (October 1997): 72.

5   Robert J. Schaefer, *The School as a Center of Inquiry* (New York: Harper & Row, 1967), 9–10.

6   Schaefer, *The School as a Center of Inquiry*, 10.

7   Richard F. Elmore and Milbrey Wallin McLaughlin, *Steady Work: Policy and Practice, and the Reform of American Education* (Santa Monica, Calif.: RAND Corporation, 1988).

8   Paul R. Mort and Francis G. Cornell, *American Schools in Transition: How Our Schools Adopt Their Practices to Changing Needs* (New York: Bureau of Publications, Teachers College, Columbia University, 1941).

9   John I. Goodlad and Robert H. Anderson, The Nongraded Elementary School (New York: Harcourt Brace Jovanovich, 1959).

10   Goodlad, *Dynamics*, 69.

11   John I. Goodlad et al., *Behind the Classroom Door* (Worthington, Ohio: Charles A. Jones, 1970).

12   Goodlad, *Dynamics*, 71.

13   Goodlad, *Dynamics*, 81.

14   Goodlad, *Dynamics*, 115.

15   Mary M. Bentzen and Associates, *Changing Schools: The Magic Feather Principle* (New York: McGraw-Hill, 1974).

16   Goodlad, *Dynamics*, 177.

17   Goodlad, *Dynamics*, 205.

18   Goodlad, *Dynamics*, 208.

19   See, for example, Matthew B. Miles, *Innovation in Education* (New York: Teachers College Press, Columbia University, 1964); Neal Gross et al., *Implementing Organizational Innovations: A Sociological Analysis of Planned Educational Change* (New York: Basic Books, 1971); Louis M. Smith and

Pat M. Keith, *Anatomy of Educational Innovation: An Organizational Analysis of an Elementary School* (New York: Wiley, 1971).

20   Schaefer, *The School as a Center of Inquiry*, 77.

21   Paul Berman and Milbrey Wallin McLaughlin, *Federal Programs Supporting Educational Change: Vol. VIII. Implementing and Sustaining Change* (Santa Monica, Calif.: RAND Corporation, 1978).

22   Elmore and McLaughlin, *Steady Work*, 24.

23   Michael Fullan and Suzanne Stiegelbauer, *The New Meaning of Educational Change* (New York: Teachers College Press, 1991), 353-54.

24   Thomas J. Sergiovanni, *Leadership for the Schoolhouse* (San Francisco: Jossey-Bass, 1996), 47.

25   Sergiovanni, *Leadership for the Schoolhouse*, 163.

26   Elmore and McLaughlin, *Steady Work*, 36.

27   Henry M. Levin, "Accelerated Schools for Disadvantaged Students," *Educational Leadership* (March 1987): 19-21; James P. Comer, *Waiting for a Miracle: Why Schools Can't Solve Our Problems—And How We Can* (New York: Penguin Books, 1997); Deborah Meier, *The Power of Their Ideas* (Boston: Beacon Press, 1995); Theodore Sizer, *Horace's Hope: What Works for the American High School* (Boston: Houghton Mifflin, 1996).

28   Amie Watson et al., "A Lab School Explores Self-Governance," *Educational Leadership* 49 (February 1992): 57-61.

29   Deborah Meier, "Can the Odds Be Changed?" *Phi Delta Kappan* 79 (January 1998): 358-62.

30   Meier, "Can the Odds Be Changed," 359.

Chapter 7

Bringing Coals to
John Goodlad in Newcastle

Seymour B. Sarason

I do not envy future historians who will try to make sense of the educational reform movement in the post-World War II era. They will, of course, endeavor to explain why, as never before, public education rather quickly became a major and continuous source of social concern. The first Russian Sputnik, racial and ethnic diversity, the 1954 desegregation decision, the civil rights movement, the women's liberation movement, the turbulent sixties, technological changes, immigration, imploding cities, drugs, juvenile delinquency and crime, television—all of these and more will be grist for the historian's mill.

How did these factors, singly or in combination, impact schools? That question, I predict, will be *the* question future historians will try to answer. Who can quarrel with the importance of that question? I do not intend to quarrel with it when I say that the question is misleading and for two reasons. The first is that the question arises from a stimulus-response perspective. That is to say, larger social forces influenced, provoked, and exposed the inadequacies of our schools. The "outside" world required and demanded school change "inside," in accord with a changed zeitgeist. The second is that the question glosses over (or ignores) how and to what degree schools contributed to that altered zeitgeist. Were they passive victims or sitting ducks, so to speak, or were they contributors to that zeitgeist? Were they contributors only in the sense that they fought against caving in to those social forces, thereby proving that the criticisms directed to them were valid? That they contributed in that way goes without saying. But it did not take long before many educators sincerely agreed with the critics of schools and sought—with federal, state, and foundation support—to change accustomed ways. That, however, has not produced the desired results, a fact dispiriting and puzzling to almost everyone, critics and educators alike.

Is it possible that there is something about schools that not only caused them to be targets for change and criticism but will continue to defeat efforts to improve them? That schools have changed in many ways is one thing but that these changes are not synonymous with improvement is quite another. Have schools been both cause (stimulus) and effect (response) of the *past and present* zeitgeist? That is not a question likely to be asked by future historians who have to wrestle with a fantastically complex social era in which every major social institution underwent criticism and change. Schools were one such institution, one among many that felt the impact of a social change of sea swell proportions. The future historian will be mightily impressed, as he or she should be, with that generalized social change, and it will be understandable if that historian will not ask if schools have features requiring them to be examined differently than other institutions.

At this point, I have to say something without which the thrust of this paper loses its force and validity. I am predicting, as I have for a long time, that in the foreseeable future, schools will not improve in accomplishing their stated purposes, and they will continue to be a source of social instability and divisiveness, especially in our urban areas. In my more gloomy moments—I do not have a dysphoric temperament—I regard schools as a kind of social time bomb waiting to explode. In my less gloomy moments, I accept the possibility that the bomb will not explode and schools will be an ever-festering, social inflammation for which different medications are dreamed up at different times, kin to the common cold but far more serious. What I am suggesting or predicting is that the future historian will have to explain more than the role of schools in the past half-century. The future historian, say in 2025, will have to explain why in his or her day schools continue to defeat efforts to improve them. It will not be sufficient for that historian to look only at forces outside of schools for explanation. There is "something" inside of schools that, if not understood, guarantees that the more things change the more they will remain the same, independent of social change.

That "something" inheres in a theory of learning. More correctly, it inheres in an espoused theory that is not reflected or respected in American classrooms, generally speaking. I have written at length about this disjunction or contradiction and I cannot repeat my position here.

(Besides, I assume that the readers of a book paying homage to John Goodlad do not require an elaboration of my position.) Briefly, then, my argument is:

1. Children who enter the school for the first time are curious, question-asking characters. They are eager to learn, to feel the sense of growth, to be competent. In an inchoate way, they want to know more about self, others, and their world; an exciting and puzzling world they have seen on television or in movies, or have been told about by parents and other adults, and by their own experiences and observations.
2. They expect the teacher to be someone who will understand them, their questions, their interests, their individuality. They expect the teacher to help them feel competent, recognized, and worthy.
3. They are eager to conform to what a teacher says or does, and they expect that that conformity will sustain their eagerness, curiosity, and motivation to learn. You might say that these young children, again inchoately, want to feel that "the more you know the more you *need* and *want* to know," i.e., that sense of growth, that sense of wanting to know and do more, that sense that you have changed and willingly so.
4. The young student does not expect to be bored by and disinterested in what he or she is learning. The expectation is that the content of learning will have personal significance—that is, it will have utility in regard to the content of past and present experience, it will in some way speak to personal hopes, problems, ambitions, questions. It will not be encapsulated content peculiar to life in the classroom but to life outside.
5. The task of the teacher is to start "where the child is," to take seriously what was said in the four previous points. It is a subversion of those points to begin with a predetermined, calendar-driven curriculum that makes the recognition of and respect for individuality at best superficial and at worst impossible. To take satisfaction from having "successfully" completed a curriculum is akin to the surgeon saying that the operation was a success but the patient died.[1]

I have pointed to *some* of the bare bones of what I have called the context of productive learning. It is a context remarkably absent in all but a few American schools. Strange to say, when I have presented my critique to groups in the educational community, I have rarely been the recipient of criticism. Nor has anyone ever denied that my argument goes a long way to explaining why, as students traverse the middle and high school years, their boredom with and disinterest in learning steadily increases.

Labaree's recent book is entitled *How to Succeed in School without Really Learning.*[2] The book is far more serious than its title suggests. It is an important book in that it is a very reasoned and scholarly analysis of how consumerism and credentialism have impacted schools, thereby subverting their intellectual-educational goal of creating and sustaining contexts of productive learning. In his final chapter, he refers to the large-scale study by Steinberg, Brown, and Dornbusch of student attitudes, quoting the following from their book:

> Most of the time, what keeps students going in school is not intrinsic motivation—motivation derived from the process of learning itself—but extrinsic motivation—motivation that comes from the real or perceived consequences associated with success or failure, whether these consequences are immediate (in the form of grades, the reactions of parents, or the responses of friends) or delayed (in the form of anticipated impact in other educational settings or in the adult world of work).
>
> Over the course of their educational careers, students are increasingly exposed to extrinsic rewards for school work.[3]

Labaree in no way disputes the argument of Steinberg and colleagues, which, he says, is a psychological one—that is, an attitudinal problem that can be ameliorated by more parental engagement in their children's schooling, establishing and respecting higher academic standards, raising the costs of inadequate school performance and failure, and using standardized transcripts that employers can use to select the most academically accomplished applicants for jobs, etc. Labaree then goes on to say that

> as a sociologist, however, I have taken a different approach in trying to explain the dysfunctional characteristics of schooling identified by Steinberg. I have focused less on the attitudes and behaviors of the actors who populate United States education than on the systemic factors that have shaped these attitudes and behaviors. From the latter perspective, I have argued that many of the central problems facing education in the United States—student disengagement for one but, also such issues as social inefficiency and persistent social inequality—are in considerable part the result of market pressures on the educational system. Each chapter of this book is a study in educational consumerism and credentialism, which shows how the market perspective has come to dominate our view of education. By redefining education as a

commodity whose acquisition can help individuals get ahead of the pack, market pressures have led to the reconstruction of the educational system in the service of a private pursuit of individual advantage. This reconstruction around the goal of social mobility is far from complete, and it has been hotly contested over the years by supporters of competing educational goals, who argue for an educational system that serves to promote social efficiency and/ or democratic equality. But as I have tried to show, in one context after another, the influence of this private perspective on United States education has been profound.[4]

Just as Labaree does not dispute Steinberg's data and descriptions, I do not dispute his sociological analysis, which in essence says that outside forces have influenced, infiltrated, and given shape to the values of the school culture, values held by students, teachers, parents, and all but a few of the general public, although for him the most influential factor has been the private sector. Unlike Steinberg, Labaree offers no concrete suggestions for action. That, of course, is understandable because so few people are at all aware of the grip that consumerism and credentialism have on schooling. Although he does not say so, Labaree's splendid analysis is the opposite of encouraging in regard to Steinberg's suggested remedies. The problem is an ingrained cultural one that will be clarified and redefined, if it ever is, only by cultural changes of sea swell proportions that, at this point, are not visible on the societal horizon. It is hard to be optimistic, and I doubt that Labaree is. However, I have to add to this gloomy conclusion.

Let us imagine—and it is wild imagining—that people read Labaree's book and agree with him that consumerism and credentialism have no or little place in schooling, and that henceforth we will take seriously that the overarching goal of schooling is to help students build, and to capitalize on, an outlook they had when they started school: To want to learn more about self, others, and the world, and to do this in a way that is self-sustaining, intellectually and socially satisfying, and respectable, and stands a chance of becoming a lifelong characteristic and source of the sense of personal-intellectual growth. What conception of productive learning is required to achieve that overarching goal? Put in another way, the revolution has occurred, the old regime has been discredited, on what basis will the revolution be secured? It is one thing to say that our schools must no longer be contexts of unproductive learning; it is another to be clear about what you mean by contexts of productive learning. I have taken this up in several of my books, and I obviously cannot repeat my argument here.[5] The grip that consumerism and credentialism have had on schools is rivaled in force only by the grip of a conception of learning that guarantees contexts of unproductive learning. A revolution that glosses this over will have the fate of most revolutions: producing the opposite of what was intended.

Whatever I have said here has been said or implied in the writings of John Goodlad. What I have said is akin to bringing coals to Newcastle. John is in the John Dewey tradition and that is the highest accolade I can pay him. I am sure that John is in agreement with Labaree's argument, as I am sure that Dewey would have been. But like Dewey, Goodlad knows that in some ultimate sense the payoff is in how we define the features of productive learning.

A final note concerns charter schools, the creation of which represents an indictment of our educational system. They, in effect, reflect the conclusion that for a school to achieve its intellectual-educational goals, it must be separated from the existing system. Charter schools (at least the bulk of them) are intended to be bulwarks against rampant, stultifying consumerism and credentialism. That is, their emphasis is on individuality, the release and sustaining of student energies, and the sense of willing engagement with what, for purposes of brevity, I shall call the life of the mind. In two of my recent books, I venture the prediction that charter schools will fall far short of their mark for a number of reasons, among which fuzziness about productive learning is one of the most important.[6] The other reasons also have nothing to do with consumerism or a credentialism but rather with the lack of a conceptual rationale for how one creates a new setting that is unfamiliar to *everyone* in it.

Notes

1   See Albert Cullum, *The Geranium on the Window Sill Died, But Teacher You Went Right On* (New York: Harlin Quist, 1971). Albert Cullum, whom I got to know thirty years ago, was the most imaginative, creative teacher I have ever known. In 1971, he published this thin, poignant, compelling book of student poems, each accompanied by a drawing. The book is dedicated "to all of those grownups who, as children, died in the arms of compulsory education."

2   David F. Labaree, *How to Succeed in School without Really Learning: The Credentials Race in American Education* (New Haven: Yale University Press, 1997).

3   Lawrence D. Steinberg with B. Bradford Brown and Sanford M. Dornbusch, *Beyond the Classroom: Why School Reform Has Failed and What Parents Need to Do* (New York: Simon and Schuster, 1996) 75

4   Labaree, *How to Succeed in School without Really Trying*, 252.

5   Seymour B. Sarason, *Political Leadership and Educational Failure* (San Francisco: Jossey-Bass, 1998); and Seymour B. Sarason and Elizabeth Lorentz, *The Creation of Settings and the Future Societies* (San Francisco: Lexington Press, enlarged edition, 1998).

6   Sarason, *Political Leadership and Educational Failure*, and *Creation of Settings and the Future Societies*.

Chapter 8
_____

Back to *A Place Called School*

Theodore R. Sizer

In August of 1981, United States Secretary of Education Terrel Bell appointed the National Commission on Excellence in Education and requested that it report on the quality of schooling in America to the newly elected Reagan administration and to the American people.[1] The Commission, led by David Gardner, then president-elect of the University of California, was a distinguished group. Its specific charge was to respond to the "widespread public perception that something is seriously remiss in our educational system."[2] The group was to assess the nature of this condition and recommend to the Secretary, the President, and the public how to address it.

During these same months, John Goodlad and his colleagues based at the University of California at Los Angeles were hip deep in one of the largest and most sophisticated studies of American schooling ever undertaken. This Study of Schooling probed deeply into the workings of schools, depending far less on expert testimony or extrapolations about the goodness of schools and children from the latter's scores on brief paper-and-pencil tests and far more on painstakingly structured and sustained visits to a carefully selected group of schools, watching, recording, comparing, and assessing. The scale of the research project gave its conclusions great weight. As the dedication of the summary volume by Goodlad cites, "more than 27,000" individuals provided data.[3] Goodlad's team was advised by an outside group with impeccable scholarly credentials and was supported by fourteen of the country's largest and most discriminating private foundations. This was a Rolls-Royce of educational inquiries.

Not surprisingly, Commission Chairman Gardner turned to Professor Goodlad for help. The Study staff met with the Commission and offered access to all of its then-gathered material. Contact thereafter apparently was fleeting. The Commission's report, *A Nation at Risk: The Imperative for Educational Reform*, was issued in May 1983. Goodlad's public report, *A Place Called School: Prospects for the Future,* was published by McGraw-Hill in 1984. To a remarkable extent, the former reflected little either of the analysis of or the conclusions of the latter.

What had the staff of the Study of Schooling put before the Commission, what had the Commission heard, and what did the commissioners choose to make of it? The outsider today can speculate only by matching what the report recommended with what ultimately appeared in *A Place Called School.*[4] The book outlines several interwoven themes. From the vantage point of the late 1990s, several stand out starkly. They bear repetition.

The Study team found "a strange, rather indefinable sameness" among schools, "seating arrangements, materials being used, teachers' roles, students' roles, teaching methods."[5] There were differences, too; one of the Study's high schools was, the researchers felt, to be "near collapse."[6]

What emerged for Goodlad was a critical distinction. "*Schools* differ; *schooling* is everywhere very much the same. Schools differ in the way they conduct their business and in the way the people relate in them to one another in conducting that business. But the business of schooling is everywhere very much the same."[7]

This pattern of schooling was not expressly a representation of clearly stated district and state policies. "My major conclusion from perusing most state guides to education in schools," Goodlad wrote, "is that this entire area is a conceptual swamp."[8] "Comprehensive lists of goals are hard to find. Instead, one finds long lists of goals and objectives for the separate subject fields and, recently in many states and districts, lists of proficiencies students are to acquire for high school graduation or grade-to-grade promotion. And in my own visits to many schools, I find little evidence of goals consciously shared by the teachers and precious little dialogue about what their schools are for."[9] "There appears to be a formidable discrepancy between the goals for schooling . . . [articulated at a school] and curricular provision for their attainment."[10] The well-intentioned mindlessness within schools that had been so devastatingly portrayed by Charles Silberman in his popular *Crisis in the Classroom* a decade earlier was clearly still a fact of educational life.[11]

A disjunction between school and society—between the schools' curricular regimens and the youngsters' real worlds—emerged in the Study's inquiries. Goodlad saw "a picture of rather well-intentioned teachers going about their business somewhat detached from and not quite connecting with the 'other lives' of their students. What the students saw as primary concerns in their daily lives, teachers viewed as dissonance in conducting school. . . . Somewhere, I suspect, down in the elementary school, probably in the fifth and sixth grades, a subtle shift occurs. The curriculum—subjects, topics, textbooks, workbooks, and the rest—comes between teacher and student. Young humans come to be viewed only as students, valued primarily for their academic aptitude and industry rather than as individual persons preoccupied with the physical, social, and personal needs unique to their circumstances and stage in life."[12] Clearly, the disjunction between school and society, carefully documented by James Coleman and his colleagues in their 1974 *Youth: Transition to Adulthood* report to President Nixon's Science Advisory Committee, was still alive and well.[13]

Goodlad saw the inadequacies of schooling increasing as the students grew older.[14] He has been often heard to remark that the best-schooled American youngster is a kindergartner and the least a high school senior.[15] He was harsh with Americans' toleration of the distance between widely articulated ends and the reality of means. "The gap between the rhetoric of individual flexibility, originality, and creativity in our educational goals, and the cultivation of these in our schools reveals a great hypocrisy."[16] "Securing the grades necessary to a high school graduation certificate appears to be more important than the actual content of schooling and the classes taken."[17] Credentials were more important than content, especially that "content" implicit in each young person's informed capabilities and the respectful commitment to use these well.

In a variety of ways, Goodlad identified the boredom experienced by students in school, especially by adolescents. "Too few of the kinds of engagements we want young people to have with knowledge occur in the classroom setting." He elaborated: "it appears that large numbers of secondary teachers resort to practices designed to keep students passive and under control just at the time when adolescents should be taking more charge of their education."[18]

Goodlad summarized:

the modal classroom configurations which we observed looked like this: the teacher explaining or lecturing to the total class or a single student, occasion-

ally asking questions requiring factual answers; the teacher, when not lecturing, observing or monitoring students working individually at their desks; students listening or appearing to listen to the teacher and occasionally respond-
ing to the teacher's questions; students working individually at their desks on
reading or writing assignments; and all with little emotion, from interpersonal warmth to expressions of hostility.[19]

The Study team "observed that, on the average, about 75% of class
time was spent on instruction and that nearly 70% of this was 'talk'—
usually teacher to students. Teachers out-talked the class of students
by a ratio of about three to one. . . . The bulk of this teacher talk was
instructing in the sense of telling. Barely 5% of this instructional time
was designed to create students' anticipation of needing to respond.
Not even 1% required some kind of open response involving reasoning or perhaps an opinion from students."[20] The error of this approach was highlighted by Goodlad, citing research extending back to
the Eight-Year Study and Project Talent: "facts students are able to
recall in classroom examinations are up to 80% forgotten just two
years later."[21]

These sorts of findings have been uncovered over and over since
the 1970s. The appalling waste of time and imagination in most
American classrooms was nicely recounted by Mihaly Csikszentmihalyi
and Reed Larson in *Being Adolescent*. In a typical mid-1980s high
school classroom, they wrote, "at least half the time the student is not
really thinking about anything even remotely related to the lecture or
to the subject matter."[22] There was little engagement, little spark, little
connection between the ideas of the classroom and the position of the
student.

Goodlad had much to say about the world of teachers. "To reach
out positively and supportively to 27 youngsters for five hours or so
each day in an elementary-school classroom is demanding and ex-
hausting. To respond similarly to four to six successive classes of 25
or more students each at the secondary level may be impossible."[23]
He wrote of the isolation and fragmentation of much of the teacher's
regimen, and of the autonomy that the individual classroom provided.
The latter was popular with teachers. He challenged the dominant
metaphor for teachers' workplaces: "Schools and classrooms cannot
be understood or accurately and usefully described by the relatively
simplistic input-output factory model so often used; they are better
understood as little villages in which individuals interact on a part-
time basis within a relatively constrained and confining environment."[24]

Goodlad's study team examined student grouping practices and found that "effective instructional practices were found to be more characteristic of high than of low classes. Students in the lower tracks were the least likely to experience the types of instruction most highly associated with achievement."[25] When tracking was eliminated, "most of the mixed classes resembled the high more than the low track classes in nearly all of the areas studied."[26] Goodlad concluded that

> popular assumptions and myths regarding headedness and handedness, good and poor students, fast and slow learners, and the like are generally accepted and at the outset built into classroom organization. Instead of creating circumstances that minimize and compensate for initial disadvantages in learning, teachers unwittingly create conditions that increase the difficulty of eliminating disadvantage. . . . Tracking . . . is perceived to be a logical and expedient way to take account of wide differences in students' academic attainments. In effect, however, it serves as an organizational device for hiding awareness of the problem rather than an educative means for correcting it.[27]

Such are samples of the argument and findings of A Study of Schooling. Many had been, or soon were to be, reinforced, extended, or challenged by the work of other researchers.[28] All are nuanced, careful, and thorough, yielding a picture that is devastatingly recognizable to those who know schools well. The picture is necessarily complex. "The realization of this complexity is a first step away from myths and simplistic notions of roads to improvement such as more discipline by teachers and proficiency tests for grade-to-grade promotion. . . . I do in fact doubt that schooling, as presently conceived and conducted, is capable of providing large segments of young people with the education they and this democracy require."[29] He concluded, "The agenda suggested by the data presented will not be carried out by a little tinkering."[30]

A Place Called School was a volume of 361 pages, plus 19 pages of notes and references. *A Nation at Risk* was a report of 36 pages—in large type and with generous margins—plus 25 pages of appendices. Both had similar audiences: the serious public, educators, and policymakers. Their strategies for dissemination, however, were strikingly different.

Goodlad called on his readers to read long and hard, a rigorous exercise that, in his view, was absolutely necessary work. *A Place Called School* was deliberately light on detailed recommendations; these were to follow state by state, district by district, school by school, college by college, with the Study's critique providing a solid platform.

Goodlad clearly wanted his readers to *think differently* about learning and schooling as a prelude to action.

On the other hand, Gardner and his colleagues clearly wanted to create a thunderclap, thus to get people's attention. And the people's attention would be caught by artful language and simple, familiar, understandable remedies. The Commission's report was to be an opening salvo for sustained reform and, while not a definitive blueprint, to provide at least a framework for action, a list of recommendations from which (say) a governor could launch his or her state's reform effort. The Commission wanted the country to move toward resolute action, *now*.

The rhetoric of *A Nation at Risk* is memorable. "Our Nation is at risk. Our once unchallenged preeminence in commerce, industry, science and technological innovation is being overtaken. . . . If an unfriendly power had attempted to impose on America the mediocre educational performance that exists today, we might have viewed it as an act of war. . . . Our concern . . . goes well beyond matters such as industry and commerce. It includes the intellectual, moral, and spiritual strengths of our people which knot together the very fabric of our society."[31]

This apocalyptic language worked. It got the attention of the nation, and even of the astonished president who had no idea of the bold message that the Commission of his administration might put before the people.[32] Goodlad received excellent reviews in important places. Gardner got on Page One.

The Commission focused on the effects of weak schooling rather than the causes of weak schooling. It produced a barrage of specific data including test scores, course enrollments, comparisons with foreign nations, and specific complaints from business and government employers about school graduates. It painted these universally mediocre indexes against a background of a new, global labor market. The commissioners quoted Paul Hurd: "We are raising a new generation of Americans that is scientifically and technologically illiterate" and John Slaughter who "warned of 'a growing chasm between a small scientific and technological elite and a citizenry ill-informed, indeed uninformed, on issues with a science component.'"[33]

The Commission identified a "national sense of frustration . . . a dimming of personal expectations and a fear of losing a shared vision for America."[34] The commissioners painted a need for what they termed a Learning Society and argued that "for too many people education means doing the minimum work necessary for the moment, then coasting through life on what may have been learned in its first quarter . . . (w)here there should have been a continuum of learning, we have none, but instead an often incoherent, outdated patchwork quilt."[35]

The Commission was no less disturbed than was Goodlad on the sloppiness in defining the purpose for the schools. The commissioners outlined four sets of "Findings." Regarding "content . . . the very 'stuff' of education," they asserted that "secondary school curricula have been homogenized, diluted, and diffused to the point that they have no longer a central purpose." Regarding "expectations," they found these to be shoddy. Regarding "time," they found too little spent on the serious matters of schooling, especially in contrast with that allocated for academic education in competing industrial nations. Finally, regarding teaching, they despaired over the weak academic background of teachers-in-training, the excessive emphasis in that training on "educational methods," poor salaries, limited professional influence over text selection, and great shortages in certain academic fields.[36]

The silences are revealing. There were no "findings" whatever about the realities of classrooms, about the boredom of students, and the disjunction between their world and that offered them up in school, about the very design and daily functioning of schools and the waste that such produces or of the lack of connection between what is known about learning and current widespread practice—that is, about the guts of Goodlad's findings.

There were five omnibus recommendations. For "Content," there were to be "Five New Basics . . . (1) 4 years of English; (2) 3 years of mathematics; (3) 3 years of science; (4) 3 years of social studies; and (5) one-half year of computer science," with two years of foreign language strongly recommended.[37] "Schools, colleges, and universities [should] adopt more rigorous and measurable standards . . . for academic performance and student conduct."[38] There was to be "significantly more time devoted to learning the New Basics."[39] Several discrete initiatives would "improve the preparation of teachers," these having to do with matters of standards, salaries, contracts, career ladders, and incentives.[40] Finally, there were recommendations for "Leadership and Fiscal Support," none suggesting a significant change in the balance of power among traditional stakeholders but expecting deep, new, and coordinated commitments from each.[41]

Was all this the "tinkering" that Goodlad urged us to avoid? Perhaps. But one person's tinkering is another's belief of what is practically doable. Clearly, the Commission believed that there had to be renewed—even unprecedented—commitments made to achieve America's needed "learning society." So did Goodlad. The differences between the two are found in the nature and scope of those commitments, and these differences may reflect more than merely choice among tactics.

Crudely put, while both Goodlad and Gardner accepted the notion of formal education—important things happening for and to children in places called schools—Goodlad, as the result of his research, recommended significant rethinking and redesign of those schools while Gardner's Commission wanted those schools, essentially structured as at present, simply to be pushed much harder. Goodlad wanted new sorts of schools. Gardner wanted the sorts of schools we currently had to do a better job. Goodlad clearly believed that without significant change inside those places called school, serious improvements were impossible. Gardner believed that an aroused public and polity could make the existing system work.

In the short run, the Commission was remarkably successful in its quest for renewed public and political concern for education. After the release of its report, every state in one form or another created commissions or task forces to respond to its call. Presidents and governors met. State "standards" and "curricular frameworks" spewed forth lists that may have largely dodged many of the deep problems of purpose that so troubled Goodlad's researchers, but at least they gave a semblance of consistency of purpose, largely in the form of curricula. The New Basics, already familiar in every high school in the country, were re-embraced. The system was ordered to shape up, and given how difficult this was to be in practice, administrators' heads rolled with striking frequency. By the mid-1990s, the nation was awash in new tests. There was talk of longer school years. The rhetoric of toughness and rigor ruled.

America appeared to be taking its "risk" seriously—a substantial accomplishment for a small commission that had been, in fact, expected to start and end in obscurity. Gardner's tactics were brilliant. The Commission had effectively sounded a call for educational reform, with concise eloquence, in acceptably familiar ways that were not too hard. The country took heed.

Why did *A Nation at Risk* spawn such a reaction? While it is tricky to write contemporary history, several explanations seem worth taking seriously.

First, the stage for fundamental reconsideration of public education had been set. The triggers were the launching of Sputnik in 1957 and the reformist surge of the Eighty-Ninth Congress and its passage of a Civil Rights Act and the Elementary and Secondary Education Act (ESEA). The former authorized the influential study of equality of educational opportunity led by James Coleman, the first sweeping study ever of education in terms of the performance of the students rather than the provision of opportunities for those students. ESEA, and its cousins found in legislation related to the so-called War on Poverty, gave national muscle to the new attention to underschooled Americans and to the inequities and incompetencies of the system.[42]

Over the next twenty years, a series of critiques and studies accelerated the pounding absorbed by the existing system. The raft of angry testimonials such as Jonathan Kozol's *Death at an Early Age* and equally angry social science studies such as Samuel Bowles's and Herbert Gintis's *Schooling in Capitalist America*, all products of the late 1960s and early 1970s, fueled the erosion of public confidence in the schools that it knew.[43] The National Assessment of Educational Progress (NAEP), a federal "thermometer" of the work of American schoolchildren launched in 1970, built on the example of the equal educational opportunity study by providing data about the performance of the system rather than merely its provision, and the NAEP results sustained the slowly growing distrust on the part of an influential public of the efficacy of the system of schools Americans provided for their children. For example, tuition tax credits—the indirect but consequential support of families choosing private schools—was a small, but interesting part of the agenda of the first Nixon administration. National attention increasingly focused on evidence of students' performance, and a major study of the meaning of the "slipping" scores on the Scholastic Aptitude Test of the College Board was conducted during the late 1970s by a commission chaired by former United States Secretary of Labor Willard Wirtz.[44]

Soon the traditionally mawkish sentiments about public education so familiar during the 1950s began to fade, and with them the post-World War II knee-jerk practice of pouring resources into the expansion of a school system whose existing design was unquestioned. The time for a trumpet call to reform had arrived. By the early 1980s, if it had not existed, the National Commission on Excellence in Education would have had to be invented.

One can say the same about A Study of Schooling. The foundations that elected to support Goodlad were as much influenced by the accelerating challenge to the educational *status quo* as any other prominent American institution. The time for agonizing reappraisal was at hand, and the public appeared to be prepared.

And yet, one wonders. While political, foundation, and business leaders, and the lions of the press were disturbed, how deep was their distress and, equally, the distress of the public?

One hazards a guess that the distress was not very deep by looking in two places: the ideas formulated by the collective, albeit usually self-appointed, leadership for the public schools; and the scale of financial resources energetically allocated by local, state, and federal governments for fundamental reform.

In neither case was there vigorous response, in the 1980s or the 1990s, with the single and interesting exception of the ultimate fallout of the Education for All Handicapped Americans Act passed and signed during the Nixon administration. There is no question that the ordinary American school pays attention differently—that is, more responsively—to the children in its midst with special physical or emotional needs in the 1990s than had been the case in the 1970s; and the notable rise in school-level educational expenditures for children who have special needs since the mid-1980s can largely be attributed to that focused and stubbornly led initiative.

However, the exception proves the rule. Beyond this legislation, the *ancien régime* persisted. One can only conclude that the public and the polity, for whatever reasons, were largely satisfied with the existing shape and routines of the familiar place called school, even though they worried about them rhetorically. What David Tyack and Larry Cuban call the "grammar" of schooling—the detailed ways and means of providing deliberate education—remained intact.[45]

What John Goodlad was addressing was this very grammar—the ideas, practices, and routines of schooling and the attitudes that lay behind them. Goodlad might have had generous cheerleaders, but the establishment, beyond its rhetoric, was only weakly behind him. On the other hand, the National Commission essentially reinforced the existing apparatus, only urging it to do much, much better. It did not recommend an initiative comparable with its rhetoric—a 1980s version for education of the 1960s war on poverty. Far from it; and the Commission probably read the country's attitudes correctly.

America wanted a new dawn to an old day. If Americans were to reinvigorate their schools, they would do so by rallying the existing army rather than recruiting any sort of new one. Even the privatizing of education, which seemed an interesting prospect to many Reagan supporters, sparked no widespread positive response. That idea, and its varied kin, for the moment went nowhere.

A second reason for the impact of *A Nation at Risk*, and the state and district steps following upon its release, was its challenge *to*, but not challenge *of*, the existing educational hierarchy. In the jargon of the time, the powers-that-be were to gather the existing stakeholders and energize them to push for new levels of excellence.

There is a paradox here, as professional educators and the bureaucracies in which they had sat for generations were under extraordinary rhetorical assault. They were frequently and unflatteringly referred to as a "blob" in the way of reform, yet by the mid 1990s had recouped most of their lost power, and, with the stick of testing, had added to it. Reagan himself pledged to disband the Department of Education, even as it grew in scale and scope over his eight-year tenure. Business leaders called for new sorts of management requiring new sorts of administrators, but no prominent business schools started substantial, focused programs for school administrators.

From all the talk, one might have expected a fundamental shift in the way public education was governed and financed. This was not to be. The momentum of existing practice was believed to be too strong to provide new arrangements with much chance for success. The sanctity of the symbols of school—graduation at age eighteen, homecoming, taking American history in the eleventh grade, Friday night football, sorting wealthier kids from less wealthy kids and kids of color, and the like—were deeply embedded in the ways the American middle class shaped its experience. Alternatives to this, however ingenious and rational, had, not surprisingly, little political traction.

The National Commission apparently sensed this reality. The commissioners recommended "that citizens across the Nation hold educators and elected officials responsible for providing the leadership necessary to achieve these reforms."[46] The Commission did not recommend changing just who these officers might be or whether power among them might be redistributed, much less even mention these possibilities. The commissioners read the political tea leaves and left the existing power relationships much as they were. Not surprisingly, the existing power groups grasped eagerly onto the report. These groups had the authority to move quickly, and move they did. The report extended their power, rather than clipping it.

Finally, there was no national, respected, and tough-minded base to rally the ideas and aspirations of the diverse constituencies within education to the cause of the kinds of reform implicit in A Study of Schooling. Public education lacked an influential community of independent academics and policymakers that characterized higher visibility professions such as those in law and medicine.

On the contrary, the university-based concentrations of people concerned with the schools were largely gathered into underfunded, overregulated (by the states), and overenrolled colleges of education, which for many institutions were at once cash cows for their university writ large and objects of scorn by the better-funded members of sister faculties. Limited persuasive and probing research was forwarded within them, and what did emerge was usually highly circumscribed and all too often shrouded in an intramural jargon that insured its limited effect.

Not surprisingly, education professors closed in on themselves, and their national associations, again while numerous, remained relatively remote from influential counterparts in related areas, neither influencing nor drawing from them in consequential ways. The political and material costs of this insularity, while difficult precisely to measure, were substantial. Nationally, there were few highly respected academics drawing on deep and wide research on learning and schooling who could insist that the National Commission pay very respectful attention to what Goodlad was saying, even if this meant shaping the Commission's ultimate report in ways that did not largely reflect the limited and limiting conventional wisdom of the times. They could have spurred the Commission to dramatic and compelling recommendations as bold as its rhetoric of the risks the nation confronted.

The National Commission's report provoked great activity, sustained for over a decade. The national problem of inadequate schooling—and inadequate learning—is now widely acknowledged. Homilies about how nice teachers are and the wonders of this year's football team are now permanently joined by harsh demands for high standards and a better academic "product."

The conventional remedies suggested by the Commission will run their course, leading to a resurgence of frustration. The existing system, even if threatened, cannot carry the load of national needs without fundamental rethinking and consequent redesign. All the testing currently in vogue will narrow instruction to what it takes to get good grades on mass-produced, machine-graded tests and will tell us once again that poor kids score less well than rich kids. It will also suggest that, if conventionally taught, neither poor nor rich youngsters will demonstrate the deep and sustained understanding of important ideas that truly matters to a nation profoundly at risk. In time, inevitably, there will be agonizing reappraisals.

It is at this point that A Study of Schooling will gain the leverage it deserves. The frustration of the moment could lead to a reanalysis of what and how young people in our time learn, and that reanalysis could inform a surge of constructive interest in a new and more effective form of schooling than the one that Americans have used for almost one hundred years. That Goodlad's data were collected twenty years ago will make little difference because the patterns he chronicles and critiques are still sweepingly familiar. The breathtaking waste of time and treasure tolerated in many schools is no less with us today than when today's middle schoolers' mothers were twelfth graders. There is a sad, almost eerie relevance to the detailed specifics of Goodlad's critique.

A Nation at Risk was crucial for its moment. *A Place Called School* is crucial for the longer haul. Gardner dramatically attracted and focused the attention of the nation. Goodlad suggested what that nation must ponder as it shapes new and better schools.

If Americans stay the course of reform, if they are encouraged to do the hard work of thinking deeply about the issues of learning and schooling, history will mark well the special—and necessarily consecutive—contributions of both grand efforts of the early 1980s.

Goodlad needed Gardner. And as the times ripen, Gardner will need Goodlad.

Notes

1 National Commission on Excellence in Education, *A Nation at Risk: The Imperative for Educational Reform* (Washington D.C.: U.S. Government Printing Office, 1983), see introductory frontmatter.

2 National Commission on Excellence in Education, *A Nation at Risk*, 1.

3 John I. Goodlad, *A Place Called School* (New York: McGraw-Hill, 1984), iii.

4 A set of internal documents produced by the Commission rests at the John Hay Library at Brown University. However, no detailed record of the internal discussion related directly to Goodlad's contribution appears there.

5 Goodlad, *A Place Called School*, 27.

6 Goodlad, A Place Called School, 28.

7 Goodlad, *A Place Called School*, 264.

8 Goodlad, *A Place Called School*, 48.

9 Goodlad, *A Place Called School*, 50.

10 Goodlad, *A Place Called School*, 280, parentheses in the original.

11 Charles E. Silberman, *Crisis in the Classroom: The Remaking of American Education* (New York: Random House, 1970).

12 Goodlad, *A Place Called School*, 80.

13 United States President's Science Advisory Committee Panel on Youth, *Youth: Transition to Adulthood* (Chicago: University of Chicago Press, 1974), Part IV especially.

14 Goodlad, *A Place Called School*, 165, 166.

15 Personal recollection of this essay's author.

16 Goodlad, *A Place Called School*, 241.

17 Goodlad, *A Place Called School*, 191.

18 Goodlad, *A Place Called School*, 192.

19 Goodlad, *A Place Called School*, 230.

20 Goodlad, *A Place Called School*, 229.

21 Goodlad, *A Place Called School*, 231.

22 Mihaly Csikszentmihalyi and Reed Larson, *Being Adolescent: Conflict and Growth in the Teenage Years* (New York: Basic Books, 1984), 257.

23   Goodlad, *A Place Called School*, 112.

24   Goodlad, *A Place Called School*, 113.

25   Goodlad, *A Place Called School*, 155.

26   Goodlad, *A Place Called School*, 156.

27   Goodlad, *A Place Called School*, 164, 297.

28   See, for example, a potpourri of studies around themes raised in Goodlad's book, *A Place Called School*; Seymour B. Sarason, *The Culture of the School and the Problem of Change* (Boston: Allyn and Bacon, 1971, revised in 1997 by Teachers College Press); Mary Haywood Metz, *Classrooms and Corridors: The Crisis of Authority in Desegregated Secondary Schools* (Berkeley: University of California Press, 1978); Sarah Lawrence Lightfoot, *The Good High School: Portraits of Character and Culture* (New York: Basic Books, 1983); Howard Gardner, *Frames of Mind: The Theory of Multiple Intelligences* (New York: Basic Books, 1983); Arthur G. Powell, Eleanor Farrar, and David K. Cohen, *The Shopping Mall High School: Winners and Losers in the Educational Marketplace* (Boston: Houghton Mifflin, 1986); Tracy Kidder, *Among Schoolchildren* (Boston: Houghton Mifflin, 1989); Milbrey McLaughlin, Joan E. Talbert, and Nina Bascia, eds., *The Contexts of Teaching in Secondary Schools: Teachers' Realities* (New York: Teachers College Press, 1990); Paul T. Hill, Gail E. Foster, Tamar Gendler, *High Schools with Character* (Santa Monica, Calif.: RAND Corporation, 1990); David Perkins, *Smart Schools: From Training Memories to Educating Minds* (New York: Free Press, 1992); Mike Rose, *Possible Lives: The Promise of Public Education in America* (Boston: Houghton Mifflin, 1995); Deborah Meier, *The Power of Their Ideas: Lessons for America from a Small School in Harlem* (Boston: Beacon Press, 1995); Linda Darling-Hammond, *The Right to Learn: A Blueprint for Creating Schools That Work* (San Francisco: Jossey-Bass, 1997). The subtitles alone tell much of the publishers' judgments about what the serious reading public might choose to read about schooling.

29   Goodlad, *A Place Called School*, 81, 91.

30   Goodlad, *A Place Called School*, 358.

31   *A Nation at Risk*, 5, 6.

32   Terrel H. Bell, *The Thirteenth Man: A Reagan Cabinet Memoir* (New York: Free Press, 1988).

33   *A Nation at Risk*, 10.

34   *A Nation at Risk*, 11, 12.

35   *A Nation at Risk*, 14.

36   *A Nation at Risk*, 18–23.

37   *A Nation at Risk*, 24.

38   *A Nation at Risk*, 27.

39   *A Nation at Risk*, 29.

40   *A Nation at Risk*, 30–31.

41   *A Nation at Risk*, 32–33.

42   James S. Coleman et al., *Equality of Educational Opportunity* (two volumes) (Washington, D.C.: U.S. Government Printing Office, 1966). The most careful contemporary analysis of this study is Frederick Mosteller and Daniel Patrick Moynihan, eds., *On Equality of Educational Opportunity* (New York: Random House, 1972).

43   Jonathan Kozol, *Death at an Early Age* (Boston: Houghton Mifflin, 1967). Samuel Bowles and Herbert Gintis, *Schooling in Capitalist America: Educational Reform and the Contradictions of Economic Life* (New York: Basic Books, 1976).

44   College Entrance Examination Board, Advisory Panel on the Scholastic Aptitude Test Score Decline, *On Further Examination: A Report of the Advisory Panel on the Scholastic Aptitude Test Score Decline* (New York: College Entrance Examination Board, 1977).

45   David Tyack and Larry Cuban, *Tinkering Toward Utopia: A Century of Public School Reform* (Cambridge: Harvard University Press, 1995), chapter 4.

46   *A Nation at Risk*, 32.

Chapter 9

Renewing High Schools:
What John Goodlad Says . . .

Janice M. Reeder

Introduction

I met John Goodlad and it changed my life. It was in 1985, the beginning of a new wave of school reform, and I was a high school principal. As part of a school-university partnership initiative sponsored by the University of Washington, I had read current books on school reform, including Goodlad's *A Place Called School*.[1] I was very intrigued with the ideas in these books and anxious to find out how to implement them. While many of the authors spoke in glowing terms of ideals, they said little about implementation.

In *A Place Called School*, Goodlad says that the school should develop the talent of each individual student. I believed in providing opportunities for success for every student, but Goodlad seemed to go beyond that. He said that we could advance the specific skills and the talents of each student. I wanted to meet John Goodlad to ask him how we could go about doing this, and finally at a social reception at the University of Washington, I got my chance. After we were introduced, I posed the question, "How can we redesign schools so that we can develop the talents of each individual student?" Goodlad said to me, "It is up to you to determine how to implement these ideas." This was a decisive moment. I realized I could read all the books on high school reform and get all of the good ideas for reforming schools, but it was going to be up to me to determine how to put these ideas into practice. That became my goal, my challenge, and my ultimate satisfaction in the remaining thirteen years of my career as a high school principal.

It was only the beginning of my relationship with John Goodlad. He continued his association with the University of Washington and, over the next several years, conducted brown bag lunch seminars for principals and presented a series of lectures, all of which I attended. It is my purpose in this essay to discuss the strategies and tactics I developed to implement the ideas I gleaned from my association with John Goodlad.

Sustaining Innovations: Understanding Change

Goodlad says that there have been thousands of innovations in education over the last thirty years, few of which are still in place today. According to Goodlad, it is *not* understanding the change process that has kept these innovations from being sustained. I was determined to implement significant, long-term improvements in my school, so I became a serious student of educational change. Through my studies, I developed some key strategies for implementing and, I hoped, sustaining significant improvements in high schools.

I listened carefully to Goodlad's ideas on the ecology of school renewal.[2] He sees school reform as needing to be embedded in the ongoing life and culture of the school. This concept urged me to implement continuous change strategies in the everyday life of my school. In the beginning, teachers were irritated when I started discussing new concerns before we had even finished our current efforts. Eventually, they, too, began to look ahead and to accept that we needed always to be working on something.

I learned from other readings that people change when they see the need to change and when they know how to change.[3] I found it important to help teachers gain an understanding of the reason for addressing any particular change being proposed. Providing data in an easily understood format and making time available to discuss and process the information builds this understanding. For example, we first began considering a new daily schedule after several task forces working on other needed improvements found the daily schedule to be a barrier. So teachers came to understand that there was a need to consider a different schedule. Later, after a new schedule was implemented, we had numerous visitors from schools also considering a different schedule. Very few of them seemed to understand what needs they were trying to meet with a new schedule. As a result, most were quite apprehensive about changing.

People must see the need for the change before they can begin considering how to change. After becoming convinced of the need for a change, teachers usually need some kind of training and time to learn to make the change. Providing this kind of professional development is a critical step in the change process. To implement the new schedule, teachers needed training on how to adapt their instruction to longer instructional blocks. Moreover, teacher concerns continued to surface and needed to be addressed throughout the change process.

Another strategy that I discovered is getting authorization or buy-in for an innovation in advance. Previously, I had helped committees significantly advance good ideas. However, there was always a glitch in the process. By the time they brought their work to the total faculty for implementation, they were too far ahead of the others, and the total faculty resisted the change. The whole group could not see the vision developed by the committee. However, when the whole staff authorizes a group to investigate an innovation right from the beginning, teachers are much more receptive to listening to proposals later on. As an example, in one of my schools, a few teachers got the idea for a "Senior Exhibition" at a conference they attended. Instead of developing a specific proposal to present to the staff, they brought the conference presenters to the school and convinced the rest of the staff of the need to pursue this innovation. Later, when members of a task force brought a specific proposal to the staff, they were quite receptive.

Implementing advising periods ("advisories") in a high school—not an easy task—is a good example of all these change strategies in action. To help staff members understand the importance of the idea, I first proposed providing more guidance to students in course selection so that they could better meet their own talents and needs. Counselors could not provide this kind of guidance to over four hundred students. Teachers agreed with the need and indicated that they would be willing to help a small number of students with course selections if they knew the students. They agreed to explore the concept of an advisory program, and since they had authorized a smaller group to develop this program, they were receptive to a specific proposal when it was presented.

The task force was deliberate about presenting dimensions of the program to the staff as they were developed. This allowed them to determine teacher concerns at every point in the process and to develop responses to the concerns. We would regularly review how advisories were going, identify concerns, and make adjustments in the structure, content, or strategies of delivery to assist teachers in dealing with their concerns. Early in the implementation of advisories, teachers were concerned with how they would prepare for the lessons they would be expected to deliver in the advisory period. Later, as they became comfortable with the presentations, they questioned how the groups were selected and requested to work with students they were most comfortable with. These very different concerns required different kinds of modifications to the implementation process.

Training was provided for teachers so that they would be better prepared for the advisory periods. In the beginning, teachers had a chance to prepare for every lesson they delivered. They participated in an afternoon of training before the very first advisory session. At that time, their colleagues demonstrated the first five lessons, providing excellent instructional models. Later, they were provided time on their own for lesson preparation. This change to advisories has been sustained over a period of ten years. This is due, I think, to the commitment that teachers had to the need for the change, the involvement they had in the design, the training they received, and the constant revisions that have been made over the years to respond to their concerns.

All of this adds up to *empowering people*. Goodlad says that the school is the unit of change and that teachers need to be agents of their own change process. I had been committed to authentic participation and had developed effective advisory councils for teachers and parents, but it was not until site-based decision making was imposed on my school—ironic, to be sure—that I learned the power of shared decision making. When advisory councils became formal decision-making groups, teachers finally joined our school reform movement. Although Goodlad never talked explicitly about the various structures that might emerge around site-based management notions in the early 1990s, he anticipated all the more important, underlying ideas that I realized were needed to implement the innovation.

Consensus decision making is the key to successful site councils. Through consensus, decisions are made that everyone can live with. To reach consensus, each participant must share his/her concerns and each concern must be addressed in the final decision. Effective site councils must include teachers, administrators, parents, and students to ensure that all relevant concerns are heard and addressed. I have found that principals play a key role in the success of consensus decision making. They are, most importantly, part of the consensus and their concerns must be addressed in the decisions made by the site council. Additionally, principals monitor policies, rules, and laws to ensure that all decisions are in compliance. Principals also play a key role in providing the information that the site council members need in order to understand and solve problems. Parents and students have special information needs since they approach the problems of education from different directions, and principals need to be aware of this. Principals also can play a critical role as "keepers of the faith." They can monitor decisions for congruence with the mission, beliefs, or goals of the school or district. Another key site council role is that of facilitator. This can be any member of the site council who is skilled in managing the typical group process functions. Much of the success of the group is due to effective facilitation, and this person should be carefully selected.

The consensus by all of these stakeholders fosters incredible ownership. Teachers, reluctant to change, feel supported because their concerns are heard and addressed. Teachers exert pressure on their peers to participate in the agreed-upon actions. When outside opposition occurs, the staff and community will present a unified and very powerful front. I have found on several occasions that when such opposition arises, it is often teachers not directly involved in designing the innovation who voice the strongest support. Having participated in making the decision, they have just as much ownership as the teachers directly involved in the development of the innovation.

I believe, with Goodlad, that shared decision making is essential for significant change to occur in schools. Engaging the expertise of teachers in school reform, creating widespread ownership by consensus decision making, and using the expertise of the principal to "keep it all moving" ensures that good decisions will actually lead to strong improvements in the school. Clearly, significant innovations are needed in today's schools. Understanding the change process is critical to implementing and sustaining these innovations.

Democracy in Education

Goodlad says that all students should have equal access to knowledge. He calls this the democratization of education. This concept has affected my work significantly in several ways as I have tried to translate this into equitable teaching and learning for all students.

I have been guided by the concept that the students with the greatest needs should receive the most resources. It is typical for schools to give their best resources and their best teachers to their best students.

This practice results in many forms of tracking and providing resources to students who can articulate their needs or who have the most assertive and demanding parents. While it is important to respond to these students' needs, it should not be done at the expense of more needy students. Extra resources should be spent on the students who are having the least success in school. If there are to be small classes, they should not be for advanced classes as much as they should be for remedial classes. All too often, schools offer small sections of advanced placement classes taught by the best teachers for their gifted students. This practice results in larger classes elsewhere on the schedule. In my schools, we were able to challenge gifted students in advanced electives open to *any* students, and these classes still prepared students for the advanced placement exams.

There are very few instances where it is appropriate to group students by ability. Goodlad says that in most honors courses, students are selected by achievement rather than by aptitude, leading to much more diversity in ability than commonly believed. Yet, according to Goodlad, teachers often teach such gifted classes as if the students all have high abilities. Because some teachers prefer to teach these "high track" classes to avoid the range of abilities they encounter in a more heterogeneous class, inappropriate pedagogy is often the result.

If we want to teach democracy, we have to model it by heterogeneous grouping of students in classrooms. Students must learn to appreciate and respect diverse views, abilities, and cultures. The biggest challenge for teachers is to respond to the wide range of ability levels of students in a heterogeneous classroom. It is important to provide teachers with resources and training to do this. There are strong and effective instructional strategies, including cooperative learning, that provide gains for students at both extremes of ability and achievement. Having students learn from each other is powerful. Removing the best and the brightest from classrooms is not fair to either end of the academic spectrum; lower ability students miss out on models to inspire them, and higher ability students miss out on the rich interaction of a more diverse environment.[4] Heterogeneous classrooms make educational sense as well as providing an environment in which to learn democratic principles.

Finally, democratic principles are best honored in a democratic process. If we want to ensure an equitable education for all children, it is more likely to occur in a process of shared decision making with representation of all stakeholders. In a site-based decision-making process that is working well, teachers and parents are informed about the needs of all students and experience first-hand the complexity of allocating resources fairly. Moreover, giving financial information to all the staff removes the impression that not everyone is getting his/her fair share. An open process of allocating resources engenders a commitment to the total needs of the school and models democracy in action.

Integrating Curriculum

Goodlad says that schools continue to attempt to "do it all," to meet an extremely wide range of educational agendas rather than focusing on a few aims. To be more successful in my schools, we had to, indeed, narrow our focus. We found that becoming clear about our primary outcomes led to more integration of courses and knowledge.

As I began observing teachers in all disciplines, I was surprised by the amount of overlap in the content as well as in the skills being taught. Teachers were not aware that someone else down the hall was teaching the same concept or using the same strategy to teach the same skills. Thus, as principal, I began to advocate a process of curriculum integration that began with asking questions about what we wanted our students to know and be able to do. Teachers were able to agree on a crucial subset of the most important outcomes for students after four years of high school. They then discussed how each course could make a specific contribution to some of the outcomes. This discussion revealed where disciplines intersected and encouraged further conversation on integration of curriculum.

Goodlad says that the divisions in the subjects encourage a segmented rather than an integrated view of knowledge. Indeed, we discovered that we had to address the issue of over-specialization in our curriculum. Interdisciplinary conversations are not easy, especially at the high school level, where teachers tend to focus narrowly on their disciplines. However, we found that high school teachers can be quite receptive to learning how their subject influences other subjects. In discussing what outcomes we wanted for students, the English and social studies teachers saw both the need and the ways to integrate their classes. Of course, English and social studies are relatively easier to work with since many teachers have some preparation in both subjects. Giving teachers adequate time to discuss their curricula reveals the common ground and enhances their commitment to integrate their courses. I once found that both ninth-grade English and social studies classes had a unit on Native Americans, but only the students were aware of this overlap. When the classes were integrated, each teacher found his/her unit enhanced by the other discipline's contribution.

It is much more difficult to combine other subjects. Goodlad says that teaching is the only profession that is modeled for students from the time they are five years old. All teachers learned knowledge in specialized courses. It is overcoming these ingrained models of specialization that makes integrating subjects such a difficult task. If we want students to develop an integrated view of knowledge, we have to start with the teachers. Assisting teachers to become focused on a few main outcomes and knowledgeable about their connection to the rest of the curriculum can help students develop an integrated view of knowledge. As a science department head early in my career, I struggled to implement an integrated science curriculum. Most science teachers were neither trained nor interested in teaching any of the content from other science classes. Integrating science with another discipline, such as math, is even more difficult. This degree of integration remains a challenge for schools.

Developing Individual Student Talents

To end where I began this essay, Goodlad says that schools should assist each student in developing his/her own talent. As obvious as it is ignored, developing individual students' talents requires that we must first get to know individual students. Ted Sizer says that we can't teach students if we don't know them.[5] But this is a constant struggle in a large high school. Since school financial restrictions make it difficult to reduce class size to a level to allow for significant individual attention, we were able to find other approaches to achieve the same end. Reducing the number of students that teachers see daily and implementing advisories were two primary strategies that worked.

First, we designed a schedule to allow for long instructional blocks. This schedule enabled students to still take six subjects, three one day and then three the next, allowing for 100-minute instructional blocks. Thus, teachers saw 60 to 90 students a day rather than 150. Teachers reported that this long block of instructional time allowed them to interact individually with each student on a regular basis. And, since they saw fewer students each day, teachers had more energy for the ones they did see. These interactions are the key to personalizing education. They provide the time for a teacher to consult with individual students, to check on their level of understanding, and to assist in motivating students to capitalize on their individual talents and interests.

The long instructional blocks also provided opportunities for using more effective instructional strategies. Goodlad says that most teachers engage in what he calls "frontal teaching" or lecturing most of the time. It is well known that this is the least effective instructional strategy. Research shows that students retain much more of what they do than what they only hear. Providing long instructional blocks of time is an effective way to encourage teachers to actively engage students in their learning. If this is combined with training for teachers on the use of more active instructional strategies, such as cooperative learning, teaching can become much more powerful. Test scores rose each year after we implemented this schedule, and we believed that the long instructional blocks—and using them well—were the reason.

Advisories personalize education for students by providing an individual advocate for each student in school. Under ordinary conditions, many students connect with at least one adult within the school. However, many of the students most needing this contact do not. Surveys of dropouts have repeatedly shown that a critical factor was the lack of connection with anyone in the school. An advisory program ensures that every student will connect regularly with an adult who will be checking to see how he/she is doing. The schedule described earlier allowed for advisories to meet every other day for thirty minutes. One primary purpose of these advisories was to provide individualized attention to students as they select courses. Another was the monitoring of the students' academic progress. Advisors sat down with individual students each quarter to look at their grades and set goals for future accomplishments. Advisories have additional dimensions and in many ways provide the opportunity for students to make connections with adults in the school.

As the principal, I, too, met with a group of students. A particular student's story sticks with me as a poignant example of the power of advisories to develop students' talents and, in this case, to keep them in school. I first met the student I shall call Jason as a tenth grader in my advisory. As we began selecting courses, he assured me that there were no courses that were of interest to him and that he intended to drop out of school. He was very interested in auto mechanics, had a job in an automotive repair shop, and as far as he was concerned, didn't need a high school education. As I talked with Jason about this,

I began to realize that the talent he was interested in developing was unrelated to many of our courses. However, I was able to show him some particular courses that I felt might be of value to him, such as a computer repair class. In addition, I helped Jason request waivers of some requirements so that he could substitute some other types of opportunities. Since Jason worked with computers at his job site to diagnose auto problems, I arranged for him to work with his computer repair teacher to earn academic credit for applying his computer skills in his automotive position. Because he knew me, Jason was willing to come to me to discuss other possible accommodations. Jason remained in school and graduated with his class. He left me the following note:

> Thank you, Dr. Reeder. You have made my last four years a little more enjoyable. You are not afraid to stand up for what you know is best. You have given me an awesome opportunity to experience this world that school prepares us for first hand. Had you not been so flexible and understanding, I would surely have discontinued my high school education. Thank you for the senior exhibition. It has meant more to me than any other part of my twelve years of public education.
> Thank you,
> Jason

Without some kind of individual attention, many "Jasons" slip through the cracks, and we lose the opportunity to help them develop their talents and prepare them for their futures.

Conclusion

Listening to John Goodlad on a number of occasions gave me very powerful ideas for improving schools. Learning to implement these ideas has been the challenge of my administrative career. My increased understanding of change has helped me facilitate the implementation of significant reform initiatives. Advisories, longer instructional blocks, senior exhibitions, and integrated curriculum can be important changes for today's schools, and putting these initiatives into practice has resulted in significant improvements in my high schools.

Goodlad's ideas continue to influence my work. I now teach prospective principals in a school of education at a local university where my students frequently hear: "John Goodlad says. . . ."

Notes

1   John Goodlad, *A Place Called School* (New York: McGraw-Hill, 1984).

2   John Goodlad, "Structure, Process, and an Agenda," in John Goodlad, ed., *The Ecology of School Renewal* (Chicago: University of Chicago Press, 1987), 13.

3   Shirley M. Hord, Gene E. Hall, William L. Rutherford, and Leslie Huling-Austin, *Taking Charge of Change* (Alexandria, Va.: Association for Supervision and Curriculum Development, 1987).

4   Jeannie Oakes, *Keeping Track: How Schools Structure Inequality* (New Haven: Yale University Press, 1985).

5   Theodore R. Sizer, *Horace's School* (Boston: Houghton Mifflin, 1992). My last job was as principal in a high school that was a member of the Coalition of Essential Schools. So we paid attention to what Ted Sizer said, too.

Chapter 10

Access to Knowledge: Challenging the Techniques, Norms, and Politics of Schooling[1]

Jeannie Oakes and Martin Lipton

The so-called common school always has served special self-interests. While doing so, however, it also has been driven by a sense of serving the common weal.[2]

Limited conceptions of what intellectual and character development mean and require by way of nurturing, accompanied by the limited instructional repertoire such conceptions reflect, seriously restrict the quality of *how* students learn. . . . Deep-seated myths and prejudices about the distribution of ability to learn contribute significantly to differentiating students' access to the array of knowledge schools provide. . . . The internal organization of schools, partly reflecting these myths and prejudices and partly designed to make the school's job easier, usually serves to create sharp differences in the educational opportunities enjoyed by students.[3]

If we need a common school to provide a common literacy, a common awareness of our democracy and the responsibility for it, a common understanding of the diversity of our heritages, and a common induction into civilized conversation, we have much to do.[4]

John I. Goodlad
Access to Knowledge

As John Goodlad notes in his opening essay in *Access to Knowledge*, a central problem for American schools is their need to accommodate the self-interests of the powerful at the same time schools serve the common good. To help manage this accommodation as the demand for universal education grew in the twentieth century, American educators differentiated their curricula. That way, students from powerful and advantaged groups could receive the education they felt they deserved and students from less powerful or disadvantaged groups could receive the education society felt they could use, while all students attended common schools.

This arrangement has been bolstered by the argument that equal opportunity in a democracy requires schools to provide each student access to the kind of knowledge and skills that best suit his or her abilities and likely adult lives. To make the argument more palatable in a culture that, rhetorically at least, values classless and color-blind policies, educators and policymakers have reified categorical differences among people. So, in contemporary schools we have "gifted" students, "average" students, "Title I" students, "learning disabled" students, and so on, in order to justify the different access and opportunities students receive. Assessment and evaluation technology permits schools to categorize, compare, rank, and assign value to students' abilities and achievements in relationship to one another (as well as to students in other schools, states, and countries—past and present).

The culture's impulse to respond in this way is not surprising, since humans seem unable to resist noticing and attempting to make sense of the differences among people and things—to categorize. Yet, as sociologist Eviatar Zerubavel writes in *The Fine Line: Making Distinctions in Everyday Life*, "The way we cut up the world clearly affects the way we organize our everyday life. The way we divide our surroundings, for example, determines what we notice and what we ignore . . . the way we classify people determines whom we trust and whom we fear. . . . Indeed, our entire social order is a product of the ways in which we separate."[5] As Goodlad notes in the opening quotes, these categories embody and perpetuate "deep-seated myths and prejudices about the distribution of ability to learn." Doing so, they enable schools to satisfy powerful self-interests while maintaining a powerful rhetoric of communitarian ideals.

This essay elaborates John Goodlad's career-long call for an analytic, moral, and democratic compass to guide our understanding and improvement of schools through the morass of compromises to the struggle for the common good in schools. Following Goodlad's lead, we consider the normative and political, as well as the technical, aspects of research, practice, and reform of educational classification and grouping.

Deep-seated Myths and Prejudices and
The Internal Organization of Schools

Those who promote ability grouping, special education, gifted programs, and the myriad other homogeneous instructional groups in
schools claim that these classifications are objective and color-blind,
rather than, as Goodlad suggests, reflecting myths and prejudices.
Advocates of grouping explain the disproportionate classification of
white students as gifted or advanced and of students of color as slow
or basic as the unfortunate consequence of different backgrounds and
abilities. They base their claims of objectivity on century-old (and older)
explanations of differences that are neither scientific nor bias-free.

Homogeneous grouping began in earnest early in the twentieth
century. It matched the prevailing IQ conception of intelligence, behavioral theories of learning, a transmission and training model of
teaching, and the factory model of school organization. It fit with the
schools' role in maintaining a social and economic order in which
those with power and privilege routinely pass on their advantages to
their children. Homogeneous grouping embodied a belief that permeated schooling during the twentieth century—that we understand most
about students when we look at their differences, and the more differences we can identify, the better our understanding and teaching.

Homogeneous grouping provided policymakers and educators a way
to "solve" an array of problems attributed to the growing diversity of
students. New immigrants needed to learn English and American ways.
Factories needed trained workers. Urban youths required supervision.
And schools needed to continue their traditional role of providing high-
status knowledge to prepare some students for the professions.
Policymakers defined equal educational opportunity as giving all students the chance to prepare for largely predetermined and certainly
different adult lives.[6] Concurrently, two phenomena shaped a uniquely
American definition of democratic schooling: (1) universal schooling
would give all students some access to knowledge; (2) IQ could justify
differentiated access to knowledge as a hallmark of democratic
fairness.

IQ and Testing

Intelligence provided a seemingly meritocratic and scientific basis for
sorting students. In the process of institutionalizing standardized psychological testing, schools also institutionalized prevailing beliefs about
race and class differences in intellectual abilities. Early testing sup-

ported the view that low-income students and students of color had vast and immutable intellectual, moral, and biological differences.

While most current grouping practices do not rely on IQ—at least exclusively—the early practices set a pattern that continues today. Standardized achievement tests, strikingly similar to IQ tests, play an important role in dividing students into ability groups and qualifying students for compensatory education programs; standardized language proficiency tests determine which class "level" is appropriate for limited English students. IQ, in conjunction with other measures, remains central in the identification of gifted and cognitively disabled students.

The Press for Universal Education

Over the course of the twentieth century, compulsory education laws and the necessity of a high school diploma drew more and more students to school—even those previously considered uneducable. States and local school systems developed an array of special programs for students who, in earlier times, simply would not have been in school.[7] By the 1960s, the federal government had turned to special categorical programs as its principal way to guarantee education for all American students. The Elementary and Secondary Education Act (ESEA) provided categorical funding for "educationally deprived" students. *Lau et al. v. Nichols et al.* was brought on behalf of Chinese students in San Francisco and led to legislation requiring that all schools provide special assistance to their students whose native language is not English. The Individuals with Disabilities Education Act (IDEA) provided funds to classify students with physical and neurological problems and provide these students with special education programs when it was believed that they could not be accommodated in regular programs. Advocates for "gifted" students increasingly used the "bell curve" logic to argue that the gifted and the cognitively handicapped are like a pair of bookends, and that those at the high end of the curve also required special support because they are as different from "normal" students as the handicapped.

Educators responded in culturally predictable ways. They identified students who were "different," diagnosed their differences as scientifically as possible, and assigned them to a category. They then grouped students for instruction with others in the same category, and tailored curriculum and teaching to what each group "needs" and what the culture expects. So, today, educators routinely assign "normal" students to "regular" classes at different levels (e.g., high, average, slow).

They place the others in "special" programs for learning disabled, behavioral problems, gifted, limited English, poverty-related academic deficiencies, and more. Within homogeneous groups, teachers assume students can move lockstep through lessons and that all class members will profit from the same instruction on the same content at the same pace. Lurking just beneath the surface of these highly rationalized practices, however, are the illusion of homogeneity, the social construction of classifications, the prevailing biases of race and social class, and self-fulfilling prophesies of opportunities and outcomes.

The Illusion of Homogeneity
In 1960, John Goodlad documented the wide range of abilities that remain in classrooms that are ostensibly "ability grouped."[8] That diversity remains today. Within classes designed for specific ability, disability, and language levels, students display considerable differences in learning speed, learning style, interest, effort, and aptitude for various tasks. Remarkably, they may also differ dramatically on the very criteria used to determine placements. Such differences mean that so-called homogeneously grouped classes are rarely that—although schools label them as such.[9] Classes designated for students at a particular ability level enroll students who span a very wide range of measured ability.[10] Moreover, categories like "learning disabled" contain highly diverse groups of students, even when they are further divided into groups of mildly, moderately, and severely handicapped. Similar difficulties arise in gifted programs.[11]

Social indicators such as maturity and cooperation also sway placements. Similarly, physical development affects personal appearance, height, and handwriting, and these in turn may bias teachers' judgments about a child's suitability for a particular class. Schools often place capable but bothersome, poorly behaved students in low ability groups.[12] Moreover, scheduling constraints wreak havoc with genuinely homogeneous classes. As Mehan, Mercer, and Rueda observe, "If there are 30 slots for LD students in a school, then there will be 30 kids to fill those slots."[13] Finally, in many schools savvy parents who want their children enrolled in the "best" classes and special programs successfully pressure educators to place them in classes "where they don't belong."[14] In a competitive system that only offers a small percentage of student slots in the high track, knowledgeable parents have few options but to pit themselves against others to get the best educational services.

Socially and Politically Constructed Categories

The considerable student differences *within* supposedly homogeneous classes are obvious and well documented. And yet, for most people, the characteristics and categories by which students are sorted remain more salient than the "exceptions" that impugn those categories. Kenneth Sirotnik reminds us that many educational constructs, including those used to classify students, began as narrowly defined, highly specialized, technical terms or measures. However, as they make their way from research to professional journals and teacher preparation programs, to popular media, to the everyday talk of policymakers and the public, they lose their narrow definitions and specialized uses. "Pretty soon," Sirotnik notes, "people talk and make decisions about other people's *intelligence, achievement,* and *self-concept* as if these attributes really existed in the same sense as, for example, people's height and weight."[15] What may have begun as specific technical concepts or as informal notions such as "at risk," "gifted," "high ability," "college prep," "attention deficit," "hyperactive," "handicapped," etc., are quickly reified and become a deeply embedded feature of students' identities in their own and others' minds.

We need look no further than official policies setting forth the definitions and the criteria used for placement for evidence that these categories are social and political constructions. States and school districts differ widely in their definitions of "high," "average," and "low" ability within the population of so-called normal students, and they have different definitions of disabilities and giftedness. A child identified as belonging in any one of these categories in one place might not qualify as such in another.[16]

Louise Spear-Swerling and Robert Sternberg argue in their book, *Off Track: When Poor Readers Become "Learning Disabled,"*[17] that the learning disabilities (LD) classification causes more problems than it solves. They claim that the distinction the category draws between LD students and other low achievers is both inaccurate and unhelpful. Not only do they remind us that IQ is a fundamentally flawed concept, but they point to research showing that most students identified as learning disabled are no more likely than other students to have biological abnormalities. They suggest that LD students and others would be better served if funding guidelines allowed teachers and other learning specialists to address specific cognitive problems such as reading difficulties without misleading teachers, students, and families with an illogical diagnosis that makes the child seem abnormal.[18]

Christine Sleeter's analysis of the learning disability category argues that social and political concerns shape the construction of categories.[19] She recounts that in the 1960s frustrated middle-class parents organized and lobbied for special LD programs in U.S. schools. These parents wanted to differentiate and protect their failing students from low-achieving lower-class and minority students whose learning problems were thought to be caused by low IQ, emotional disturbances, or cultural deprivation. The LD classification made additional resources appear scientific and fair, and it was much easier for affluent parents to accept than either retardation or problems of culture or family background. In fact, the vast majority of students labeled as LD during the first ten years of the classification's existence were white and middle class. Similar accounts could be told about "gifted" as a categorical program, the recent push to establish Attention Deficit Disorder as a disability, and the emergence of "at risk" students.

Ironically, some categories do the opposite of what they intend. Instead of providing rationality and organization to the schooling enterprise, they add ambiguity and controversy even for the categories' strongest advocates. For example, a research overview produced by the federally funded ERIC Clearinghouse on Disabilities and Gifted Education entitled "ADHD and Children Who Are Gifted," cautions against confusing gifted students with those who have hyperactivity disorders.[20] Another ERIC summary describes learning disabled/gifted students. This category is typified by "an extremely bright student who is struggling to stay on grade level." Such students may not be noticed, the summary asserts, because "their superior intellectual ability is working overtime to help compensate for an undiagnosed learning disability. In essence, their gift masks the disability and the disability masks the gift."[21] Very disruptive students may fall into this category: "They are frequently off task; they may act out, daydream, or complain of headaches and stomachaches; they are easily frustrated and use their creative abilities to avoid tasks."[22]

Race and Social Class Bias

African American, Latino, and low-income students are consistently overrepresented in low-ability, remedial, and special education classes and programs. They are less likely to participate in "gifted" programs. This is not surprising, given that grouping practices grew from the once-accepted practice of preparing students of different racial, ethnic, and social-class backgrounds for their separate (and unequal) places in society. The belief in whites' genetic superiority has largely fallen from favor, and grouping explicitly by race and social class has become a schooling taboo. However, the persistent stratifying effects of schools' grouping practices continue to make deep, unquestioned sense to many in schools and society. The burden of defending such practices has simply shifted from racial superiority to competitively based notions of merit.[23]

Segregated schools serving low-income and minority students typically have proportionately fewer academic classes than do schools serving predominantly white, more affluent students—a pattern that disproportionately consigns students of color to low-track classes. In desegregated schools, African American and Latino students are assigned disproportionately to low-track classes. For example, in a 1990 study for the National Science Foundation, we found a pattern of "racially identifiable" math and science classes in both segregated and racially mixed schools. In racially mixed schools, many classes had larger percentages of white students than one would expect at the school; and many other classes had larger than expected percentages of students of color. Nationwide, for every six high-ability "white" classes, there was only one high-ability "minority" class. At the same time, for every seven low-ability "minority" classes, there was only one low-ability "white" class.[24] Similarly, a study by the Urban League found that while 23 percent of the minority middle school students in big city districts were in low-track math classes, only 8 percent of white students were. In contrast, 56 percent of white students were in high-track classes, compared to only 36 percent of the minorities.[25] A third study of two hundred school districts in the late 1980s found that white students were more than three times more likely than blacks to be identified as gifted.[26]

In part, these placement patterns reflect differences in minority and white students' learning opportunities that affect their preparation and achievements. But they also reflect the fact that U.S. schools use white, largely middle-class standards of culture and language styles as they screen for academic ability and talent. Teachers and school psychologists sometimes mistake the language and dialect differences of Hispanic and black students for poor language skills, conceptual misunderstandings, or even bad attitudes. An additional hazard for students of color is that schools often confuse cultural differences with cognitive disabilities, particularly retardation.

But, more blatant discrimination also takes place. In racially mixed school systems, African American and Latino students are much less likely than white or Asian students *with the same test scores* to be placed in high ability classes.[27] For example, in one West Coast school system, white and Asian students with average scores on standardized tests were more than twice as likely to be in "accelerated" classes than Latinos with the same scores. While only 56 percent of very high scoring Latinos were in accelerated classes, 93 percent of whites and 97 percent of Asians with comparable test scores were. Nationally, students identified as gifted and talented come disproportionately from white, economically and socially advantaged families.

Researchers have noted for the past twenty-five years that students with identical IQs, but different race and social class, have been classified and treated very differently in special education placements.[28] By the late 1970s, the misidentification problem triggered both federal and state court decisions requiring that potentially disabled students receive due process. In a far-reaching decision, the California courts ruled in *Larry P. v. Wilson Riles* (1979) that schools could no longer use intelligence tests to identify minority students as mentally retarded. However, substantial problems remain and new ones emerge, including recent evidence that African American boys are disproportionately identified as ADHD.[29]

Despite increasing attention to cultural differences and civil rights actions, grouping ideologies and practices persist in connecting intellectual aptitude and prospects for success to race and class. Moreover, high-achieving, affluent, white parents are more willing to "push the system" if they are displeased with the course assignments, while parents of low-achieving and mid-range students (often nonwhite and lower-income) are frequently less comfortable and skilled at challenging the system.[30] When a status preference or other advantage exists, efficacious, high-income parents will use their considerable political capital on behalf of their children. For example, they might pay a private psychologist to re-test their child if the child missed a "gifted" cut-off on the school's test. So might a well-off parent of a struggling child who learns that a "learning disabled" identification allows students extra time to take tests, even in high-ability classes. While the process of discovering a student's disability, identifying it, and deciding what to do is a complex and emotionally wrenching experience for any parent, poor parents who might not be native English speakers, or who may be cautious about public institutions, face additional obstacles. As a result, their children may not receive the same careful screening (and repeat diagnostic services) as the children of white, middle-class parents.

Self-fulfilling Prophecies

Placement in a low-ability class becomes a self-fulfilling prophecy—a cycle of low expectations, fewer opportunities, and poor academic performance. "Poor performance," then, begins the cycle anew, giving additional justification to the schools to lower expectations and reduce opportunities. [31] Extensive research makes clear that in every aspect of what makes for a quality education, children in lower tracks typically get less than those in higher tracks and gifted programs.[32] Some of these differences are listed below. [33]

Sometimes, alternatives for learning disabled students simply become the lowest track in the school. Often, specialists working with disabled students are not subject-matter experts but focus on study skills or adjustment, putting further distance between the learning opportunities of regular and special education students. Moreover, regular classroom teachers often falsely assume that all special needs are taken care of elsewhere and make fewer efforts to tailor instruction to the individual learning needs that all students have.

Often limited English-speaking students in separate programs suffer the same fate. While the evidence is clear that they learn better with strong support in their own language, the shortage of qualified, bilingual teachers frustrates this approach. Many students in these

Grouping-Related Differences in Learning Opportunities

Higher-Group Advantages	Lower-Group Disadvantages
Curriculum emphasizing concepts, inquiry, and problem solving	Curriculum emphasizing low-level facts and skills
Stress on students developing as autonomous thinkers	Stress on teaching students to follow rules and procedures
More time spent on instruction	More time spent on discipline or socializing
More active and interactive learning activities	More worksheets and seat-work
Computers used as learning tools	Computers used as tutors or electronic worksheets
More qualified and experienced teachers	More uncertified and inexperienced teachers
Extra enrichment activities and resources	Few enrichment opportunities
More engaging and friendly classroom atmosphere	More alienating and hostile classroom atmosphere
Hard work a likely classroom norm	"Not working" a likely classroom norm

programs must learn from teachers who are not fully able to teach either English or academic subject matter using the students' languages. Other students work mostly with teachers' assistants. While these assistants may be fluent in the language, they will not have either the subject-matter or pedagogical knowledge of a fully qualified teacher.

Finally, grouping practices help shape students' identities, status, and expectations for themselves. Both students and adults mistake labels such as "gifted," "honors student," "average," "remedial," "LD," and "MMR" for certification of overall ability or worth. These labels teach students that if the school does not identify them as capable in earlier grades, they should not expect to do well later. Everyone without the "gifted" label has the *de facto* label of "not gifted." The resource classroom is a low-status place and students who go there are low-status students. The result of all this is that most students have needlessly low self-concepts and schools have low expectations. Few students or teachers can defy those identities and expectations.

These labeling effects permeate the entire school and social culture. Thus, we have frequent references to "gifted parents." Teachers talk about "my low kids." Parents and educators alike confer greater status on those teaching high-achieving students. Teachers of low-ability classes may be admired for how "tough" their job is, but it is often assumed that they are not—or do not need to be—as well qualified. Often highly qualified special education and bilingual teachers are not thought to have the expertise to work with highly able students.

Over the years of schooling, students who are initially similar in background and skills become increasingly different in achievement when they are put into separate classes. In three school districts where we studied ability grouping, students who were placed in lower-level courses—disproportionately Latino and African American students—consistently made smaller achievement gains than classmates *with the same abilities* who were put in higher-level classes.[34] This happened consistently; students with both high and low test scores did better in higher-level courses.

Among the most consequential effects of homogeneous grouping is that it masks the essential problem of teaching any group of twenty to thirty-five people. Such instruction always requires, and should require, a variety of teaching strategies. Not all students will benefit from the same tasks, materials, and procedures, even if the school grouped them because of their similarities. Multiple criteria for success and reward benefit all students, regardless of grouping practices. Unfortunately, conventional grouping practices and the illusion of homogeneity deflect attention from these instructional realities. When instruction fails, the problem is too often attributed to the child or perhaps to a wrong placement.

We Have Much To Do

Arguments about whether to "fix" or largely abandon homogeneous grouping raise deep questions about how democratic schools should grapple with the differences among students. In a postmodern age— one with increasing student diversity and expanding conceptions of competence—it becomes extraordinarily difficult to specify what is mainstream (or normal) and what is "different." It is increasingly hard to distinguish between who is "special" and who is simply out of sync with traditional practices. Do we accept the current grouping structure and culture of schools as neutral and consider their inequalities to be anomalies in an otherwise fair and workable system? Or should educators try to change the structures and norms? If so, how will educators accommodate student diversity without classifying and sorting?

Since the late 1980s, policymakers, educators, and advocacy groups have responded to problems with homogeneous grouping by recommending that schools dismantle it. These recommendations reflect growing support for heterogeneous grouping as necessary to ensure that all students have access to high-quality curriculum, teachers, and learning experiences. For example, early analyses of the disappointing performance of United States students on the Third International Mathematics and Science Study (TIMSS) support mounting concerns that the low scores stem, in part, from the tracking of most American students in less academically demanding math and science classes.[35] Increasingly, educators and policymakers are developing an awareness that schools cannot teach or achieve social justice unless they eliminate grouping practices. A number of school desegregation cases have cited the practice as a source of continuing racial discrimination.[36] However, this goal will not be accomplished quickly, and policy reports will simply gather dust unless enlightened educators understand and act to change the norms and political relations these grouping practices embody. There is a long, hard road ahead.

Technical Skills, Politics and
Power, Norms and Beliefs

Many schools around the country have altered their grouping practices by reducing or eliminating ability grouping, by adopting schoolwide
reform instead of targeting groups of students for compensatory education programs, by including gifted and disabled students in regular
classes, and by developing two-way bilingual programs. They have
found that heterogeneous grouping requires far more than simply mixing
students in classrooms and proceeding with "business as usual." Such
teaching requires new learning theories, curricular designs, pedagogy,
and assessment, along with new ways of connecting students with
teachers, with resources, and with one another. Without bold changes,
new grouping practices will clash with established practices, and before long, the new groupings will change to fit those old practices,
rather than the school adjusting to fit the new practice. For example,
many have returned to Goodlad and Anderson's still-promising work
from the late 1950s that supports the possibility of inclusiveness offered in nongraded elementary schools.[37]

To support the organizational changes, many teachers are struggling to devise ways for diverse students to learn productively together
and to align their teaching with sociocognitive perspectives on learning. Using such techniques as Socratic seminars, experiential curriculum (e.g., project-based science and interactive math), and cooperative small-group learning, these teachers promote instructional
conversations and scaffolding in their classes. They craft multidimen-
sional assignments to challenge students of varying abilities. Some
stress assessments that they can justify as providing students with
useful information and inclinations to work hard and successfully.
Others include multicultural content to make knowledge accessible.[38]
Many find the structures, curriculum, and pedagogies that are advocated for separate gifted programs to be workable practices for heterogeneous groups.

However, most educators who attempt heterogeneous grouping also
run headlong into community values and politics around race and social class that combine with beliefs and ideologies about intelligence.[39]
Without attention to these underlying issues, the inequalities currently
associated with grouping inevitably resurface in a new organizational
guise.

144   Access to Knowledge

Attention to the Political

Grouping and its consequences have meaning and exchange value beyond school. After all, homogeneous grouping, accompanied by public labels and status differences, signals which students should gain access to the university and the status and life chances that higher education can bring. Thus, tracking becomes part and parcel of the struggle among individuals and groups for comparative advantage in the distribution of school resources, opportunities, and credentials that have exchange value in the larger society. Therefore, it is not surprising that there are those with a clear personal stake in maintaining homogeneous grouping. Efforts to move away from it nearly always confront resistance from those whose children are advantaged by it.

Educators worry about the political consequences of abandoning homogeneous grouping, in particular the loss of support of parents of high-track students. This concern has been fueled by advocates for separately funded, categorical programs for the gifted and talented. In local forums, such as school board meetings and in popular practitioner journals, these individuals and groups lobby strongly against policy changes that may threaten special opportunities now available to high achievers. In many communities, this political dimension encompasses issues of race and social class stratification.

One highly publicized example of these politics took place in Calhoun County, Georgia, where Superintendent Corkin Cherubini attempted to dismantle the tracking system that he considered a form of "education apartheid." Tracking by ability began in Calhoun County in the third grade, placing students in racially disproportionate groups that stayed together for most of their schooling. Federal civil rights officials whom Cherubini invited to visit the district supported his actions, saying that some of the practices were illegal as well as unfair. However, the white community reacted with outrage. A white businessman and a former member of the school board told an *Education Week* reporter, "I don't think anyone is more disliked here than Dr. Cherubini. At the rate we're going, we'll be back to the 60s with whites in private schools." Mr. Cherubini's enemies made threatening phone calls to his home and office and tried unsuccessfully to recall him.[40]

Successful heterogeneous grouping requires that groups that now see themselves as competing—such as the white and black families in Calhoun County, Georgia—come together across a deep political divide to make common cause around the issue of serving all students well. However, building coalitions among these divergent constituencies requires that educators making changes guarantee that their new practices will provide all students with opportunities that are at least as rich and rigorous as those they previously enjoyed. No parent would sensibly agree to less. But, it also requires that educators confront less rational opposition to the changes. Some parents will object to changes that take away the *comparative* advantages enjoyed and effectively used (both in school and beyond) by students whose parents are privileged by race and class—no matter how good the new approach might be. Confronting these issues is a political process that requires astute political leadership and considerable risk-taking by educators.

Attention to the Normative

The critical lesson learned from school reform efforts since the 1960s is that new, equity-minded practices must make sense to teachers and communities, and that it matters *how* they make sense. Genuine and equitable school reform cannot stand side by side with existing and entrenched views of human capacity, conceptions of individual and group differences, traditions for organizing schools and classrooms, and beliefs that schools should sort and train students for a differentiated workforce with unequal economic rewards.

The convention among reformers has been an attempt to define equity according to whether all students have access to good schooling. They assume that by starting with a conception of good schooling, all students will find access and be well served. We need a different reform convention—one that begins with students and defines good schooling by whether all students actually become well educated. Thus, as with John Goodlad's work, the proper study of schooling goes beyond simply documenting practices and identifying the best ones. The study of schooling must carefully monitor the alignment of practice with equitable schooling norms and values. Such study must engage educators and communities, as well as researchers, if it is to alter what "makes sense" to those who must change practices. This approach holds much promise, though it surely frustrates critics and bureaucracies bent on linear, rational progress and five-year reform programs.

Genuine reforms, such as those that encourage and alter inquiring relationships among schools and communities, are elusive and follow unpredictable timelines. Like democracy itself, these reforms must be judged, in part, by the quality of the struggle to achieve, refine, and redefine equitable schooling. And so, while we do not expect a "victory" of community interests over parochial and self-interests, Goodlad and others struggle to gather and analyze the data, to fashion the arguments, and to study the alternatives. As a result of this work, fewer schools and individuals will view students whose home culture and knowledge are "different" as less intelligent. Traditional sorting and homogeneous grouping will come to be seen as compatible with and an unwanted outcome of behavioral and individualistic theories of learning. Norms supportive of cognitive and sociocultural approaches to learning will demand heterogeneity.

Without a doubt, heterogeneous grouping is an extraordinary reform to undertake, and those in schools attempting it are the first to agree. The success of their efforts requires solid empirical research that documents the problem and points to efficacious alternatives. Yet, grouping reforms will never succeed or fail based on empirical evidence alone. Thanks to John Goodlad's juxtaposition of the moral imperatives of American education with his own considerable empirical research on schooling, others who study schools (like us) have a path to follow as we struggle alongside educators who seek a firm foundation for their enormously complex work of creating equitable schools.

Notes

1 This essay is drawn from material more fully developed in Jeannie Oakes and Martin Lipton, *Teaching to Change the World* (New York: McGraw-Hill, 1999).

2 John I. Goodlad, "Common Schools for the Common Weal: Reconciling Self-Interest with the Common Good," in John I. Goodlad and Pamela Keating, eds., *Access to Knowledge: The Continuing Agenda for Our Nation's Schools*, revised edition (New York: College Entrance Examination Board, 1994), 6.

3 Goodlad, "Common Schools for the Common Weal," 7.

4 Goodlad, "Common Schools for the Common Weal," 11.

5 Eviatar Zerubavel, *The Fine Line: Making Distinctions in Everyday Life* (Chicago: University of Chicago Press, 1993), 1–2.

6 Jeannie Oakes, *Keeping Track: How Schools Structure Inequality* (New Haven, Conn.: Yale University Press, 1985).

7 John G. Richardson, "Common Delinquent, and Special: On the Formalization of Common Schooling in the American States," *American Educational Research Journal* 31 (1994): 695–723.

8 John I. Goodlad, "Classroom Organization," in Chester Harris, ed., *Encyclopedia of Educational Research* (New York: Macmillan, 1960).

9 Hugh Mehan, Jane Mercer, and Robert Rueda, "Special Education," in *Encyclopedia of Education and Sociology* (New York: Garland, 1997).

10 Jeannie Oakes, "Two Cities: Tracking and Within-School Segregation," in L. Miller, ed., *Brown Plus Forty: The Promise* (New York: Teachers College Press, 1995); Jeannie Oakes, "Report to the Court," *New Castle County*, 1995.

11 For example, one desegregating school district identified 70 percent of the white students from the most affluent neighborhoods as "gifted." Kevin Welner, "Mandating Equity: Rethinking the Educational Change Literature as Applied to Equity-Minded Reforms" (Ph.D. diss., University of California at Los Angeles, 1997).

12 Donald L. MacMillan and Daniel Reschly, "Over-representation of Minority Students: The Case for Greater Specificity or Reconsideration of the Variables Examined," *Journal of Special Education 32* (1997): 15–24.

13 Mehan, Mercer, and Rueda, "Special Education."

14 This phenomenon has been documented in tracked classes and in gifted programs. See, for example, Elizabeth Useem, "Student Selection into Course

Sequences in Mathematics: The Impact of Parental Involvement and School Policies," *Journal of Research on Adolescence* 1 (1991): 231–50; Susan Yonezawa, "Making Decisions About Students' Lives" (Ph.D. diss., University of California at Los Angeles, 1997); Marilyn Ann Verna and James Reed Campbell, "Distinguishing Ingredients of Talented and Gifted Programs at the Elementary and High School Levels" (paper presented at the Annual Meeting of the American Educational Research Association, San Diego, April 1998).

15   Kenneth Sirotnik, "Equal Access to Quality in Public Schooling: Issues in the Assessment of Equity and Excellence," in John I. Goodlad and Pamela Keating, eds., *Access to Knowledge: The Continuing Agenda for Our Nation's Schools*, revised edition (New York: College Entrance Examination Board, 1994), 162.

16   Jeannie Oakes and Gretchen Guiton, "Matchmaking: The Dynamics of High School Tracking Decisions," *American Educational Research Journal* 32 (Spring 1995): 3–33.

17   Louise Spear-Swerling and Robert J. Sternberg, *Off Track: When Poor Readers Become "Learning Disabled"* (Boulder, Colo.: Westview Press, 1996).

18   See, for example, Thomas Armstrong, *The Myth of the ADD Child* (New York: Dutton, 1985).

19   Christine Sleeter, "Learning Disabilities: The Social Construction of a Special Education Category," *Exceptional Children* 53 (September 1986): 46–54; Christine Sleeter, "Why is There Learning Disabilities? A Critical Analysis of the Birth of the Field in its Social Context," in Thomas S. Popkewitz, ed., *The Formation of School Subjects: The Struggle for Creating an American Institution* (New York: Falmer Press, 1987).

20   James T. Webb and Diane Latimer, "ADHD and Children Who Are Gifted," *Eric Digest #E522* (Reston, Va.: Council for Exceptional Children, ERIC Clearinghouse on Disabilities and Gifted Education, 1993.)

21   Susan Baum, "Gifted But Learning Disabled: A Puzzling Paradox," *Eric Digest #E479* (Reston, Va.: Council for Exceptional Children, ERIC Clearinghouse on Disabilities and Gifted Education, 1990).

22   Baum, "Gifted But Learning Disabled."

23   For a compelling elaboration of this argument regarding merit and competition, see Nicholas Lemann, "Rewarding the Best, Forgetting the Rest," *New York Times*, 26 April 1998, 15.

24   Jeannie Oakes, *Multiplying Inequalities* (Santa Monica, Calif.: RAND Corporation, 1990).

25   Ana Maria Villegas and Susan M. Watts, "Life in the Classroom: The Influence of Class Placement and Student Race/Ethnicity." (Paper presented at the Annual Meeting of the American Educational Research Association, Chicago, Ill., April 1991).

26 Kenneth J. Meier, Joseph Stuart, and Robert E. England, *Race, Class, and Education: The Politics of Second-Generation Discrimination* (Madison: University of Wisconsin Press, 1989).

27 Oakes, "Two Cities."

28 Megan, Mercer, and Rueda, "Special Education."

29 Luanna H. Meyer, Beth Harry, and Mara Sapon-Shevin, "School Inclusion and Multicultural Education," in James A. Banks and Cherry A. McGee Banks, eds., *Multicultural Education: Issues and Perspectives* (Boston: Allyn and Bacon, 1996).

30 Useem, "Student Selection." See also, Amy Stuart Wells and Irene Serna, "The Politics of Culture: Understanding Local Political Resistance to Detracking in Racially Mixed Schools," *Harvard Educational Review* 66 (Spring 1996): 93–118; and Yonezawa, "Making Decisions."

31 Jeannie Oakes, Adam Gamoran, and Reba Page, "Curriculum Differentiation," in Philip Jackson, ed., *Handbook of Research on Curriculum* (New York: Macmillan, 1992).

32 This is not to say that *particular* low-ability classes do not have wonderful facilities, a solid curriculum, and qualified teachers, but such situations are clearly exceptions to the rule.

33 Summarized from Oakes, *Keeping Track*; Oakes, *Multiplying Inequalities*.

34 Oakes, "Two Cities."

35 Jo Thomas, "Questions of Excellence in Consortium Ranking," *New York Times*, 22 April 1998, 11.

36 Oakes, "Two Cities"; Jeannie Oakes, "Report to the Court"; Kevin Welner, Jeannie Oakes, and Gilbert FitzGerald, *Report to the Woodland Hills School District* (Los Angeles: Graduate School of Education and Information Studies, University of California at Los Angeles, 1998); Kevin G. Welner and Jeannie Oakes, "(Li)Ability Grouping: The New Susceptibility of School Tracking Systems to Legal Challenges," *Harvard Educational Review* 66 (Fall 1996): 451–70.

37 John I. Goodlad and Robert H. Anderson, *The Nongraded Elementary School*, reissued with a new introduction (New York: Teachers College Press, 1987).

38 Jeannie Oakes, Amy Stuart Wells, Susan Yonezawa, and Karen Ray, "Equity Lessons from Detracking Schools," in Andy Hargreaves, ed., *Rethinking Educational Change with Heart and Mind* (Arlington, Va.: Association for Supervision and Curriculum Development, 1997), 43–72.

39 Jeannie Oakes, Amy Stuart Wells, Makeba Jones, and Amanda Datnow, "Detracking: The Social Construction of Ability, Cultural Politics, and Resistance to Reform," *Teachers College Record* 98 (Spring 1997): 482–510.

40   Robert C. Johnston, "Effort to Do the Right Thing Upsets Ga. County," *Education Week,* 14 December 1994, 1.

Chapter 11

John I. Goodlad and John Dewey: Implications of Their Ideas for Education and Democracy in China

Zhixin Su

John Goodlad and John Dewey are both highly respected education theorists and reformers in the twentieth century. Goodlad was a student of Ralph Tyler, who was a student of Dewey at the University of Chicago. Not surprisingly, there are many similarities in their educational ideas and practices. Goodlad and Dewey have both been recognized as among the foremost scholars, master teachers, prophets, and reformers in American education.[1]

Goodlad's and Dewey's contributions to education development in other parts of the world are also well known. Dewey visited many nations during his lifetime and wrote extensively on the political, social, and educational changes in other nations. His works, especially *Democracy and Education*, *The School and Society*, and *My Pedagogical Creed*, have been translated into many different languages and his ideas have been widely implemented in the educational practices of foreign lands. During his long professional career, Goodlad has also consulted frequently with educators in other nations and held important positions in prominent international education organizations including UNESCO Institute for Education, International Bureau of Education, and International Association of Educators for World Peace. His early book on an educational innovation, *The Nongraded Elementary School*, coauthored with Robert Anderson, was translated into Japanese, Spanish, Italian, and Hebrew, and was used as a reference for educational reform in different international settings. His more recent research reports, *A Place Called School*, *Teachers for*

Our Nation's Schools, and *Educational Renewal: Better Teachers, Better Schools,* have also found their places in the libraries and class-rooms in foreign schools and universities.[2]

One of the countries significantly influenced by visits from both Dewey and Goodlad is China. Although Dewey visited China much earlier in the twentieth century, between 1919 and 1921, than Goodlad's visit, which took place in 1981, they exerted equally important influence on the development of education and democracy in China. In this chapter, I will describe Goodlad's and Dewey's historical visits to China, evaluate the impact they have had on Chinese education, and explore further the implications of their ideas for the development of education and democracy in China.

Historical Visits to China

Goodlad and Dewey visited China at very different, but both critical and historical, times. Early in the twentieth century, when the May 4 Movement in China ended the feudal system, the Chinese politicians and intellectuals eagerly looked toward the West for ideas and models in developing its new social and educational systems. Several higher education leaders, who were formerly Dewey's students at Columbia University, invited Dewey to visit China in 1919 on an extensive lecture tour because they regarded him as the great apostle of philosophic liberalism and experimental methodology, the advocate of complete freedom of thought, and the man who, above all other teachers, equated education to the practical problems of civic cooperation and useful living.[3]

Dewey traveled to twelve provinces and lectured on social and political philosophy, philosophy of education, ethics, and the main trends of modern education. His visit and lectures had a tremendous impact on the development of democracy and education in China at that time. For many years after Dewey's visit, his philosophy of education dominated the teaching of educational theory in all Chinese teachers colleges and in university departments of education. The Chinese educational aims in the 1920s were reconsidered in light of Dewey's thought: while the old educational aims emphasized military education modeled after the Japanese pattern, the new goals embraced the aim and spirit of American education—"the cultivation of perfect personality and the development of democratic spirit." In practice, the national school system in China was reformed according to the American pattern—the 6-3-3 plan—and governed by a set of principles advocated by Dewey that were "to promote the spirit of democracy," "to develop individuality," "to promote education for life," and "to facilitate the spread of universal education."[4] Child-centered education predominated in the revision of the curriculum and new methods of teaching in accord with Dewey's pragmatic theory were initiated. Dewey's former students, then education leaders in China, also established numerous experimental schools and colleges, the most famous being the Morning Village Normal School, which literally implemented Dewey's philosophy in Chinese teacher education and rural education reform.[5] Therefore, Dewey's influence on Chinese education was both profound and extensive.

Goodlad visited China in 1981, also a very significant historical moment in the modern history of China. Goodlad was then the dean of the Graduate School of Education at the University of California at Los Angeles and was designated as the leader of the American Education Foundation Delegation to China. The Delegation's visit to China was a part of the exchange programs organized and sponsored by the United States National Committee on United States–China Relations and the Chinese National Ministry of Education. Before the early 1980s, China was a fairly closed country without much contact with the outside world, the least of which was the United States, which was considered the arch-enemy of the Chinese people in the 1950s through the mid-1970s. Despite Dewey's earlier influence, the Chinese education system now followed the former Soviet Union models and was guided by the Marxist-Leninist and Maoist thought. After the normalization of diplomatic relations between the United States and China in the late 1970s, the Chinese educators became very eager to learn from the educational experiences of American educators. In 1981, the Chinese National Ministry of Education organized the first Teacher Education Delegation to the United States, which consisted of key administrators from several major national teacher training institutions as well as selected officials from the Chinese National Ministry of Education.

While in the United States, the Chinese delegation visited the colleges/schools of education in several major public and private universities—the University of California at Los Angeles, Stanford University, Harvard University, Columbia University, the University of Michigan, among others—observed innovative educational reform practices in both public and private schools, and engaged in fruitful conversations with prominent American educators including John I. Goodlad, Lee Shulman, and Lawrence Cremin. The Chinese delegation was deeply impressed with the modern theories and practices in American education. Although Bruner's discovery method had been introduced in China, little else was known about educational thought and practices outside of China. On this visit, the Chinese delegation took home not only their impressions of the schools and schools of education in the United States, but also fresh ideas and books on education reform from Goodlad, Shulman, and Cremin.

The American Education Foundation Delegation's visit to China followed the Chinese Teacher Education Delegation's visit to the United States in 1981. It was an intensive twenty-day trip to ten different regions in China. Before Goodlad's delegation visited China, the Chinese National Ministry of Education had a fixed format for treating distinguished visiting educators from other countries: warm hospitality, fantastic food, beautiful sightseeing, and visits to the best of the educational institutions across China. However, Goodlad's visit significantly altered this routine.

Although this was his first visit to China, Goodlad was very shrewd in his observations. After a few trips to the key schools (the major academic-track schools) where they saw the elite among China's more than two hundred million students, Goodlad asked how delinquent children were educated and where they were schooled. The Chinese officials were quite surprised at first. They were so used to showing the best schools and best students to the foreign visitors, they never thought of presenting the guests with the less glorious side of Chinese education. Given Goodlad's clear concerns, the Chinese hosts decided to make an exception and led the delegation to an alternative school, where students with various delinquent behaviors (theft, violence, prostitution, etc.) were educated. The Chinese believe in the value of hard work and resort to manual labor and hands-on work as a vehicle to re-educate and reform the delinquent children and youths. Goodlad and other American visitors visited the toy and bicycle assembling workshops for boys and girls in the school; they asked many questions and made constructive suggestions.

The second important change that Goodlad made in the United States-China exchange programs was the attention he called to the education of children in the rural, minority areas. China has fifty-five minority nationalities, most of whom dwell in the special minority autonomous regions and rural, border areas. When Goodlad's delegation visited China, they were taken to the border province of Yunnan, where their hosts from the Chinese National Ministry of Education planned for them to tour the Stone Forest, a famous sightseeing spot. While most delegates were looking forward to the sightseeing trip, Goodlad had something else in mind. When he learned that Yunnan has more than twenty minority nationalities, many of whom live in the Stone Forest Region, he insisted on visiting a rural school for the minority children. Again, this had never before been arranged for foreign visitors in the routine exchange programs of the Chinese National Ministry of Education. The conditions in the rural schools, especially for those in the minority areas, were not very good and the quality of education was much lower than that in the major key schools in China's large cities. The Chinese always want to show their best to their guests, and Goodlad's suggestion sent another ripple of change through the established exchange programs.

Again, the Chinese officials made special arrangements for his delegation to visit an ordinary rural, minority school in the Stone Forest Region. During the visit, the Chinese hosts noted Goodlad's clear concern for the minority children and their families, his detailed questions regarding the curriculum, instruction, and reform in the minority school, and his constant observation and comparison of the differences between this school and the other schools he visited in the large cities in China. Many questions were raised regarding whether children in China's rural and minority areas received the same access to knowledge as the mainstream children living in large cities.

Sometimes it takes an outsider to help open the insider's eyes. When John Dewey and Paul Monroe visited China in the early 1920s, their former students in China took them to visit China's schools in both urban and rural areas, which helped the Chinese educators themselves to see the tragic conditions of education in China at that time—over 80 percent of the people lived in poverty in the countryside and over 77 percent of the population was illiterate. As a result of these visits and discussions with their American mentors, some Chinese intellectuals went through fundamental personal transformation; some even gave up their positions and comfortable lives in the cities, went to the countryside to live the simple life of farmers, and devoted their lives to developing rural education for the ordinary working people.

Goodlad's visit to China, although a short one, exerted similar kinds of influence on his Chinese counterparts—he impressed upon them the importance of education for the disadvantaged and the less fortunate, and urged them to focus more attention on the education for children with special needs and problems. His suggestions prompted the Chinese National Ministry of Education to make a significant change in its policy and practice in international education exchange programs—from then on, education delegations from other countries would have the opportunity to visit not only the best but also the ordinary and special education schools so that they could obtain a more balanced view of Chinese education and engage in active discussions on education for all children.

Influence on Chinese Educators

Both Dewey's and Goodlad's visits to China left deep impressions on Chinese educators and, as a result, many came to the United States to conduct study and research under their guidance. When Dewey was on the faculty at Columbia University, Teachers College led all other American colleges and universities in Chinese graduates. Several nationally famous modern educators in China—Chen Heqing, Tao Xingzhi, and Hu Shi—were former students of Dewey. They spearheaded the spread and implementation of Dewey's philosophy on education and democracy in Chinese practices. Dewey also kept close and frequent correspondence with his Chinese students and encouraged them to commit to the cause of democratic development in China. His Chinese followers always sought him for lessons from American educational and political experiences and regarded him as "a most dear friend to the Chinese people, one who understands what China needs the most."[6] During the Chinese anti-Japanese movement, Dewey signed, together with Einstein and fourteen other renowned American scholars, an open letter to the Chinese government, urging it to release seven patriotic Chinese intellectuals, one of whom was the first translator of Dewey's *Democracy and Education* from English to Chinese.

In the 1980s and 1990s, Goodlad, like Dewey, also mentored Chinese intellectuals, including graduate students, visiting scholars, and visiting Chinese education delegations. After his historical visit to China in 1981, he has received standing invitations from Chinese education institutions to visit and lecture there, and he has kept active correspondence and communication with education administrators and university professors in China. Two Chinese doctoral students participated in the national Study of the Education of Educators in the United

States directed by Goodlad. They have translated and published re-search papers and books by Goodlad and introduced his ideas to Chinese education reformers, and they have designed and conducted comparative studies of teacher education in the United States and China. To the Chinese educators who have worked with him, Goodlad is a master mentor in educational inquiry and a role model in implementing changes in educational institutions.

Goodlad recommended many readings to Chinese students and scholars including works by John Dewey, R. S. Peters, Alfred North Whitehead, contemporary United States philosophers, and philosophers from other cultures. His own position is that education is a process of inquiry through which individuals come to understand physical and social phenomena, organized subject matter, and ultimately, themselves. This is the direct opposite of assimilating information as facts or truth—the only mode of learning that most Chinese educators have been familiar with in their upbringing and education in China.

In Chinese students' schooling, they were exposed to Marxist-Leninist and Mao Zedong thought, and were taught to accept these theories as truths and gospels. Goodlad helped open his Chinese students' eyes to a different world with different ways of thinking, different ways of schooling, and very different ways of life.

The inquiry method is very different from the rote learning method in the Chinese educational system. Increasingly, the Chinese educators, especially those who have studied in the United States, are introducing the inquiry method into the Chinese schools and colleges.[7] Goodlad is an excellent role model in educational inquiry, not only for American scholars but also for the Chinese educators. Inquiry—particularly *critical* inquiry—is the necessary first step to help Chinese educators understand some of the wrenching problems, such as inequality of educational opportunity, in Chinese education.[8]

Implications of Goodlad's and Dewey's Ideas for Education and Democracy in China

Goodlad's and Dewey's educational philosophy and mankind perspectives have significant implications for the development of education and democracy in China. In fact, both Dewey's and Goodlad's visits to China were partially responsible for the democratic movements and educational reform in China, at two of the most important historical periods in modern Chinese history.[9] Dewey's former students from

China tried to establish Dewey experimental schools and normal schools in China, some of which still exist today as the hotbeds for developing democratic and progressive educational practices. There are many similarities in the education philosophies of Dewey and Goodlad. In some ways, Goodlad's ideas are more applicable to the modern Chinese educational practices, especially to the development of a more equitable education for all children in China.

A consistent theme in Goodlad's educational philosophy is the emphasis on achieving excellence and equity for all children. As noted above, during his visit to China, he requested to see schools for children with special needs and problems and for children from the rural and minority areas in China because he was concerned about their access to schools and to knowledge. In *A Place Called School*,[10] Goodlad refers to his visit to the key schools—exemplary and experimental schools often affiliated with teacher training institutions in China—and suggests that the word "key" can be used to describe centers and schools for developing innovative educational practices in American educational reform. While acknowledging the role of the Chinese key schools in pioneering the implementation of new policies and sometimes cooperating with the universities in conducting modest education experiments, Goodlad points out that there were some controversies surrounding their presence and designation because of the elitist connotations.[11]

Key schools in China were first established in 1953 at the suggestion of Mao Zedong. The Chinese government's rationale for establishing key schools was that a fairly large amount of resources should be mustered to run a number of key schools in order to train for the state a small group of high-quality, specialized personnel so as to rapidly upgrade China's scientific and cultural level.[12] The educational system thus established formed a new relationship that was generally described as one between big and small pagodas: the formation from elementary through secondary to tertiary schools resembled a pagoda—the higher the level, the fewer the schools. And the key schools at all levels were the core and mainstay of this big pagoda, namely, the small pagodas. As the key schools developed in the 1950s and 1960s, inequality of educational opportunity became a controversial issue among the Chinese educators and parents. Children admitted to key schools experienced a higher quality curriculum and better quality teachers and had a much greater chance of passing the national examination for university entrance.

Although the key schools were destroyed during the Cultural Revolution in the late 1960s and early 1970s, they were restored in 1978 on a national scale. Again, the government deems it a measure of strategic significance to re-establish the key school system so as to concentrate the limited resources in a relatively small number of schools in order to expedite the training of outstanding personnel. Key schools were established not only in secondary level, but also at the university, elementary school, and kindergartens, although the latter two were abolished in the early 1980s due to strong protests from the parents. Some key schools still serve as lab schools for teacher training and educational experiments, but most are run as academic-track schools preparing students for the passage through the national examination for entrance into higher education. The promotion rate from key secondary schools to universities is extremely high—90 percent in some schools—compared with the average promotion rate—4 to 5 percent—of the whole country. In ordinary schools, there are also academic and vocational (or fast and slow) tracks, and those assigned to vocational (or slow) tracks based on test scores have few chances of receiving higher education and obtaining higher-status jobs in the society. Many teachers, students, and parents in ordinary schools feel depressed, frustrated, and victimized, and consequently, there has been heated debate over the necessity of running key schools.[13]

The nature of the debate over tracking in China, however, is very different from that in the United States because the official argument for it is that "everyone is equal in front of test scores," a long-standing popular saying that few dare to challenge. To many Chinese education policymakers, key schools and tracking are the rational and commonsense solutions to the problem of limited resources and the urgent need for a small cadre of highly educated scientists for modernization purposes. In the United States, it is a matter of equality of educational opportunity—whether all have equal access to excellent schooling and knowledge.

The Chinese education policymakers can be persuaded to change their policies and practices regarding key schools and tracking in order to provide better education for all children if they study carefully the findings from Goodlad's A Place Called School,[14] which demonstrate the detrimental effects of tracking on children, especially those from disadvantaged backgrounds—in the United States these are children from the urban, minority, and poor families, and in China they are children from the rural and minority areas and remote regions as well as urban children attending ordinary schools. In fact, both in China and in the United States, studies have shown there to be lower self-esteem, more school misconduct, higher dropout rates, and higher delinquency among students in lower tracks.[15] As Goodlad observes, track placement affects whether or not students plan to go to college and the probability of their acceptance, over and beyond the effects of aptitude and grades.[16] This is also very true in China. There is in China, as in the United States, a huge gap between our highly idealistic goals for schooling in our society and the differentiated opportunities condoned and supported in schools.[17]

Goodlad has envisioned and implemented many changes in order to create excellence and equity in American education. Some of these are also highly relevant for Chinese educational reform. First, all of the major problems in schools need to be addressed as a system, rather than one by one or piecemeal.[18] The debate on key schools in China should be expanded into a serious, reflective inquiry into all aspects of education, including the overall goals, curriculum designs, the examination system, the connection between education and work and between lower-level schools and higher education.

Second, it is a moral imperative to provide equal access to good schools and high-status knowledge to all children, not just some children who, because of where they live and who their parents are, are placed in high tracks or academic-track/key schools. Goodlad and his colleagues have demonstrated with sufficient empirical evidence the detrimental effects of tracking on children from disadvantaged backgrounds. They have also offered promising alternatives to tracking: agreement on a common core of studies from which students cannot escape through electives; mastery learning, which emphasizes a combination of large-group instruction and small-group peer tutoring; elimination of any arrangements designed to group students in separate classrooms on the basis of past performance; and random assignment of students to heterogeneous classes that can offer the most equity with respect to gaining access to knowledge while still preserving the more advantageous content and teaching practices of the upper tracks.[19]

In fact, comparative studies have found that the Chinese and other Asian nation students employ more cooperative learning, peer tutoring, and teamwork in their studies.[20] The Chinese schools may even have a better chance to succeed in implementing Goodlad's reform agenda. After all, the Chinese educators have had their success in creatively and critically experimenting with John Dewey's philosophy in Chinese educational practices. They can be equally successful in adapting Goodlad's ideas in their educational reform. Both Dewey and Goodlad are now considered "The Great Western Educators" in modern Chinese education literature.[21] They certainly deserve the titles and the respect from the Chinese people.

Notes

1 See, for example, Ralph Tyler, "Introduction," in Judith S. Golub, ed., John I. Goodlad, *Facing the Future: Issues in Education and Schooling* (New York: McGraw-Hill, 1976), 1-3; M. Frances Klein, "John I. Goodlad: Essential Characteristics of His Teaching," *Teaching Education* 4 (1992): 155-60; and the other chapters in this book.

2 Tokyo University, for example, has forty-four references (books, reports, articles) by Goodlad. The two top universities in education in China—Beijing Normal University and East China Normal University—also have ten of the most important works by Goodlad in their libraries. The book by Kenneth A. Sirotnik and John I. Goodlad, *School-University Partnerships in Action: Concepts, Cases, and Concerns* (New York: Teachers College Press, 1988) was translated into Japanese by Takeaki Nakadome in 1994. In addition, in 1987, I collaborated with Liangfang Shi in translating "Schools and Universities as Partners in Educational Reform," by John I. Goodlad from English to Chinese, and in 1989, I collaborated with Jianping Shen in translating chapter 6 from *A Place Called School* from English into Chinese. Both translated papers were published in the prestigious Educational Science Edition of the *Journal of East China Normal University*, which is widely distributed to educators throughout China. Most recently, Jianping Shen translated Goodlad's book, *What Schools Are For*, from English to Chinese, which is currently in press in Taiwan.

3 Zhixin Su, "A Critical Evaluation of John Dewey's Influence on Chinese Education," *American Journal of Education* 103 (May 1995): 302-325. See, for example, John I. Goodlad and Pamela Keating, eds., *Access to Knowledge: The Continuing Agenda for Our Nation's Schools*, revised edition (New York: College Entrance Examination Board, 1994).

4 Robert W. Clapton and Tsuin-Chen Ou, "Introduction," in John Dewey, *Lectures in China*, 1919-20 (Honolulu: University of Hawaii Press, 1973), 22-23.

5 Zhixin Su, "Teaching, Learning, and Reflective Acting: A Dewey Experiment in Chinese Teacher Education," 98 *Teachers College Record* (Fall 1996): 126-52.

6 Su, "Teaching, Learning, and Reflective Acting."

7 For comparisons of the teaching and learning methods in American and Chinese schools, please see Zhixin Su et al., "Teaching and Learning Science in American and Chinese High Schools: A Comparative Study," *Comparative Education* 30 (1994): 255-70.

8   For what it means to make inquiry critical see, for example, Kenneth A. Sirotnik, "Critical Inquiry: A Paradigm for Praxis," in Edmund C. Short, ed., *Form of Curriculum Inquiry: Guidelines for the Conduct of Educational Research* (New York: SUNY Press, 1991).

9   Zhixin Su, "A Critical Evaluation of John Dewey's Influence on Chinese Education," *American Journal of Education* 103 (May 1995): 302–25.

10   John I. Goodlad, *A Place Called School: Prospects for the Future* (New York: McGraw-Hill, 1984).

11   Goodlad, *A Place Called School*, 300.

12   Ximin Pan, "A Preliminary Discussion of Problems Involving Several Aspects of Key Schools," *Inner Mongolia Social Sciences* 3 (1982): 27–30.

13   Lu Bing and Wang Zhaojie, "It Is Improper to Lay Lopsided Emphasis on Promotion Rate," *Guangming Daily*, 5 November 1982, 1; From the Editor, "Is It Proper to Divide Senior High School Textbooks into Two Categories?" *People's Daily*, 3 November 1984, 5.

14   Goodlad, *A Place Called School*; and Jeannie Oakes, *Keeping Track: How Schools Structure Inequality* (New Haven: Yale University Press, 1985).

15   Walter E. Schafer and Carol Olexa, *Tracking and Opportunity* (Scranton, Pa.: Chandler Publishing Co., 1971); and Editor, "Is It Proper to Divide Senior High School Textbooks into Two Categories?" *People's Daily*, 3 November 1984, 5.

16   Goodlad, *A Place Called School*, 152.

17   Goodlad, *A Place Called School*, 161.

18   Goodlad, *A Place Called School*, 271.

19   Goodlad, *A Place Called School*, 296–97.

20   Zhixin Su, "Teaching and Learning Science in American and Chinese High Schools: A Comparative Study"; and Harold Stevenson and James Stigler, *The Learning Gap* (New York: Summit Books, 1992).

21   See, for example, Zhixin Su, "A Critical Evaluation of John Dewey's Influence on Chinese Education"; and Jianping Shen, "John I. Goodlad: A Great Educational Researcher and Practitioner," *Information on Educational Research* 5 (1997): 41–51; Jianping Shen has also written a chapter, "John I. Goodlad and His Educational Ideas," to be published in the book, *Great Western Educators*, by the Shanghai East China Normal University Press.

Chapter 12

Connecting Education and Community

Paul E. Heckman

A group of mothers travels to Phoenix, Arizona, to meet with the governor's assistant to express their concern for their neighborhood and children and to request state resources for childcare services for families in their neighborhood. At first glance, this is not an unusual event. Mothers often have access to and request assistance from a governor's office—if they are influential. What is different about this story is that these mothers are from an economically poor Latino community in southeastern Arizona. These mothers have little experience with visits to politicians' offices or with influencing policymakers at the local or state level. Yet, after the conversation with the governor's assistant, they receive a commitment of support for their request for financial resources. On the return trip home to Tucson, Arizona, they are lively, delighted, empowered. They understand that through their efforts to clearly communicate their wants to a high-level politician, they have garnered "state" support for their neighborhood and school. They also understand that political influence is possible for them, if they and their neighbors politically organize themselves.

Prior to this meeting, these mothers, their children, other community members, and the teachers and principal of their neighborhood school have been a part of the Educational and Community Change (ECC) Project at the University of Arizona, which has encouraged changes in their schools and neighborhoods.[1] One component of the Project's work has been promoting neighborhood organizing activities that urged adults to identify problematic conditions in their neighborhood, analyze those conditions to find out what problems may lie beneath them, and investigate alternatives that may address these problems. Together, they have sought changes for what they previously believed were unchangeable problems. In addition to the trip to the governor's office, for example, the children, their parents, other neighborhood members, and the teachers and principal of their neighborhood school were concerned about a vacant house that was across the street from the school. Homeless individuals were sleeping in this house and, from time to time, fires erupted from inside. At other times, the house was a place for drug use and drug selling. Children feared going by the house and parents feared for the well-being of their children and the overall effects that such a house posed for the neighborhood. Parents and their neighbors investigated and found out that the City of Tucson owned the property and building because of the property owner's default on taxes. They also found out that the City of Tucson could demolish the house, ridding the neighborhood of at least this one vacant house, and they called for meetings with a local city council member and requested that the city board up the house and put a fence around the building. The city complied and eventually demolished the house.

What follows in this chapter is an elaboration of some of the ideas and activities that guided the ECC Project and encouraged the above two examples. What is clear is that many ideas that John Goodlad has elaborated about educational change, conceptions of education, and the relationship between education and community heavily influenced the ECC Project and the concepts that guided it. In brief, the ECC Project sought the creation of new connections between families, neighborhood, and school in a low socioeconomic community and urged new schooling experiences for the children who lived in this community so that they could be successful in elementary school, future schooling, and in their lives beyond precollegiate schooling. In addition to the aforementioned neighborhood organizing, creating these connections required changes inside the school. For example, attention needed to be given to inventing a different kind of schoolwork for students and teachers in which school time and effort were used to identify both interesting and problematic conditions in the community. Children would work as scientists, historians, mathematicians, and writers in their efforts to understand a real-world problem in their community and what possible solutions might address it. Knowledge and resources that existed in the families and in the school's neighborhood would be used to attend to those problems. We believed that in these kinds of studies, children could more readily bring their existing knowledge and resources to bear and that it would provide motivation for conducting these studies because the interests of their neighborhood and families were being directly affected.

During the seven years of Project work that promoted connections between education and community, the individuals involved contributed their insights and ideas. Consequently, the initial ideas of the Project evolved in ways that we could never have anticipated at the beginning. This chapter will explore this evolution during the Project's work in the first two of the eventual five Project sites in Tucson, Arizona. Lessons learned from what can happen when education and community are understood as interconnected concepts include this fundamental idea: education happens in a community among all the educational institutions that exist there, and by studying real community problems that need improvement, children's academic knowledge and skills are furthered.

Guiding Ideas about Education and Community

The Goals and Purposes of Education

The ECC Project grew out of considering what it might take to answer the questions: Can *it* be done? Can schools fundamentally alter the modal ideas, beliefs, actions, and structures that typically exist in most schools and classrooms? And if so, can schools then create new ideas and practices that promote achievement and success for *all* children—both in their elementary and secondary schooling experiences and for their years beyond formal schooling?

The Project began with particular conceptions of education and its connection to community. One definition of education is to stimulate or develop the growth of an individual. In this sense, when we speak of educating children, we are talking about furthering children's development in line with an intended set of purposes and values. Bowman discusses a view of development that focuses on the importance of the social environment of the child, that shapes the child's development, and the contribution that the child individually makes to her environment and hence her development.[2] In this view, development involves the accrual of knowledge and skills, that arises from the child's interaction and activity with others and involves dialogue and experiences with older and younger members of the community. Hence, children's development and achievement are rooted in their community contexts and those with whom they spend their time in these settings.

Different definitions of development as well as different goals and purposes have focused public schools at various times. Each has had more or less prominence during different periods of American educational history. Labaree discusses three goals that have been in conflict with each other throughout the history of American schooling: the goals to promote democratic equality, social efficiency, and/or social mobility.[3] The first goal, democratic equality, seeks to prepare children in schools "to play constructive roles in a democratic society."[4] The second goal, social efficiency, asks children to adapt to "the requirements of a hierarchical social structure and the demands of the occupational marketplace."[5] The third goal, social mobility, seeks educational credentials for students that "they need in order to get ahead in this structure (or to maintain their current position)."[6] Labaree further contends that these conflicts are inescapable and even necessary.

> The fact that educational goals are in conflict, however, is not in itself an unmanageable problem. We cannot realistically escape from it by just choosing one goal and eliminating the others. Any healthy society needs an educational system that helps to produce good citizens, good workers, and good social opportunities. Preparing young people to enter into full involvement in a complex society is itself a complex task that necessarily requires educators to balance a variety of competing concerns, and the educational institutions that result from this effort necessarily are going to embody these tensions.[7]

The ECC Project sought ways in which schools might focus on several goals or purposes of education, similar to those identified by Labaree. The Project used as one of its guides the four purposes of education that Goodlad had articulated following an examination of the educational goal statements from the fifty states and a review of the literature, that focused on a historical examination of the goals of American education: 1) intellectual development; 2) social development; 3) vocational development; and 4) personal development.[8] These goals, we believed, could guide the development of new schooling and classroom activities in Project sites if they were treated as equally important and tended to in concert. In the Project's view, public schools were indeed created and now exist to promote democratic citizenship; successful citizens fully participate in and benefit from the political, economic, and family lives of their community. This requires, however, that attention be paid to all four of the goals suggested by Goodlad. In short, intellectual development involves encouragement of children and youths to further their cognitive abilities and insights into what have been called the academics. Social development seeks children's insights and actions about working, interacting, and achieving with others and suggests the importance of cooperation and interpersonal relationships. Vocational development focuses on enlarging individuals' dispositions to productively work in a job or career and be successful in the economy. Personal development encourages individuals toward creativity, self-expression, and a positive sense of self.

As Labaree suggested, however, there are tensions among these various purposes of public schooling, that often compete with each other for the attention of educators. Moreover, these tensions have important implications for guiding what schools focus on as they consider what the nature of the educational experiences should be for children. For the ECC Project, each of the four goal areas had equal importance; all were believed to contribute to each and every child's development as a productive citizen of our democracy.

An Understanding of Prior Knowledge and Cultural Wealth

While the conceptions and purposes of education were important guides for what might happen in Project schools, there were other considerations as well. The Project was based on a conception of prior knowledge that took into account the fact that children develop physically, emotionally, and intellectually prior to the time that they begin schooling. Children bring important knowledge with them to school and important human resources and knowledge exist in their neighborhood. This prior knowledge could direct schooling activity and inform what knowledge and skills were to be promoted in the classroom. However, it was clear that sometimes schools and those involved in education did not consider all forms and conceptions of knowledge to be equally valid. Often, the knowledge that educators are encouraged to promote does not take into account the students' prior knowledge that they bring with them to school from their interactions at home and in their communities. The cultural wealth found in many communities, especially the cultural wealth that exists in economically poor neighborhoods, is often disregarded, or at best, undervalued, because it differs from the "high-cultural" wealth more often found in upper-middle class communities.[9] This has several effects. First, when one kind of cultural wealth has greater value than another, what is understood to be culture narrows and no longer encompasses, for example, all learned behavior or "the whole range of human activities which are learned and not instinctive."[10] Second, when the conception of cultural wealth narrows to a high-cultural wealth notion, those individuals with various kinds of cultural wealth have fewer educational opportunities to fully participate in and benefit from their personal and community resources.

The ECC Project believed that the generally held narrow conception of cultural wealth in schools could be one explanation for the long-standing empirical relationship between socioeconomic status, race, and measures of school achievement. A persistent interpretation of this relationship suggests that the problem is the inadequacy of economically poor families, their human resources, and the knowledge that the children bring to school. If economically poor families would be like middle-class families, the argument goes, and if the children of these economically poor families knew what middle-class children knew, then economically poor children would have higher achievement scores and the correlation would vanish. For example, they argue that more books need to be in the homes and that middle "classness" has to pervade or else children cannot learn in school. An even more pernicious interpretation suggests that the children and their families who are economically poor and of color cannot learn as much as middle-class white children because these children are not smart enough. Such interpretations, however, are either blatantly wrong or they undervalue the importance of human and material resources in particular communities and the knowledge that resides in them. These persistent views have kept educational policy and practice stagnated during the past two decades, and the relationship between socioeconomic status, race, and student achievement has remained unchanged.

The Educational Ecology of the Child
The ECC Project sought an alternative interpretation and explanation for why economically poor children, usually of color, did not succeed in school. One alternative is Bronfenbrenner's idea of an ecology of human development as a way to understand the multiple interactions from which children develop.[11] Goodlad has extended the idea of an ecology of human development to education by calling the various educational experiences of a child—the set of experiences and interactions that children have with individuals, objects, and activities in various places in their neighborhood and community—the "educational ecology" of the child.[12] Cremin agrees and refers to the multiple educational influences in a child's life as the "configuration of education."[13] Thus, we considered the entire "educational ecology" of the student as opposed to the more common practice of looking at the school as the sole place of education. Moreover, the ecological metaphor served

as a conceptual organizer of how we thought about and enacted education, more generally.[14]

Formal, Nonformal, and Informal Education

Cremin and LaBelle delineate three kinds of educational institutions that make up any given educational ecology.[15] For them, the three major parts of any ecology or configuration of education are formal, nonformal, and informal educational activities and institutions. Formal education consists of schools and the activities under way in them that are guided by formal curricula and structures, that either further or impede the development of children in these settings. For example, children experience a "graded" curriculum with delineated objectives that they are to learn in age-specific grouping arrangements with materials that correspond to their grade level.

Nonformal education involves those organized activities in which children and youths regularly engage outside of formal education—before and after school as well as during summer and holiday recesses. Nonformal education activities happen in clubs and other voluntary associations, that also have explicit guidelines to suggest the nature of the activities in which children and youths are to engage. For example, Boy Scouts and Girl Scouts, 4-H Clubs, summer camps, after-school childcare, and youth activities like the American Youth Soccer Organization have guidelines, and activities occur regularly after school, on weekends, and during the summer.

Informal education happens outside of formal and nonformal education and consists of all of the other experiences that children have in their families and in interaction with other individuals in their neighborhood and community. These activities are more often unplanned and have fewer explicit goals than do the activities of nonformal and formal education. For example, when parents and children sit at the dinner table, they eat and talk. Those involved in these interactions have not planned the outcome of these discussions or the general format for what will happen first or second or third. Nonetheless, particular forms of discourse are learned and used in these discussions as well as ways of understanding the world and ideas about that world. For example, family stories that are told convey guidelines for what is important in life and how to best live that life. William Whyte's *Street Corner Society* describes activities and guidelines that were conveyed to children in the North End of Boston in the late 1930s. He describes how he came to understand the importance of the Italian language in the neighborhood and the manner in which roles for men and women are established and thus learned. This study and more recent ones, such as David Simon and Edward Burns' *The Corner,* further illustrate the nature of the informal educational system and confirm that learning happens within neighborhoods.[16]

For some children, their experiences within and across the institutions and activities of the educational ecology—formal, nonformal, and informal education—are smooth and congruent. For example, a middle-class child in her family learns a standard English dialect. When she goes to school, the teachers and most of her classmates also use this language. She fits in nicely and usually knows this immediately. No one asks her to change her language or the stories that she learned in her informal education at home and in her neighborhood. Instead, she is often asked to use what she already knows about her language. When she tells a story about a summer vacation or a family tradition, for example, she conveys her story in the language that she knows— the same language of most of her teachers. When the child leaves school and goes to a nonformal educational after-school activity, be it childcare or a club program, she also experiences a "fit." In other words, she routinely experiences an uninterrupted flow in using her home language, experiences, and discourse patterns across the educational ecology.

However, other children, usually those who are economically poor and of color, have a different experience. Because of the differences between the various parts of the ecology, these children experience incongruity and conflict, especially between their formal and informal and sometimes between their informal and nonformal educational experiences. For example, a child of color who lives in an economically poor community often experiences a language other than standard English at home and in his neighborhood. If the child learns a primary language other than English, let's say Spanish, or a nonstandard dialect of English, he will find that this language and the discourse patterns work well in the informal setting. The child is understood by the members of his family and neighborhood when he speaks, and he understands what others are communicating. When the child goes to school, however, standard English is exclusively used by the child's teachers and sometimes his peers. The adults in the school expect all of the children in the school to understand and be understood in the language of standard English. The child who learned nonstandard English, however, experiences a conflict. What has seemed normal and expected in his informal education at home and in his neighborhood is now considered incorrect. The child finds himself being negatively challenged, at worst, or ignored, at best. He cannot use what he knows from his informal education at home and in his neighborhood, and he comes to believe that what he knows is less important than what the teacher knows. In some cases, if the child leaves school and goes to a nonformal educational activity, he may or may not experience a similar conflict. For example, in an after-school program, a child's language may also be challenged because in some of these settings efforts are under way to "bring the child into the mainstream society."

Because of the perceived lack of value of what some children bring to school, schools have often advocated for changes in students' informal education—as if somehow the informal education in the ecology of these children could better align with the values and ideas that have guided schools (formal education) and that have existed in middle-class communities for decades. In order to succeed, the conventional line of thinking goes, these children have to become "ready" for school, in effect, to be more like white and middle-class children.

The ECC Project sought alternatives to this view. We agreed that if the relationship between the informal and formal educational institutions could be altered, economically poor children of color would benefit and demonstrate greater learning. But the focus of change was not to be on the informal education—namely changing the parents, their family interactions, and the community—but instead on the school. In particular, we sought changes in the ideas and practices of schooling that would take advantage of the knowledge and resources that children bring with them to school. Our hope was that children's knowledge and what they thought about from their informal educational experiences could focus the curriculum and activities of both nonformal and formal activities. While we acknowledged the tremendous task being proposed, we also knew that if the Project could encourage continuity among these three parts of the educational ecology, then children who have different informal educational experiences than white middle-class children would finally experience advantages in school that they never before had.

Enacting the Ideas

The Work inside the School
During the first year of the Project, efforts were undertaken to lay the groundwork for fundamentally new connections between the families and neighborhood and the first project school. Two issues surfaced

from time to time that stimulated attention to what children knew and the resources they had in their families and neighborhood and focused people's thinking and actions inside of the school. These issues arose in the context of weekly "dialogue" sessions that took place in the school. In these sessions, the teachers, principal, and Project staff met for three hours and inquired into what each person thought about and practiced in their classrooms. We named these meetings "dialogues" because of the manner in which these group examinations happened. During these dialogues, all of the participants engaged in discussion and debate about the ideas underlying practices under way in classrooms, the problems with these ideas and practices, and the alternatives that could be pursued in classrooms. These dialogues had their bases in an inquiry and change process earlier identified by Goodlad and his colleagues as involving dialogue, decision making, action, and evaluation (DDAE).[17]

The first issue pertained to student behavior and the amount of time that teachers seemed to be using in their classrooms in getting students to "behave." In addition, these educators believed that they could predict who among their students would have behavioral problems. Their ability to make such predictions rested on what they thought they knew about a child's family and her siblings. For example, many of the siblings of those students who had "behavioral problems" were reported by these teachers to also have had behavioral problems. The younger siblings were behaving just like their older counterparts, and the older siblings had dropped out of school before completing high school.

The second, related issue focused directly on the fact that the children who attended this school appeared not to know what middle-class children knew (e.g., colors, the alphabet, certain stories and nursery rhymes). Since these children did not have this kind of knowledge, the children had more difficulty with schooling activities and were not successful with the classroom materials with which most middle-class children had success. The teachers' explanations about why the children knew little of what they expected them to know—and why they behaved poorly—focused on the inadequacy of the families and the neighborhood where these children lived. In their view, family members did not promote expected school behaviors nor did they urge children to learn concepts and ideas that were valued in the school. The teachers believed that these children did not have the appropriate dispositions or knowledge because the parents did not spend time with them exploring the names of the colors, for example, or expressing their support for their education in the school.[18]

In dialogue sessions, these explanations, theories, and beliefs were explored and alternative explanations sought so that new thoughts and actions could arise in the school—and, increasingly this happened. For example, during one of the dialogue sessions in which several teachers were putting forth the belief that children did not know anything when they came to school, we decided as a group to conduct an experiment during the forthcoming week. In this experiment, we would ask children what they knew about whatever teachers were going to be exploring or "teaching" before the children did or were taught the activity. The questioning of the teachers' prevailing beliefs and the idea for the experiment arose in light of discussions about human cognition and the existence of prior knowledge, as well as Eleanor Duckworth's view that children have "wonderful ideas."[19] The experiment to be conducted in classrooms would investigate what and how much children knew and what they thought about when presented with a task or learning situation in school. In general, a view existed among many in the dialogue group that children would not know much about what they were to be taught, because that is why they needed to be taught. In addition, another question to be investigated in the experiment was whether or not students would reveal more knowledge if they were asked to express this knowledge in their first or second language (in the case of this school, Spanish or English).

During the week, most teachers went back to their classrooms and, at some point, asked children what they knew about a particular subject that was going to be studied, and they sought expression of this knowledge in either English or Spanish. When the dialogue group next met, a number of participants brought in comments from the children about what they knew, in both languages, recorded on large sheets of chart paper. As teachers discussed what they found out, they expressed surprise at how much students knew. Moreover, when children's primary language was Spanish and when they expressed their knowledge in that language, the list of what these students knew and expressed grew substantially. This fact also surprised the teachers.

The revelation that the children both knew a lot and expressed more of their knowledge when using their primary language generated questions about the existing belief that these children did not know much of anything. After additional discussion and examination, many of the participants decided to explore the issue further, even as they tentatively retained their conventional view. Throughout the next several months of discussion and additional investigations, attention turned to the importance of students' interests and whether or not engagement increases and misbehavior decreases when students pursue their interests. This latter question arose since some members of the dialogue group reported that they had seen such results already in their classrooms.

These developments in the thinking and actions of teachers in the first Project site continued throughout the first year of work. This in turn was beginning to affect the relationship between the school and the community in that the work inside of the school was promoting questions in the minds of educators about the prevailing, taken-for-granted ideas about the prior knowledge of the children (or their cultural wealth), the knowledge and resources that existed in the families and the neighborhood, and the importance of altering some of these old, heretofore unexamined, assumptions and theories.

The Work in the Neighborhood

More direct focus on the neighborhood and the relationship between the school and the community occurred in the second year. Our assumption was that important human and material resources existed in the families and the neighborhood but that individuals and other resources were underutilized because parents and their neighbors remained isolated from each other and not involved in political activity. One of the neighborhood organizations with which the Project was developing a connection was known as the House of Neighborly Service (HNS). The director of the HNS supported the Project, its assumptions, and its objective to promote the success of neighborhood children in school and beyond. The discovery of these shared ideas was serendipitous. When the Project began, we anticipated that we would seek connections among different educational institutions in Project communities so that we were addressing various aspects of the children's educational ecology. However, at that time, we were unclear about which agencies we would connect with and what the nature of those connections would be. We assumed that we would find many nonformal educational institutions within this one project neighborhood and that collaborating with HNS was simply one of many collaborations to be found. As we were to later learn, however, in this and many other economically poor communities in Tucson, few of the nonformal institutions wanted to collaborate on objectives like ours. Instead, many were focused on a single objective, such as the prevention of substance abuse and their particular methods for addressing substance abuse, and they were not interested in broadening their focuses and their methods of relating to children and their families.

Eventually, we hired an individual who would coordinate project work in the neighborhood, encourage connections among the educational institutions including the school and families, and visit key parents and community members one-on-one in their homes. The purposes for these home visits focused on getting to know these parents and neighborhood members, finding out what they wanted for their children and themselves, and understanding their views of their school and neighborhood. The hope was that common interests and issues would surface, and further meetings with all of those who had these common interests would lead to useful action. As this work unfolded with the intended consequences, teachers saw parents as resourceful, knowledgeable, and motivated citizens eager to make their neighborhood better and educate their children.[20]

For example, as noted in the introduction, parents were instrumental in having the City of Tucson board up and erect a fence around an abandoned house across the street from the first Project school. In order for that decision to be made, parents and students investigated various options for removing transient individuals from this house with a City Council member and other city departments. In addition, parents organized a large neighborhood meeting with over sixty community members, children, and teachers from the school and designed and coordinated a number of speeches that presented their requests and arguments in support of the City taking action to board and fence the house.

After the meeting with the City Council member, teachers commented on their positive impressions of the students and parents, their ability to orally present their requests for action, the power of the arguments that were presented, and the resulting decision by the City to grant the requests of the parents. These impressions, in turn, challenged the prevailing view held by those inside of the school that parents did not care and did not have the necessary skills from which children could learn. They also saw a motivated and articulate group of students who could present arguments to a City Council member that yielded positive results for the community.

The Creation of the Coalition

Another development in the Project also promoted stronger connections between the school and neighborhood and a more positive assessment of the parents, students, and neighborhood. An organization that became known as the Coalition was created by parents, other community members, teachers, the principal, several Council members from the City of South Tucson, a member of the governing board of the school district, an assistant superintendent of the school district, several business people from the greater Tucson community, and staff members of several community organizations in the City of South Tucson and the City of Tucson.

At first, the Coalition focused on matters of neighborhood safety, which is why political action in the neighborhood centered on vacant houses. Subsequently, the Coalition sought ways of creating and connecting after-school and summer childcare activities to what was happening inside of the school program as it became reinvented through its work with the Project. After-school and summer school activities were important to the parents and to the Project's interest in promoting a more powerful educational ecology. For parents, the interest in the after-school activities arose because they wanted activities for their children that would promote their success and more productive use of their time when school was not in session. For the Project, its conception of education sought connections among nonformal, informal, and formal education.

Space limitations do not permit detailing the many features and activities of this Coalition.[21] Suffice it to note that because of the Coalition's construction, political actions benefiting the community and the school, teachers' views of parents and the neighborhood became more positive. In turn, these more positive views of the informal and nonformal institutions of the neighborhood encouraged positive views of the children as capable and interested in learning in school. Teachers saw parents analyze situations, find alternatives, argue for alternatives with politicians, find resources, and enact political influence in securing the resources and changes in characteristics of their neighborhood; and teachers concluded that the parents were smart, skillful, knowledgeable, and interested in improving their own circumstances. Consequently, if parents were like this, then, the potential of their children also being this way was more likely. Moreover, as parents experienced teachers interacting with them and their children in more positive and collaborative ways, parents trusted teachers more and would, in turn, come to school more often to just talk and discuss what they were thinking and understanding about their children, the neighborhood, and the school. Parents were also being asked more

and more to come to school and share their many skills and knowledge in classrooms. Parents and other community members were being seen as resources, rather than a group of individuals who were in
deficit and in need of being remediated through parent education or
other kinds of help.

As the fourth year of the Project came to a close, it was becoming
apparent that the ECC Project neighborhoods and schools in the City
of South Tucson were developing into what Goodlad had earlier referred to as an "educative community."[22] In this sense, the school
(formal education), after-school and summer programs (nonformal
education), and the interactions among family members and other
community members (informal education) interconnected. In such an
educative community, education starts with the knowledge and skills
and resources of the child and his or her family and, from these, new
knowledge and skills are built.

Developments Between the School and the Community

Connections Between the Classroom and the Community

In the two schools where the Project had now focused its work, connections between education and community developed in ways we
had anticipated. First, student interests and prior knowledge directed
what children focused on and investigated in their schoolwork. Second, students and their families were viewed as knowledgeable resources. Third, important schoolwork focused directly on students,
teachers, and parents working together to investigate, understand, and
alter problematic circumstances in their neighborhoods.

Teachers now experienced first-hand that when students have a
high degree of interest in their schoolwork, their considerable prior
knowledge in what they are studying and investigating becomes apparent. Consequently, teachers more readily connected students' motivation and success to their interests and prior knowledge, and
more classroom work was initiated with this in mind. This kind of
teaching usually took several days of discussion and negotiation about
questions that students wanted to explore and what they knew about
the phenomenon that might focus their questions. These initial explorations were often punctuated with visits to known locations that were
also of interest to students. Teachers discovered that important educational goals could be met by replacing textbook–centered topics and activities with more relevant, neighborhood-focused learning opportunities.

Because of these changes, a number of student investigations coincided with the actions that their parents were taking in the work of the Coalition. For example, at Mission View Elementary School, the citizens of the school district had passed a school building renovation bond. Mission View was in a later group of schools to undergo renovation. Parents and the Coalition became concerned that their wishes with regard to how the renovation would proceed were being overlooked and that less of the bond money was going to their school than to some in wealthier neighborhoods. In taking action on these concerns, the location and design of the playground became one of the negotiating points. At about the same time, children in several of the classrooms in the school were also expressing dismay at the condition of the existing playground. Consequently, the students began a study of various playgrounds: playground designs, how to estimate costs of playgrounds, and what would have to be done to rebuild them.

As the Coalition worked on the overall renovation design of the school building, the children interacted with Coalition members about their study and findings of playgrounds. Their work contributed to the negotiations between the Coalition and the school district about the allocation of resources and the scope and design of the school renovation work to be undertaken at this school. The adults saw that students knew something and that what they knew made a contribution to resolving an important adult and community issue in this neighborhood.

Interestingly, as students pursued their interests and added to their prior knowledge, there were less of what many in the schools referred to as "discipline problems." In turn, students viewed their school and classrooms as more engaging and interesting places and experienced teachers as liking and respecting them more. Parents saw their children as more interested and engaged and, consequently, saw the school as a more inviting place to be. The number of hours parents spent at school significantly increased. Teachers and parents became more connected, furthering the positive views of each other and of schooling.[23]

A New Relationship Between the School and the Community

Goodlad focuses on the educational ecology of communities because it is folly to ignore neighborhood context and assume that all that is educative happens in schools. Thus, he argues, educators must consider how communities can become more educative.[24] What this chapter has hoped to demonstrate is that when schooling and neighborhood become more interconnected, a more educative community can evolve. In the case of the ECC Project:

1. The beliefs and actions of educators in schools and in educational institutions in the Project neighborhoods changed; educators came to see that what happens in neighborhood families, and what children bring as knowledge from their home to the school are valuable resources and equivalent to those found in upper- or middle-class children, families, and neighborhoods.
2. Parents, educators, and students of these schools and neighborhoods participated in the democratic life of their community by identifying problematic neighborhood conditions, determining which ones could be addressed and solved, figuring out what changes were necessary, and taking political action by acquiring the needed funds and other resources.
3. Parents, students, and educators expressed positive views of the relationships and connections in the educational ecology and saw decreases in student discipline problems and increases in student motivation and learning.

These developments, as well as others, have encouraged those involved in the ECC Project work since its inception to embrace the importance and possibility of altering educational ecologies to enhance the lives of children, their families, and educators in neighborhood schools. Educative communities can be created and nurtured and will likely be necessary if we truly desire *all* of the nation's children to learn and succeed.

Notes

1 Paul E. Heckman, "Altering Patterns for Success" (A Proposal to the Charles Stewart Mott Foundation for the Redesign of Education for Children at Risk, University of Arizona, 1990); Heckman et al., *The Courage to Change: Stories from Successful School Reform* (Thousand Oaks, Calif.: Corwin Press, 1996).

2 Barbara Bowman, "Early Childhood Education," in Linda Darling-Hammond, ed., *Review of Research in Education* (Washington, D.C.: American Educational Research Association, 1993), 102.

3 David F. Labaree, "Public Goods, Private Goods: The American Struggle Over Educational Goals," *American Educational Research Journal* 34 (Spring 1997): 42.

4 Labaree, "Public Goods, Private Goods," 43.

5 Labaree, "Public Goods, Private Goods," 46.

6 Labaree, "Public Goods, Private Goods," 50.

7 Labaree, "Public Goods, Private Goods," 73.

8 John I. Goodlad, *What Schools Are For* (Bloomington, Ind.: Phi Delta Kappa Foundation, 1979).

9 Jane Roland Martin, "There's Too Much to Teach: Cultural Wealth in an Age of Scarcity," *Educational Researcher* 25 (March 1996): 4–10; Luis C. Moll, *Vygotsky and Education: Instructional Implications and Applications of Sociohistorical Psychology* (New York: Cambridge University Press, 1991).

10 John Beattie as quoted in Martin, "Cultural Wealth," 6.

11 John I. Goodlad, "Education, Schools, and a Sense of Community," in Don Davies, ed., *Communities and Their Schools* (New York: McGraw-Hill, 1981), 331–53.

12 Urie Bronfenbrenner, The Ecology of Human Development: Experiments by Nature and Design (Cambridge, Mass.: Harvard University Press, 1979).

13 Lawrence E. Cremin, "Family-Community Linkages in American Education: Some Comments on the Recent Historiography," *Teachers College Record* 79 (1978): 701.

14 See, for example, Kenneth A. Sirotnik, "Ecological Images of Change: Limits and Possibilities," in Andy Hargreaves, Ann Lieberman, Michael Fullan, and David Hopkins, eds., *International Handbook of Educational Change* (Hingham, Mass.: Kluwer Academic Publishers, 1998).

15   Thomas J. LaBelle, "Formal, Nonformal, and Informal Education: A Holistic Perspective on Lifelong Learning," *International Review of Education* 28 (1982): 159–75.

16   William Whyte, *Street Corner Society* (Chicago: University of Chicago Press, 1981, originally published in 1943); David Simon and Edward Burns, *The Corner: A Year in the Life of an Inner City Neighborhood* (New York: Broadway Books, 1997).

17   John I. Goodlad, *The Dynamics of Educational Change* (New York: McGraw-Hill, 1975).

18   Viki L. Montera, "Bridging the Gap: A Case-Study of the Home-School-Community Relationship at Ochoa Elementary School" (Tucson: University of Arizona, Ph.D. dissertation, 1996).

19   Eleanor Duckworth, *"The Having of Wonderful Ideas" & Other Essays on Teaching & Learning* (New York: Teachers College Press, 1987).

20   Montera, "Bridging the Gap."

21   Actions included neighborhood safety issues, childcare programs, after-school activities, health care, affordable housing, and summer programs.

22   John I. Goodlad, *A Place Called School: Prospects for the Future* (New York: McGraw-Hill, 1984), 349–57.

23   Montera, "Bridging the Gap."

24   Goodlad, "Education, Schools, and a Sense of Community."

Chapter 13

Teaching on Both Sides
of the Classroom Door

Gary D Fenstermacher

There is, in the Goodlad corpus, a fascinating implication about where teaching occurs. For most of us, teaching occurs on only one side of the classroom door. The side the students are on. However, as one reads the writings of John Goodlad, there is a growing sense that teaching involves more than working with students. It also involves working with one's colleague teachers, with members of one's community, with fellow citizens of the state and nation, and with the human species. This is the other side of the classroom door, the side that faces out to the school, the community, the nation, and the planet.

The thought seems almost counterintuitive. We understand how teaching can take place on the classroom side of the door, but how does it take place on the other side? Perhaps the reason this question is perplexing is that we think of teaching solely as instructing, as conveying information to or facilitating understanding in students. For Goodlad, teaching is more than that. In addition to instructing, teaching is also serving as a good steward of one's school, keeping one's community informed about education, being an effective citizen in a democratic nation, and being a transformational learner. Thus there are at least five critical roles for a teacher, only one of them (albeit in many ways the central one) performed on the classroom side of the door.

Before exploring these roles in any depth, it is important to note that I am interpreting, not describing, Goodlad's work when I assert that for him teaching amounts to more than what goes on behind the classroom door. As already noted, Goodlad places a great deal of emphasis on the role of steward, but he does not directly argue that the roles of informant to the community, citizen in a democracy, and transformational learner are nonclassroom roles. My doing so here is more an interpretation of Goodlad than it is of how he presents his own ideas. However, that is part of the charm of rich scholarship; it expands and alters the thinking of those who engage it. It is the rich scholarship of John Goodlad that creates the occasion for me to wonder whether our conceptions of teaching are not enhanced by breaking the boundaries set by the walls of a classroom, thinking of teaching as extending to the school, the community, the nation, and to humanity at large.

It may be that I am abusing the definition of "teaching" by having it cover activities outside the classroom. Perhaps it would be more correct if I argued that the *work* of the *teacher* encompasses far more than what takes place behind the classroom door, and restrict the term "teaching" solely to what occurs when the teacher meets students on the classroom side of the door. This more precise construction does no harm to the argument here, so we may let it stand. However, rather than refer awkwardly to "the work of the teacher," as if I were engaged in a sociological inquiry into the occupational nature of teaching, I prefer to simply write about the notion of teaching, in all its simultaneous simplicity and complexity.

With this modest caveat out of the way, let us turn our attention to that side of the door most of us are on when we think about the activity of teaching.

On the Classroom Side of the Door

In 1970, Goodlad coauthored *Behind the Classroom Door.*[1] It is this informative (and discomforting) little book that creates the occasion for my thinking of teaching as taking place on both sides of the door. In this book, Goodlad and his colleagues report on what they found in 150 classrooms in 67 schools around the nation. Although the findings are depressing, they offer much insight into what is involved in examining teaching as it occurs in the role of instructor. This study tells us a great deal about what teachers do on the classroom side of the door[2] —even though what they do is not, for the most part, consistent with the ten "reasonable expectations" that Goodlad and his colleagues established for teachers in their role as instructors of children and youths.

Of particular interest here is how often, when we find that teachers do not meet our expectations as instructors, we are unable to break the boundaries of the classroom in order to find a remedy. If fault is found in the role of instructor, then it is the role of instructor that we try to repair, when it might be that the role of instructor would change for the better if we attended to other roles that assuredly accompany it. Attention to these accompanying roles carries us to the other side of the classroom door.

On the Other Side of the Door

The role of instructor is not the only one a teacher performs, even if it is the one that garners most, sometimes all, of our attention. In making this claim, it is useful to distinguish between *incidental* and *connected* roles. Incidental roles are those that may influence the work of teaching, but are not essential to or tightly linked to the activities of teaching. For example, a teacher may also be a sister, a worshiper, a wife, and a mother, but these roles are incidental to teaching.[3] In contrast, there are roles that are tightly connected to the work of teaching, and these are the roles of interest here. As noted earlier, there are at least four that one might extract from Goodlad's work. They are steward to the school, informant to the community, citizen in a democracy, and transformational learner.

To contend that these roles are tightly connected to teaching is to argue that there are close conceptual links between the role of instructor and the four other roles, between the role behind the classroom door and the roles performed on the other side of the classroom door. These conceptual links are forged by the historical evolution of school teaching in American society, by the theories we prize as setting the foundations for education in a democracy, and by the social traditions that have come to characterize the nature of teaching in United States society. Hence, to contend that there are teaching roles that transcend the classroom role of instructor is to argue that there is a conceptual, and interdependent, relationship between good work as an instructor and good work as a steward, informant, citizen, and learner. In a moment we will turn to an examination of each of these roles. But before doing so, I want to reiterate a point made a moment ago.

When what teachers do fails to live up to our expectations for them, there are a number of responses at our disposal. One is to address the conditions under which the teaching occurs, such as when facilities are in disrepair and teaching resources are scarce.[4] Another is to address the circumstances of student life, as in the case of highly impoverished or racially different learners.[5] A third is to rethink the work of teaching, as we have done in so many of the national reports about educational reform over the last decade and one-half.[6] In the case of so many of these reports, teaching is understood exclusively as instructing, as an activity that takes place behind the classroom door. This conception accords with our commonsense view of the activity and causes little consternation under most circumstances. When, however, we seek to change what teachers do behind the classroom door, we might experience far more success examining roles conceptually connected to instructing, rather than focusing exclusively on instruction itself.

Looking beyond, not only behind, the classroom door is one of the more exciting and provocative implications of Goodlad's work on teaching. As roles beyond the door are described below, consider their connections to instruction, and the extent to which the nature of classroom instruction might be advanced by cultivating more profound understandings of these other roles. We begin with the role that Goodlad himself has addressed so often, that of steward to the school.

In the Role of Steward to the School

It comes as no secret to anyone that a teacher does not spend his or her entire professional life in a classroom. That teacher is a member of a school faculty, an employee of a school district, and often, a public servant. There are duties and obligations incurred by membership in a faculty and employment by a school system. They pertain to the exercise of what Goodlad calls "good stewardship."[7] The notion of a steward is derived from that of caretaker, one who looks out for or manages the affairs of an estate, club, or other organization. Teachers are stewards of their schools, looking after the school as an educational entity committed to the advancement of both its students and the larger human ecology. In this role, teachers have responsibilities beyond their respective classrooms and beyond their personal preferences as teachers. These responsibilities include the character and quality of learning experienced by all students in the school, the mission and conduct of the school as a whole, as well as the place of the school in the community it serves.

Among the reasons Goodlad stresses the notion of teacher as steward is his conception of the role played by the school as an organizational and physical entity. He has consistently argued over the many decades of his scholarly work that the school is the critical unit of change. It is not the school district, the state, or the individual classroom that successfully serves as the focal point for educational change, but the school site. He marshals extensive empirical data in support of this view, as well as a good bit of theory.[8] Assuming he is correct, the role of steward is profoundly important, for it will determine, to a large extent, the capacity of a given school to renew itself or to respond thoughtfully to the efforts of others to reform the school.

Just what are the duties and responsibilities of a steward and how do we prepare teachers to exercise them responsibly? There are few ready answers to this question because we have given so little attention to it. For example, most of the teacher preparation programs with which I am familiar attend almost entirely, if not exclusively, to preparing the prospective teacher for the role of instructor. Once hired, the new teacher experiences an induction into the school, but it is often unplanned and its subtext is more likely to be about how to get along by going along than it is about the responsibilities of exercising care for the sustenance and advancement of the school as a whole.

Indeed, to fully appreciate the responsibilities of stewardship, a teacher must have a deep and thorough understanding of the nature and purpose of formal education in a free society. Good stewardship is less a matter of maintaining a happy workplace or having effective means for resolving interpersonal tiffs (although these are not unimportant features) than it is a matter of serving as a constructive and helpful colleague in the joint aspiration of making the school a good place for children to learn and teachers to work. To have this understanding of the school as a place engaged in education as an ideal is to incur obligations beyond stewardship. It places the teacher in the role of helping those outside the school understand what education is about and what schools are for.[9]

In the Role of Informant to the Community

How do parents and other members of a local community learn about the purpose and the practice of schooling in a free society? Through their own experiences, of course, and by means of newspapers, magazines, books, radio, and television. However, as anyone who has ever read a newspaper account or seen a television report on something with which he or she is intimately familiar, these media are unable to offer much in the way of history or context for an event, and they quite often assume a specific editorial perspective. Thus, the larger public's view of what schools are for and what happens in them may be and often is slanted by the print and broadcast media.[10] This distortion is not always negative, but it is frequently unbalanced and typically far too truncated to serve as the basis for thoughtful deliberation.

If a community is to receive a complete and balanced report on the work of its schools, it is most likely to obtain such a report from the people who work there, particularly teachers and school administrators. For teachers, the major opportunities to inform arise from communication with parents, from participation in local professional associations, and from forging relationships with school officials who are specifically charged with public affairs and community relations. For example, letters carried home by students are often an excellent opportunity to inform parents not only about homework, but about the larger point and purpose of what will take place in the classroom. Local chapters of teacher professional associations also have opportunities to assist teachers in serving as informants, but this role is often overshadowed by more insular matters. As such, opportunities are often lost to tell stories or share insights that might be far more effective, in the longer run, for relieving the stresses of more "interior" problems faced by both teachers and their schools.

The geographic area in which I presently reside is served by several different school districts (including an intermediate school and a community college district). Each of these entities issues newsletters to the community, but few contain articles about the more substantive tasks of education in a democratic society. These publications are almost always about boundaries, buses, buildings, and budgets, with little said about why these "b-words" are vital to the larger undertaking in which we are mutually engaged. Increasing the awareness and understanding of the teacher's role as informant to the community could have a salutary impact on what now passes for "information to the community about our schools." It is, however, a role for which few teachers are prepared, and in which few members of the community are willing to acknowledge teachers.

Gaining a better understanding of the next role offers additional insight into the informant role, and a more powerful justification for it. Indeed, there is a close connection between the two, as will become evident in a moment.

In the Role of Citizen in a Democracy

Why is the role of citizen so special to teaching? This question is a natural one, given that we are all likely to hold the status of citizens in a democracy. As we all hold it, why place such stress on it for teachers? The answer lies in the intimate and critically important relationship between democracy and education. As Benjamin Barber remarks, "Democracy is not a natural form of association; it is an extraordinary and rare contrivance of cultivated imagination."[11] To sustain democracy, education is essential. It cannot be any form of education, but must be an "apprenticeship of liberty," where one is engaged in "learning to be free."[12] A central task of formal schooling in American society is this apprenticeship of liberty, teaching the meaning of freedom and the means of preservation and enhancement.

While there are likely to be few dissenters to this high-minded prose, there are many who believe that these noble goals are achieved with courses in American history, civics, and social studies. Although such courses may help us succeed in mastering the *procedures* of citizenship, they do not cultivate the *qualities* of a good citizen. Once again, Barber is helpful, as he describes these qualities: "The literacy required to live in civil society, the competence to participate in democratic communities, the ability to think critically and act deliberately in a pluralistic world, the empathy that permits us to hear and thus accommodate others, all involve skills that must be acquired."[13] The cultivation of these qualities makes exceptional demands on teachers, demands that differ from those made on persons in most other occupations.

Fulfillment of these demands requires that teachers understand the qualities of a citizen as well as the procedures of citizenship, and that they fully meet the conditions imposed by both. Thus it is not only vital that teachers engage in enacting the procedures of citizenship, such as jury duty, voting, public deliberation, and other forms of participation in the political life of the community, state, and nation, but that teachers also cultivate and practice the qualities of citizenship, such as openness, tolerance, mutual respect, reflective thought, considerate speech, and compromise. The teacher, in contrast to many others, not only must possess and practice these qualities, but must do so in ways that cultivate their acquisition by those who are their students.

Goodlad puts the point well when stating that "the public purpose of schooling in a democratic society should be the teaching of those altruistic dispositions that cultivate the transcendent self in the democratic community."[14] In this statement, Goodlad connects the teacher as democratic citizen to the teacher as transcendent self. That is what I propose to do in considering the teacher as a transformational learner.

In the Role of Transformational Learner

When we think of the teacher solely in the role of instructor, we may easily lose sight of the fact that the teacher must also be a learner, and that being good at learning may call on different capacities and skills than being an instructor. Certainly we will have no difficulty believing that a teacher must be a learner of pedagogy (the art and science of teaching) and of his or her content areas (such as mathematics, history, or language). In matters of method and content, all of us, I think, are prepared to view the teacher as a learner. Yet this sense of the teacher as learner is not transformational.

Transformational learning is learning that changes or transforms the learner in profound ways. It is, as well, learning that enables the learner to share the transformation with other learners. In other words, transformational learning changes both the learner and the learner's capacity to change other learners. In *Teachers for Our Nation's Schools*, Goodlad remarks that teachers must learn their content twice: "The first time in order that it be part of their being, the second time in order to teach it."[15] This delightful notion of having to learn your material twice touches on what I mean by transformational learning.

Part of the work of teaching is modeling learning. It is being a learner so that your students can see what is involved in learning the material that you are teaching. Too often students have the impression that the teacher is not learning the material but has already mastered it and is engaged solely in conveying it. So often, in this modality, the learners have no sense of what it means to be deeply engaged in and fascinated by the content, or of how the pursuit of this content slowly alters the minds and hearts of those who study it. In so stating, I am not contending that the students can encounter the material at the level the teacher is encountering it, but I am urging that the teachers share the character of their encounters with content with their students. If the students are to become fascinated with what is taught, the person teaching must also be fascinated with what is taught.

There is more. It is not only a matter of the teacher conveying a measure of his or her own engagement with the material to be learned, but conveying as well how this material is transformative for the teacher, how the teacher is different because of this material and how students are likely to be different as a result of their coming to appreciate and master it. How am I different because of the music I listen to, the art I perceive, the mathematics I understand, the history I know, the languages I speak? For a teacher to learn transformationally is to learn twice, but with a slightly different spin than Goodlad gives it (though I believe he would welcome this difference). The first time is to gain a sense of how the teacher is transformed by the learning; the second time, to gain a sense of how students may be transformed by learning this material. A transformational learner is one who sets out to learn something not only to teach that thing, but to change oneself and to change one's students. In William Ayer's language, teaching is "world-changing work."[16] Changing the world begins first with changing oneself, then others. Until we have looked into our own minds and hearts with serious and constructive intent, we are little qualified to peer into the hearts and minds of our students.

In the agenda of educational renewal espoused by Goodlad and his colleagues, there are nineteen postulates that stipulate the conditions necessary for the education of all those engaged in the formal schooling of the young. Two of these postulates are relevant to the role of transformational learner. Postulate Eight calls for "future teachers to move beyond being students of organized knowledge to become teachers who inquire into both knowledge and its teaching."[17] Postulate Nine calls for "a socialization process through which candidates transcend their self-oriented student preoccupations to become more other-oriented in identifying with a culture of teaching."[18] These two postulates stipulate the initial conditions for transformational learning. I would add a third, calling on teachers to see that before they can become engaged in "world-changing work," they must be engaged in self-changing work.

Teachers ought to be students themselves, and students in the presence of their students. And they should do this as a part of the work of teaching. It is this effort that contributes to making teaching endlessly fascinating for both teachers and students.

To Teach on Both Sides of the Classroom Door

If I have succeeded in making my point, you may now see teaching a bit differently. It is more than instructing. It is also being a steward, an informant, a citizen, and a special kind of learner. These additional roles are cultivated and practiced on what I have called "the other side" of the classroom door. Yet because of their close conceptual connection to instruction, they are roles that enhance and enlarge the role of instruction. The teacher who is an exemplary steward, informant, citizen, and learner will be a very different kind of instructor from one who is none, or only some, of these. These differences will ceaselessly redound to the benefit of the teacher's students.

Thinking of teaching as being engaged in multiple roles conceptually connected to instruction adds another dimension to the work. Those who instruct others gain a special purchase on the roles of steward, informant, citizen, and learner. To instruct is to experience these other roles in extraordinary dimension, for not only does a teacher have the chance, as so many others of us also do, to be a steward, informant, citizen, and learner, but the teacher—unlike the others— has the opportunity to constantly see his or her reflection in these roles as the effort is made to educate one's fellow human beings. The resulting synergy provides what may be the greatest gift of teaching, for it is work that not only helps us instruct, but also to grow as stewards, informants, citizens, and learners. John Goodlad does not say it in exactly this way, but what he says enables me to say it. I hope these thoughts on a portion of his work do justice to that work, while perhaps adding a wrinkle to it that otherwise may have been hidden for some. It is a wrinkle that has offered me many hours of pleasurable contemplation, as I think about the many ways to advance the work of teaching without restricting myself solely to the view that teaching is what takes place on one side of the classroom door. I find it much more invigorating and fascinating to think of teaching occurring on both sides of the door.

Notes

1   John I. Goodlad, M. Frances Klein, and Associates, *Behind the Classroom Door* (Worthington, Ohio: Charles A. Jones Publishing Company, 1970).

2   In the same spirit as other studies of classrooms, see Dan Lortie, *School Teacher* (Chicago: University of Chicago Press, 1975), and Philip Jackson, *Life in Classrooms* (New York: Holt, Rinehart, and Winston, 1968).

3   There are readers who will surely object to this formulation of incidental and connected roles, believing that, for example, the role of parent is vital to success in the role of teacher, or that of parishioner is a great aid to promoting the moral development of the young. In the United States, however, there is little in our history, our theory, or our educational practices that argues for a tight connection between being a teacher, on the one hand, and being a parent, sibling, or member of a religious community, on the other.

4   A case in point is the description of the hideously deprived school settings described by Jonathan Kozol, *Savage Inequalities* (New York: Crown Publishers, 1991).

5   Kozol, cited immediately above, does this in the book that followed *Savage Inequalities*, entitled *Amazing Grace* (New York: Crown Publishers, 1995). One may also read soul-shaking accounts in such works as Alex Kotlowitz, *There Are No Children Here* (New York: Anchor Doubleday, 1992) and Daniel Coyle, *Hardball* (New York: G. P. Putnam's Sons, 1993).

6   The most recent, which includes useful commentary on many prior reports, is the National Commission on Teaching & America's Future's, *What Matters Most: Teaching for America's Future* (New York: National Commission on Teaching & America's Future, 1996).

7   John I. Goodlad, *Teachers for Our Nation's Schools* (San Francisco: Jossey-Bass, 1990), 51.

8   See John I. Goodlad, *A Place Called School* (New York: McGraw-Hill, 1984), and prior research cited in that work.

9   Once again I am indebted to the title of a Goodlad book for the phrasing of an idea. In this case, it is John I. Goodlad, *What Schools Are For* (Bloomington, Ind.: Phi Delta Kappa Educational Foundation, 1979, 1994). Although this book is not specifically addressed to performing the roles of steward or informant, its content would be of great value to those acting in these roles.

10 A telling case for such distortion is made by David C. Berliner and Bruce J. Biddle, *The Manufactured Crisis* (Reading, Mass.: Addison-Wesley, 1995).

11   Benjamin Barber, *An Aristocracy of Everyone* (New York: Ballantine Books, 1992), 5.

12   Barber, *Aristocracy of Everyone*, 4.

13   Barber, *Aristocracy of Everyone*, 4.

14   John I. Goodlad, *In Praise of Education* (New York: Teachers College Press, 1997), 43. As in the case of stewardship, there is much that Goodlad has written on the democratic obligations of schooling and teaching. In addition to *In Praise of Education* (particularly chapter 2), see his contributions in John I. Goodlad and Timothy J. McMannon, eds., *The Public Purpose of Education and Schooling* (San Francisco: Jossey-Bass, 1997); and Roger Soder, ed., *Democracy, Education, and the Schools* (San Francisco: Jossey-Bass, 1996).

15   Goodlad, *Teachers for Our Nation's Schools*, 52.

16   William Ayers, *To Teach: The Journey of a Teacher* (New York: Teachers College Press, 1993), 8.

17   John I. Goodlad, *Educational Renewal: Better Teachers, Better Schools* (San Francisco: Jossey-Bass, 1994), 82.

18   Goodlad, *Educational Renewal*, 83.

Chapter 14

Partnerships, Centers, and Schools

Richard W. Clark and Wilma F. Smith

A group of school- and university-based educators gathered to consider John Goodlad's ideas related to the simultaneous renewal of the education of educators and schools. One participant, obviously frustrated with what was new terminology to him, complained, "Why all this talk of partnerships, partner schools, and centers of pedagogy? Why don't you just use one term? After all, don't they all mean the same thing?" The answer to the last question was an easy "no," but the answer to the first question was longer and more complex than the listener wanted to hear on that warm afternoon.

John Goodlad calls for the establishment of *centers of pedagogy* as necessary vehicles to the renewal of the education of educators.[1] He has also called for the creation of symbiotic *partnerships involving school districts and universities*—School-University Partnerships (SUPs).[2] In addition to his work in school-university partnerships, Goodlad has written extensively about the importance of the individual school as the primary unit for renewal and, specifically, of *partner schools* as key to the simultaneous renewal of schools and the education of educators. Our question in this chapter is similar to that raised by the frustrated meeting participant: are these three terms really one or are these three separate but related ideas? If they are related ideas, in what ways are they different and how do they (should they) interact?

In this chapter we will explore these concepts, drawing upon our experience in working with *partnerships, centers of pedagogy,* and *partner schools* in the National Network for Educational Renewal (NNER) during the past twelve years. We will discuss definitions and describe some models that depict their relationships.

School-University Partnerships

The first element is the school-university partnership. Goodlad reported results of in-depth investigations in more than 1,000 classrooms and interviews of 1,350 teachers, 8,624 parents, and 17,163 students in *A Place Called School*.[3] He described actions needed to renew schools and called for the creation of a national network of local school-university partnerships. After describing "*The Partnership*" he had initiated with surrounding school districts while he was dean at the University of California at Los Angeles (UCLA), Goodlad went on to say that what is needed is

> a critical mass large enough to make a visible difference—a really sizable network of partnerships, if you will. Each partnership must be small enough to be conceptually and logistically manageable and large enough to include the essential components of the community arena—but no more. The network to which the partnerships belong must be a binding, communicating one sharing a reasonably common agenda.[4]

On August 2, 1985, John Goodlad invited thirty-two educators representing higher education, public schools, state departments, the federal government, and interested private foundations to a work conference in Chicago. Among the issues considered at this conference was "linkage of eight to twelve school-university partnerships, each with a focus on simultaneous reconstruction of preparation and practice, and each with a small agenda of areas where self-interests overlap."[5]

At this conference, he elaborated on his concept of partnerships, emphasizing that:

> successful partnerships have at least three essential characteristics: a degree of dissimilarity between or among the partners; the mutual satisfaction of self-interests; a measure of selflessness on the part of each sufficient to assure this satisfaction of self-interests by all involved.[6]

He suggests that school-university partnerships can fulfill these three characteristics if they begin with *recognition* that the responsibilities of these two institutions for the quality of schooling are "virtually inseparable."[7] To demonstrate this point, he reminds us of the report from *A Study of Schooling* that the range of pedagogical methods is exceedingly narrow, with teachers generally employing the same methods that had been used with them when they were students:

The argument for school-university partnerships proceeds somewhat as follows. For schools to get better, they must have better teachers, among other
things. To prepare better teachers (and counselors, special educators and
administrators), universities must have access to schools using the best practices. To have the best practices, schools need access to new ideas and knowledge. This means that universities have a stake in school improvement just as
schools have a stake in the education of teachers.[8]

Such a view is clearly consistent with the notion of James Thompson concerning reciprocal interdependence;[9] therefore, it is not surprising that Goodlad, like Thompson, emphasizes the complexity of
the effort to provide coordination for such a partnership. He points
out that "the rather casual rotation of management responsibilities
among members will not suffice for active partnerships,"[10] even if it
might work for networks. He identifies other ways in which such partnerships differ from networks—in their purposes, structure, ambiance,
and evaluation, as well as staffing. Goodlad's view of the structure of
partnerships has not varied. Writing in 1995, he described the structural characteristics of these partnerships much as he had ten years
earlier:

> A school-university partnership represents a formal agreement between a
> college or university (or one or more of its constituent parts) and one or more
> school districts to collaborate on programs and projects in which both have a
> common interest. This agreement includes designation of a governing body,
> commitment of resources (usually varying in nature and amount over time),
> an executive officer, a secretariat (usually modest, in our experience), and an
> approved budget.[11]

Partnerships such as those Goodlad describes are not easy to lo-
cate. In a 1988 discussion of school-university collaboration, Clark[12]
observed that there were many instances of collaboration, but few, if
any, examples of symbiotic relationships that meet the tests established by Goodlad for those that he contended can make a difference.
At the same time, it is necessary to remember that the network that
Goodlad created (the NNER) is not a "partnership" but a linking of
partnerships in a binding relationship that facilitates conversations
about a common agenda of school and teacher education renewal.

Developmental Stages of Partnerships
As a result of their observations of the first five years of the NNER,
Wilson, Clark, and Heckman posited the existence of a developmental

process for school-university partnerships.[13] They identified five developmental stages of partnerships: getting organized, early success, waiting for results, major success and expansions, and mature partnership. The following discussion of these stages draws on their occasional paper.

Just as a two-year-old may suddenly seem old for his or her age, or an adolescent to be reverting to the "terrible twos," partnerships seem to move forward in a jerky, messy fashion, rather than progressing predictably in a linear manner. Thus the flow of developmental stages can best be visualized as a series of overlapping events rather than a linear path.

Stage 1: Getting Organized

During this first stage, partnership founders seek to determine who will be involved, ask why the partnership is being formed, draw up rules for operation and governance, and determine what resources will be invested. Goodlad described this stage when he observed that "the delegated institutional representatives often spend a lot of time seeking to uncover the initial purposes before coming to the realization that they must assume the task."[14] It is this realization by the participants that they must shoulder the burden, not recommend what others should do, that is critical to leaving this first stage behind. If all goes well, the outcome is a commitment to the mission and an acceptance of their shared responsibilities.

Stage 2: Early Success

Excitement spreads as participants join in conferences and seminars, discover that there are common interests, meet with outsiders who reinforce them as being on the right track, and recognize the really significant challenges that face them. This excitement is often recognizable as the glow that new acquaintances share at the end of a conference during which they have joined in extended conversations about common concerns. They are often heard to say, "We need to do this more often," "I didn't realize school (university) people were really worrying about the same thing I was," or "This is so much more stimulating than attending a conference or a class where someone lectures to me."

Stage 3: Waiting for Results

As the first blush of success and satisfaction fades, there is a lull while participants struggle to achieve some real results from their labors.

Impatient participants bail out. Self-doubt is expressed. During this stage, partnership leaders frequently retreat to discussions of structure, convene meetings that ask, "What are our real goals?" or change the people assigned to formal leadership roles.

Stage 4: Major Success and Expansion
In this stage, results that are significant to the participants are achieved, and (sometimes in a separate stage, sometimes as part of this stage) the base of participation expands to include teachers, administrators, and professors from multiple areas of interest. The initiators of the partnership discover that success breeds success. Recognition accorded the partnership by outsiders leads others to seek admission, opens up sources of additional funding, and permits a wider inclusion of all segments of the schools and universities in partnership activities. All participants commit additional resources.

Stage 5: Mature Partnership
Participants provide leadership to major renewal efforts in the schools and higher education. Critical inquiry into progress of partnerships on substantive issues dominates the conversation. Schools and colleges/universities involved are visibly engaged in restructuring that goes beyond tinkering. All the elements of a truly symbiotic relationship are present. Significant resources are committed on a long-term basis. Relationships become truly interdependent. The general theme is productivity, resulting in high achievement and pride in successes.

Given the nature of institutions, it also seems likely that there may be a sixth stage, which is not a reversion to earlier discussions of structure and purpose, but is a stage of decline and decay anticipating (and eventually actualizing) the demise of the partnership. In other instances, personal agendas of individual members may take the partnership in a different direction, as happened with at least one of the partnerships that was originally part of the National Network for Educational Renewal.

Examples of Partnerships
The evolution of four partnerships—all described in *School-University Partnerships in Action*, edited by Sirotnik and Goodlad[15]—help clarify the complexity of these developmental stages. As of this writing, two of the partnerships have terminated. They are very much at "stage six." Two are advanced stage-four partnerships. When described in 1988, three of the partnerships would best have been characterized

as being at stage four, while one that had been at stage four reverted to stage one and then advanced again to the early success stage. It should be apparent from what follows that "making school-university partnerships work is . . . not a list of 'how-to-do-its'. . . , it is an amalgam of principles and concepts, beliefs and values, conditions and processes, people and programs, and hard work . . . in context."[16]

Partnership A, one of the two now at stage six, was created at a major research university by the dean of the graduate school of education and some of his colleagues in 1980.[17] After its first five years, the dean left and the faculty and leadership who remained showed little interest in continuing the work. Consequently, the school-based members of this vibrant, stage-four partnership went in search of new university partners. As might have been anticipated, the new alliance they found needed to move through the first stage again. However, the school personnel involved were used to the high support level that had been attached to the original partnership, and their new university colleagues found them to be too demanding for the limited faculty resources they had to commit to the partnership. The university faculty anticipated rich dialogue involving the school leaders, but the school people expected the university people to carry the load in organizing, leading, and providing "experts" for these dialogues to a greater extent than seemed to the university faculty to be indicative of a true partnership arrangement. More to the point, the new partners never developed the congruity of purpose—similarity of philosophy—that seems to be necessary for successful partnerships. The continuing school members saw the partner schools they were creating as places where inquiry into practice could occur; the university faculty saw them more as an opportunity for the promotion of the critical theories in which they believed.

By 1991, this partnership was no longer a member of the NNER, and the seminars and school renewal efforts that had been its main strength had ceased.

Partnership B, the second stage-six partnership, began in 1984, and a relationship between the institution of higher education and the NNER continues. From the original experience, school people learned to value partnering efforts—several alliances among former districts persist, and at least two new partnerships involving school districts and universities have emerged from the earlier partnership effort. However, the overall partnership that began as one of the ones most heavily invested in by both school and university participants no longer exists. Moving quickly to stage four, this partnership had created renewing schools, sponsored the development of professional development schools, and gained considerable notoriety as a locus for the development of teacher leadership and for exemplary programs for the education of principals. Leadership changes in the school and college were accompanied by philosophical changes. The partnership slipped back to phase three and remained there for three years. The bond of agreement regarding educational purposes was shattered as new superintendents joined the partnership but advocated very different approaches to education than the original partners. While early leaders had been committed to constructivist notions of learning, new ones focused on implementing external, top-down standards and expressed the belief that there were few at the university who could help them in this work. Simultaneously, college of education faculty turned from the work in the field to more traditional kinds of scholarship, which they found to be surer sources of academic recognition and reward. They concentrated on writing about subjects such as content pedagogy, multicultural education, theories concerning technology in this country, and on developing new teacher education programs that would be an exemplary model for a select few candidates. Financial difficulties experienced by both levels of the partnership finally became the excuse for dissolution of the long-term agreement in 1995.

Partnership C, in contrast to the previous two settings, flourishes after a dozen years of work. Initiated by a university professor who had served as the early director of Partnership A, this partnership has reinvented itself several times. During its lifetime, it has contributed to the creation of a major revision of a teacher education program at the university, but most of its efforts have been focused on school renewal. There have been two executive directors of this partnership, both well received by the teachers and administrators in the field and both skillful in conceptualizing school and teacher education reform. One of the remarkable characteristics of this partnership has been its ability to adapt various reform efforts to its purposes rather than be a slave to the dogma of a particular movement. In a similar fashion, it has adopted, then adapted, such initiatives as the NEA Mastery Schools Project, the Coalition of Essential Schools, the Atlas Project, Foxfire, and systemic reform efforts of the National Science Foundation. During one year, when the same person had responsibility for the directing of the partnership and the teacher education program, this partnership represented a stage-five structure in many ways. Subsequent leadership changes and the development of differing philosophies within the college of education (or perhaps expression of dormant differences) moved the partnership back to stage four, where it sits as if waiting for the freedom of an agenda unfettered by external expectations.

Partnership D is the second oldest of the four. The same person who played a key role in creating it was also instrumental in the development of A and B. However, it continues to this writing as what may be the closest to an example of a stage-five partnership currently in existence. It has continued through four deans and a complete turnover of superintendents in the five partner districts since its beginnings in 1984. It features a sophisticated engagement of partner schools, a complexly structured center of pedagogy, school renewal seminars, and budding participation of arts and sciences faculty in the work of the partnership. It is probably no accident that this partnership exists at a large, private, religiously affiliated institution of higher education where there is considerable sharing of values between the university and the community around it. From the beginning, the partnership has devoted substantial attention to both the process and substance of its existence. Competent, issue-focused leadership, a clear vision of the purpose of the partnership, and specific activities designed to overcome resistance to change have helped partnerships C and D move forward.

Additional information about these four partnerships and others in the NNER could shed light on why some have succeeded and some have failed. Answers to questions such as the following should provide some of the necessary clues:

1. What processes and structures now exist in partnership schools for examining existing conditions, practices, and knowledge, and for creating these anew? How are these processes and structures being used for such purposes?
2. What examples can be identified that demonstrate that the principal and superintendent have encouraged teachers and others at a school to engage in inquiry and proceed with needed changes?
3. What provisions are made to ensure that teachers have time to engage in inquiry and subsequent action?
4. What examples show that teachers have engaged in renewing activities (alternative schedules, alternative curricular and grouping practices, etc.)?
5. Is the university climate conducive to changes that encourage a symbiosis between the university and the schools?

6. What steps are being taken to identify and develop sites such as partner schools (professional development or key schools) where future teachers, administrators, and others are educated?
7. What processes are in place for college faculty to inquire into their own programs?
8. How are those in the schools involved in renewing preparation programs?
9. How is the dialogue being extended to the community regarding the reshaping of schools and preparation programs?

In addition to defining the basic elements of partnerships, Goodlad suggests that successful school-university partnerships are important to the development of centers of pedagogy:

> The establishment of such partnerships is not a necessary prerequisite to seeking partner schools as integral components of centers of pedagogy—but it helps enormously. . . . The partner school becomes just another collaborative endeavor—albeit one to be entered into very deliberately and carefully, since its success depends on fine-tuned human connections.[18]

Elsewhere in the same book, he speaks more emphatically, saying "we believe . . . that the prior existence of a school-university partnership eases the journey along this road to the creation of centers of pedagogy."[19]

And in a third reference to partnerships and centers of pedagogy, he was even more direct: "it is necessary to move ahead with school-university partnerships that provide the essential resources, including partner schools, for the centers of pedagogy."[20]

In order to explain why such partnerships may either be helpful or necessary for the establishment of centers of pedagogy, we first need to be clear about what such centers are.

Centers of Pedagogy

According to Goodlad, the intent of a center of pedagogy

> is to bring together into a single faculty a sufficient number of the three groups of actors requisite to developing coherent preparation programs. A center of pedagogy, whether located organizationally inside or outside of an SCDE, is characterized by all the conditions necessary to its healthy functioning—conditions comparable to those in professional schools or institutes. Most of the faculty members divide their time between the needs of such a center and their home departments or, in the case of personnel from the schools, in their

home schools or organized units within their schools. Each center has a core group of faculty members who devote all or more than half of their time to it. There are clear guidelines with respect to voting privileges, criteria for advancement and merit awards, and the like.[21]

Goodlad introduced centers of pedagogy in *Teachers for Our Nation's Schools*. While the definition quoted above and the extended discussion of the concept in *Educational Renewal* are straightforward, the differences among various institutions of higher education and the different circumstances attached to the states in which they operate and their school district partners have meant that all of the evolving centers are quite different.

Montclair State University created the first "official" center of pedagogy in the fall of 1995. Since then, centers have been created or are under development at a number of other NNER settings. Some have concentrated on form, such as at Hawaii and, to some extent, at Brigham Young University. In other instances, initial attention has been given to collaborative discussions of ideas in the belief that form will follow. In other instances, simultaneous attention has been given to form and function.

At the University of Connecticut, steps toward the development of a center of pedagogy have focused on working sessions involving partner schools and arts and sciences and college of education faculty, who have been developing interdisciplinary curriculum. The partnership, affiliated with the NNER during the late 1980s, created professional development schools in keeping with precepts of both the NNER and the Holmes Group. These efforts produced the school foundations for the conversations. Supported by a DeWitt Wallace-Reader's Digest Fund incentive award, the college of education faculty who had been working in the schools began to pull arts and sciences faculty into their discussions.

In Hawaii, through the instigation of the Hawaii School-University Partnership, legislation was passed in 1995 creating a teacher education center that was to be their version of a center of pedagogy. In 1997, funding was secured for the center. In the interim, there has been considerable discussion over the role of the center and the place it should have within the university. Should it be tied to the dean of the college of education? Be a unit within curriculum and instruction? Be attached to the office of the academic vice president? Be located in the state department of education? Such questions concerning form continue as of this writing.

Meanwhile, at Brigham Young University, the BYU-Public School Partnership was instrumental in work led by the dean to establish a complex center of pedagogy. Following extensive university-wide review, BYU's center was established with a three-person leadership team (one faculty member from the schools, one from the arts and sciences, and one from the college of education) reporting to the dean of the college of education. The dean was, in turn, to be responsive to guidance from a partnership board consisting of school district superintendents, from a representative from the university, and from the state department of education. After its first year of operation, the day-to-day management of the center of pedagogy was simplified with the appointment of the school member of the tripartite leadership team as its executive director. The stage-four partnership at BYU facilitated the evolution of the center as it assumed responsibility campus-wide for the education of educators.

At Montclair State University, the agenda for education in a democracy, built on earlier institutional concentration on critical thinking, formed the ideological basis for the structuring of their center of pedagogy. The New Jersey Network for Educational Renewal (NJNER), begun in 1987 as a school-university partnership known as "the clinical schools network," has many of the characteristics of a stage-four partnership. The center of pedagogy was defined from the outset as

a place where the education of educators is conceptualized, planned for and carried out. Its members include all those committed to, and whose participation is necessary for, that endeavor. Its goal is the facilitation of the ongoing simultaneous renewal of the education of educators, the educational program of the University, and the educational program of the schools in the interest of student learning.[22]

Led by a tenure-line MSU faculty member, the center has negotiated agreements with the faculty union that allows joint appointment between academic departments and the center, allowing for formal input from the center in faculty applications for reappointment, tenure, and promotion. The center of pedagogy has been instrumental in helping develop sixty school and university leaders who are identified as members. The university's first doctoral program is to be housed in the center. Clearly, participants engaged in substantial discussion of ideas that created the momentum for the development of the center and the growing recognition across campus of the center as a very strong entity. As representatives from MSU report:

> Montclair State University and the NJNER had a choice: either establish a
> Center and then put pieces into place, or, put the pieces into place and then
> establish the center. We chose the latter course. . . . Perhaps most important,
> the New Jersey Network for Educational Renewal had emerged as a mature
> partnership involving the University and surrounding school districts.[23]

While these examples are representative of the progress being made
in the establishment of centers of pedagogy, they are also alike in that
none of them includes all the faculty responsible for teacher education
or the protected budget for the education of educators required in
Goodlad's definition. As of this writing, none can report that it is fully
engaged in what Goodlad describes as the main task of the center of
pedagogy:

> There are no substitutes, however sensible and enticing they appear to be, for
> the institution-based curriculum development process of setting and holding
> to a mission, determining the nature and needs of the student body, sorting
> out the most fundamental curricular themes, projecting the necessary array
> of organizing centers for developing these themes, sorting out faculty com-
> mitments and responsibilities, and engaging in formative evaluations and re-
> visions of the whole.[24]

Generally speaking, other elements of the university and schools
have retained such responsibilities. The emerging centers of pedagogy are similar in that they have built upon established school-university partnerships and include as a key part of their work the creation
and operation of professional development or partner schools. As
Goodlad noted, "to be whole, a center of pedagogy requires teaching
schools in the same way most medical education units and programs
require teaching hospitals. . . . These schools are variously referred to
in educational literature and practice as professional development, clinical, and practice schools."[25]

These partner schools are a critical part of, but not the same thing
as, a center of pedagogy.

Partner Schools

Major organizations agree on four basic purposes as defining the work
to be accomplished by partner or professional development schools
(PDS). The National Network for Educational Renewal (NNER), the
Holmes Group, the National Center for Restructuring Education,
Schools, and Teaching (NCREST), and the National Council for the

Accreditation of Teacher Education (NCATE) are among groups con-
curring in these purposes.[26] Although the wording varies from organization to organization, most agree that such schools 1) provide a
clinical setting for preservice education, 2) engage in professional development for practitioners, 3) promote and conduct inquiry that advances knowledge of schooling, and 4) provide an exemplary education for some segment of pre-kindergarten through grade twelve
students.

The National Network for Educational Renewal (NNER) includes
more than five hundred such schools in its most recent directory, and
there are many others that are part of other initiatives. The schools
reported are substantially different from each other. The agreement
regarding purpose that is apparent in the national statements is not as
evident when the practices in the schools are examined. Almost all
schools calling themselves professional development schools emphasize some element of preservice education. A few focus only on re-
training existing teachers or some other form of staff development.

For many, staff development activity is limited to incidental learning
by the teachers in the PDS. That is, teachers are said to benefit from
their exposure to the preservice candidates and their mentors without
any added thought to the cumulative effect of such exposure on the
individual teachers or the relationship of such exposure to the reforms
a school may need. Only a few partner schools assume responsibility
for aiding the growth of teachers in a district or a region.

Inquiry efforts tend to feature projects carried out by individual professors or school faculty rather than being institutionally driven. Occasionally, inquiry projects are featured in a course in action research
taught by a university faculty member that is also available to people
in the partner schools. Whether schooling is—or even should be—
exemplary for the children enrolled in the partner school is not at all
clear. Few data exist concerning P–12 educational practices in PDSs;
most published case studies focus on the training being provided for
preservice candidates. University- and school-based educators often
worry about whether preparing preservice students in an "exemplary"
setting will leave them unprepared for the *real world* of schools. Others point out that preparing teachers in settings that are not at least
seeking to be good schools ensures that new teachers will enter the
profession having been socialized into schools that merely perpetuate
the status quo.

The gap between advocated purposes and the real life being experienced in the schools motivates various standard-setting groups to

separate the "wannabes" from the real professional development schools. NCATE is advancing the most ambitious of these standard-setting efforts under the leadership of Marsha Levine.[27] The NCATE project proposes to build on work done earlier by Holmes, NNER, NCREST, AFT, and NEA, as well as on alternative models of quality review such as the School Quality Review Process in New York and the private sector's Malcolm Baldridge Awards.[28]

Thus far, each effort to develop standards has made good progress as long as it has remained at the committee level. When the preliminary work products are brought before the parties who are apt to be measured by the standards, the reactions become defensive and explanations abound as to why each site must be judged on its own merits. This has been vexing for both policymakers and funding sources who want to know what PDSs are actually accomplishing. As NCATE moves ahead with twenty PDSs that will be piloting its draft standards, it may be able to move beyond this barrier.

In summary, nationally stated purposes have been developed that have limited presence in the practices of individual partner schools. Also, there are several groups at work on national standards for such schools, but there is resistance to external measurement of progress in relation to those standards. This resistance extends to the notion that external standards might serve to define the characteristics of local partner schools.

Partner or professional development schools are by definition the product of collaboration between one or more schools and one or more universities. Therefore, there is considerable sensitivity to the appearance of one partner knowing at the outset what the final shape of the partnering endeavor should be. This was reflected in a developing partner school relationship that included Temple University and an urban high school. The relationship was initiated by the university as part of its effort to revise its teacher education program. Some of the Fillmore High School faculty involved believed that they were being used by the university, as revealed by the following statement from an English teacher. While she acknowledged that progress had been made during the first two years of the project, she reported that

the program's connection with Temple's College of Education was perhaps less successful. Temple's students reported uniformly positive experiences in their Lab School field placements. But the College of Education alternated between paying no attention to Fillmore and demanding that Fillmore (and other PDS) teachers holding university adjunct appointments assume the far-reaching responsibilities on the university campus listed in the original Carnegie proposal. The original proposal did not, of course, foresee the enormous commitment in time and energy that teachers would have to invest in the high school component of the program. It may have been naïve to expect too easy an integration of university and high school. It is unfortunately not clear that the College of Education has the flexibility to recreate a program already committed to paper even as that program evolves.[29]

Either a sound school-university partnership or a center of pedagogy would have provided ongoing support for Fillmore and Temple and many other partner schools that are struggling to find common ground for partnering. Their experiences highlight the interdependence of the three entities—partner schools, colleges of education, and departments of arts and sciences—and the need to provide a vehicle for collaboration among the partners.

The Interaction of School-University Partnerships, Centers of Pedagogy, and Partner Schools

We propose three models as appropriate to advancing the cause of the simultaneous renewal of the education of educators and schools. While there may be other arrangements that will work, these three offer strong possibilities for success.

Model 1: A Single Institution of Higher Education (IHE) Working with One or More School Districts

In this arrangement, the IHE and one or more school districts create a school-university partnership with the broad purpose of simultaneous renewal. This partnership creates a center of pedagogy with participants from partner schools, the school districts, the school/college/ department of education (SCDE), and the department of arts and sciences (A&S). There should be sufficient partner schools within the center of pedagogy to provide for clinical experiences for all prospective teachers. The partnership creates a league of cooperating schools that includes the partner schools and other schools within the district(s) who wish to participate in either general renewal activities or specific projects involving collaboration between the IHE and the school.

Model 2: Multiple IHEs Working with One or More School Districts

The arrangement could be the same as in Model 1 with all the IHEs sharing in a single center of pedagogy. The IHEs and partner schools consider their relationships as reciprocal and interdependent. Joint cohorts of preservice teachers (from the various IHEs) participate in some coursework and field experiences together and are mentored by faculty teams comprised of members of different IHEs and partner schools.

A less complex model calls upon the school-university partnership (SUP) to provide an overall umbrella for renewal activities. Each IHE would create a center of pedagogy that involved a number of partner schools. In this arrangement, it is possible that university students from more than one IHE may be assigned to a particular partner school. In this instance, the SUP would be performing an additional function of coordinating experiences of students involved from different centers of pedagogy.

Model 3: A Single School District Working with One or More IHEs

This model occurs in settings where closely proximate IHEs work with a single partner school. Success is dependent upon a thriving center of pedagogy or SUP, which assumes a coordinating and communication function to bring together the various faculties and preservice students for cohort reflective seminars and like activities.

Whichever of the three models (or others) is adopted, there are some common interactions that occur within the partnership, the center of pedagogy, and the partner schools.

The partnership, defined in the fully symbiotic way Goodlad has defined it, is necessary to establish a common philosophy—or at least a common language for talking about the ends and means of the collaboration. Unless this conversation occurs and the parties come together in agreement about the ends of education and the processes of learning, it is unlikely that trust will be built by the partners.

The center of pedagogy is necessary if the schools and arts and sciences faculty concerned with teacher education are going to be legitimately engaged in the work. It is also essential if the education faculty members directly concerned with the education of educators are going to have control of their work rather than being controlled by other senior faculty. Only if the broader partnership has helped develop a common language and understanding can the center effectively meld these three groups into a coherent, well-functioning entity.

The partner school is the locus of the essential clinical training component of the education of educators, but more, it is the source for school-based educator participation in the partnership and the center. It is the location where university- and school-based inquiry can gain better understanding of what it takes to be successful in schooling children and youths. But the partner school cannot be effective if the faculty who work with the education of educators are reduced to the role of second-class members of the academic community rather than given the collegial status of fellow members of the center of pedagogy.

A critical element of the partnership in all three models is the provision made for the support of schools that are not partner schools. In earlier writings, Goodlad refers to these as key schools. The partnership must arrange for supportive activities for all interested schools in participating districts even if these schools are not identified formally as partner schools. This function should be seen as a responsibility of the partnership, not of the institution of higher education. Thus, school and university members of a partnership may work with an elementary school on improving a literacy program, with a high school on implementing a new interdisciplinary curriculum, and with a middle school on age-appropriate instructional techniques. In each case, the schools would be benefiting from their district's participation in the partnership. Politically, unless school districts can see this kind of benefit as a potential for all schools, it is difficult for them to identify a select group of schools as partner schools. Ideally, partner schools will also evolve so that they have a role in helping with the staff development of teachers in other schools. This will work best if there is the shared language in the district and university that has grown out of a broader partnership.

In short, it is our contention that each of these entities—partnership, center of pedagogy, and partner school—is essential to the other and that all are essential to the successful, simultaneous renewal of the education of educators and schools. As educators throughout the country work to advance these concepts, they owe a considerable debt to John Goodlad for his pioneering efforts in defining them and helping to explain the relationship among them.

Notes

1   Centers of pedagogy are described by John I. Goodlad in *Teachers for Our Nation's Schools* (San Francisco: Jossey-Bass, 1990), 276–82, and further explained in detail in *Educational Renewal: Better Teachers, Better Schools* (San Francisco: Jossey-Bass, 1994), 235–73.

2   School and university partnerships create an avenue for collaborations to improve schools, as John I. Goodlad points out in *A Place Called School* (New York: McGraw-Hill, 1984), 353–57. Such partnerships are further explained in John I. Goodlad, "School-University Partnerships for Educational Renewal: Rationale and Concepts," in Kenneth A. Sirotnik and John I. Goodlad, eds., *School-University Partnerships in Action: Concepts, Cases, and Concerns* (New York: Teachers College, 1988), 3–31. Partnerships are further delineated as critical to the simultaneous renewal of schools and the education of educators in John I. Goodlad, *Educational Renewal*, 96–130.

3   Goodlad, *A Place Called School*.

4   Goodlad, *A Place Called School*, 356.

5   Goodlad, *Summary: Work Conference on School-University Partnerships, Chicago, August 2, 1985* (Seattle: University of Washington, unpublished manuscript, 1985), 2.

6   John I. Goodlad, *Summary: Work Conference on School-University Partnerships*, 1.

7   John I. Goodlad, *Summary: Work Conference on School-University Partnerships*, 7.

8   John I. Goodlad, *Reconstructing Schooling and the Education of Educators: The Partnership Concept* (Seattle: University of Washington, unpublished manuscript, 1985), 6.

9   James D. Thompson, *Organizations in Action* (New York: McGraw-Hill, 1967).

10   John I. Goodlad, *Summary: Work Conference on School-University Partnerships*, 4.

11   Goodlad, *Educational Renewal*, 114.

12   Richard W. Clark, "School-University Relationships: An Interpretive Review," in Kenneth A. Sirotnik and John I. Goodlad, eds., *School-University Partnerships in Action* (New York: Teachers College, 1988), 32–66.

13   Carol Wilson, Richard Clark, and Paul Heckman, "Breaking New Ground: Reflections on School-University Partnerships in the NNER," Occasional Pa-

per No. 8 (Seattle: Center for Educational Renewal, College of Education, University of Washington, 1989).

14   John I. Goodlad, "School-University Partnerships: A Social Experiment," *Kappa Delta Pi Record*, 24 (Spring 1988): 77–80.

15   Kenneth A. Sirotnik and John I. Goodlad, eds., *School-University Partnerships in Action* (New York: Teachers College Press, 1988).

16   Kenneth A. Sirotnik, "Making School-University Partnerships Work," *Metropolitan Universities* 2 (Summer 1991): 15.

17   See Paul E. Heckman, "The Southern California Partnership: A Retroactive Analysis," in Kenneth A. Sirotnik and John I. Goodlad, eds., *School-University Partnerships in Action*, 106–123, and also Paul E. Heckman, "Exploring the Concepts of School Renewal: Cultural Differences and Similarities Between More and Less Renewing Schools," Technical Report No. 33 (Los Angeles: Laboratory in School and Community Education, Graduate School of Education, University of California at Los Angeles, 1982).

18   Goodlad, *Educational Renewal*, 115.

19   Goodlad, *Educational Renewal*, 109.

20   Goodlad, *Educational Renewal*, 98.

21   Goodlad, *Educational Renewal*, 113.

22   Montclair State University/New Jersey Network for Educational Renewal, "Mini-Exhibition" presented at the Annual Meeting of the NNER, August 1997, 2–3.

23   Montclair State University, "The Center of Pedagogy" (Upper Montclair, NJ: Montclair State University, January 1997), 2.

24   Goodlad, *Educational Renewal*, 155–56.

25   Goodlad, *Educational Renewal*, 114.

26   For detailed information, see Richard W. Clark, "Evaluating Partner Schools," in Russell T. Osguthorpe, R. Carl Harris, Melanie F. Harris, and Sharon Black, eds., *Partner Schools: Centers for Educational Renewal* (San Francisco: Jossey-Bass, 1995), 229–62; Holmes Group, *Tomorrow's Schools: Principles for the Design of Professional Development Schools* (East Lansing, Mich.: Holmes Group, 1990); National Council for Accreditation of Teacher Education, *Draft Standards for Identifying & Supporting Quality Professional Development Schools* (Washington, D.C.: NCATE, September 1997); and National Center for Restructuring Education, Schools, and Teaching, "Vision Statement: Professional Development Schools Network," *PDS Network News* 1 (1993), 3.

27   National Council for Accreditation of Teacher Education, *Draft Standards for Identifying & Supporting Quality Professional Development Schools.*

28   National Council for Accreditation of Teacher Education, *Draft Standards for Identifying & Supporting Quality Professional Development Schools.*

29   Morris J. Vogel and Essie Abrahams-Goldberg, "The Professional Development School as a Strategy for School Restructuring: The Millard Fillmore High School–Temple University Connection," in *Chartering Urban School Reform: Reflections on Public High Schools in the Midst of Change* (New York: Teachers College Press, 1994), 50.

Chapter 15

Reflections on Renewal: The Research University and Teacher Education

Allen D. Glenn

Introduction

Colleges of education in major research universities are complex crea-
tures. On one hand, faculty in these institutions are often highly criticized for their emphasis on scholarship at the expense of teaching,
service, work with the public schools, and an interest in teacher preparation.[1] On the other hand, it is the research generated by these same
faculty that provides the basis for the continual renewal of teacher
education. For example, the Holmes Group's agenda was created by
faculty at large, research institutions, and the foundation for the National Network for Educational Renewal was laid at the University of
California at Los Angeles and completed at the University of Washington in Seattle. Both are well-known research institutions. Colleges of
education in research universities have always struggled to balance
their research focus and their commitment to educator preparation.

In the mid-1980s, education faculty, once again, were being asked
to rethink their commitment to teacher education. National attention,
supported by the work of the Center for Educational Renewal, was
focused on a variety of major weaknesses in how teachers were prepared to begin their careers. The argument was that if America were
to meet the demands of the twenty-first century, teachers had to be
better prepared.

The challenge for a research-oriented college of education was to
decide on a course of action that would address the issues being raised
about teacher education and yet keep it linked to the overall mission

of the broader university. Without such a link, the unit would be in a weakened position when seeking resources and support. For the faculty at the University of Washington, the question was "What type of teacher preparation program is appropriate for a college of education in a large, research-oriented university?" To answer this question, we needed to engage in a thoughtful, and sometimes painful, examination of core values and norms of behavior.

This chapter chronicles the journey. Special attention is given to the examination of core values and norms and how our participation in the National Network for Educational Renewal influenced the renewal process. The reader should be aware that looking back after almost a decade illuminates events much beyond their original clarity and also causes some to lose their initial brilliant glare! While what is written is based on a review of college documents, position papers, reports, and notes, much of it comes from a personal perspective. Therefore, the voice will be that of the dean attempting, as best as possible, to place the events into some historical perspective.

Teacher Education: Beginning Again

The University of Washington had come through some very difficult times in the 1970s. By the late 1970s, it had reassessed its mission and set a course for the next decade. The decision was to recast the university into a major research institution known for cutting-edge research and creative, model programs. To achieve this goal, all units across campus came under careful review.[2]

The college of education did not fare well in this institutional rethinking of mission. It had a large undergraduate teacher education program and expended considerable resources on preparing individuals to enter teaching and related fields. This internal mission was now at odds with the university's, and the college was asked to rethink its future. In 1981, with pressure from the university, the faculty decided that the college would focus on the development of new ideas for teacher preparation and the creation of training models that were innovative or exemplary. Retained programs would serve as demonstration projects and incorporate research on learning, curriculum, and supervision.

Dramatic downsizing followed. Programs were eliminated, the number of faculty members was diminished, enrollment in teacher education programs was reduced, and teacher education became a fifth-year program. It was a difficult period in the college and for the many faculty who had created an award-winning (from AACTE) teacher education program in the 1970s. To be an accepted member of the university community, the college needed to enhance its research productivity and infuse that research into model programs.

It was, however, also a time of renewal. In 1985, a well-known scholar from the University of California at Los Angeles joined the faculty—John Goodlad—bringing with him a research agenda that has influenced teacher education at the University of Washington and across the nation. Other faculty with both excellent research and teaching skills and an interest in teacher education also began to join the faculty.

During the mid-1980s, Goodlad and associates continued their research initiatives that would lead to the publication of *Teachers for Our Nation's Schools* (1990) and *Educational Renewal: Better Teachers, Better Schools* (1994). At the same time, other faculty in the college were establishing creative programs based on the current research and thinking about education. The Puget Sound Educational Consortium (PSEC), a consortium composed of the college and ten school districts, was formed. The PSEC began to address critical educational issues that were impacting the schools. It soon became a national model and drew considerable attention to the college. Emerging from the PSEC activities and with initial support from the Danforth Foundation, other faculty members created an innovative educator program designed to prepare principals.[3] Another faculty effort established the college's first model for professional development schools. The seeds of simultaneous renewal were beginning to sprout and reshape the environment.

By the late 1980s, the time when I joined the faculty, the renewal of teacher education was on the national agenda. The college faced an interesting dilemma. What should it do about teacher education? Housed within the college was Goodlad's Center for Educational Renewal (CER), the research center that provided the data about the woeful status of teacher education nationally. Could we ignore these findings? Opinions varied. Some faculty members remembered that it was the commitment to a large teacher education program that precipitated the massive cut in the college less than ten years earlier. Others, who had been instrumental in creating the "old" program, had serious misgivings about "throwing away" what currently existed. Others said, "Let's do it!" All, however, were concerned with the same question: "Could we maintain our research productivity and legitimacy in the university and at the same time focus considerable resources on program renewal?" We were on our way to becoming a strong, research-oriented college. Would we put this effort at risk? More importantly, should we put younger faculty members' careers at risk by asking them to also focus on the renewal of teacher education?

These were very serious issues and questions. But, the reality was that we really had little choice about what to do. The education and political climates in the state demanded that we step forward and assume a leadership role in the area of teacher education. Looking back, Gary Wills's words that "leadership is always a struggle; often a feud" would prove to be prophetic.[4] We began small, with informal discussions among a group of faculty interested in teacher education renewal. We began, however, with two advantages.

First, we were not without some experience. A number of faculty had been involved in the creation of the PSEC, the principal preparation program, and the professional development school concept. Some of the essentials we learned were: (1) don't do "business as usual" and with current program parameters; (2) create a vision with essential themes, but don't ponder all the little details; (3) ensure that the core of the program is not mechanics but reflection on practice; and (4) don't hold back on starting a program.[5] Faculty began informal discussions about teacher education and spent almost a year talking about issues, building new coalitions, and floating ideas out to the broader faculty and staff. During the initial stages, we focused more on ideas, people, and the serendipities that arise from interactions (chaos) rather than a rigid flow chart of activities. Better organization would come later.

Second, we were awash in the research findings from the Center for Educational Renewal, and several staff of CER were faculty in the college. While wholesale adoption of the Center's initiatives was unrealistic at this stage of our development process, the research and philosophy underlying the Center's work provided the grist for many initial discussions and, in the end, became planks in a renewed teacher education program. The process was under way.

Essential Elements of Renewal

In the early 1990s, there were a variety of reform initiatives under way across the country. Renewal trumpets were being sounded from many quarters. Some offered simple solutions; others demanded more sweeping changes. What was most appealing about the philosophy and agenda of the Center and the National Network?

First, the work focused on the moral and intellectual aspects of being a teacher and the mission of schooling a democratic society. Laid out carefully as "reasonable expectations," the agenda set high standards for America's teachers.[6] Far too often, teacher education programs have become lost in a focus on technique of instruction and teacher behavior. Here was a clarion call to raise expectations and to make teachers a "strong intellectual and moral force in the community."[7] Faculty could identify with such a call.

The moral and intellectual aspects of teaching became core concepts that focused faculty discussion beyond instructional strategies, created a philosophical base from which the program could be developed, and stimulated thinking that was not business as usual. In fact, the power of these ideas emerged later when the faculty developed a brochure for prospective students about the new programs. In part the philosophy states:

> We believe that the process of educating teachers for a democratic and inclusive society implies the responsibility for ensuring that our graduates have high standards for both their own conduct and that of their students. We are committed to the development of ethical, caring teachers who understand their responsibility to educate all students and to believe in each student's ability to learn and grow.[8]

It was the struggle to create a vision around these ideas that brought faculty, staff, students, and teachers together. The discussion was not about direct instruction, cooperative groups, or technology, but about core ideas—ideas that would provide important mental "hooks" throughout the renewal process.

Second, the postulates were powerful organizers for renewal because of their research base. We had a love-hate relationship with the postulates. Some faculty were put off by the term postulates and their implications. Others were opposed to using anyone's "checklist" to guide renewal efforts. And yet, all found the essential ideas useful in raising important questions to consider and ones that had specific programmatic implications. The postulates also laid out the conditions for assessing renewal efforts and became important markers during the change process. Their value can be illustrated in the following manner.

1. **Postulates One and Two** call for a commitment from the institution to the preparation of teachers. Examining these postu-

lates and being reminded of them during the early years of development caused us to think carefully and strategically about how we wanted to approach the university's central administrators.[9] Educating the university's central administration about the renewal agenda and our part in a national effort was especially critical because of the administrative changes that took place. In nine years, the university had two presidents, three provosts and an acting provost, and three budget officers! Continued support from the president (and others in central administration) was an important component of the renewal process.

2. **Postulates Three and Four** called for us to rethink our organization and budgeting. Program renewal was the driving force, but organization is needed to institutionalize programs. For a number of reasons, we weren't ready to adopt the center of pedagogy concept; the ideas presented in postulates three and four reminded us as administrators and faculty that, if the new program was to sustain and renew itself, a stronger, better-functioning organizational structure was needed.[10]

3. **Postulates Five through Nineteen** became standards for assessing the emerging program. While we never sat down as a faculty and discussed the postulates, the essential concepts floated in and out of curriculum discussions, emerged as we prepared for NNER events, and were the focus of discussions when we met with colleagues from other sites.

Third, participation in the NNER provided an external perspective. It is easy to become self-absorbed in renewal and convinced of the uniqueness of one's situation. "Yes, but we are" is a comfortable rationalization for doing what one is doing. Participation in a national effort added perspective, reality, and insights into the renewal process. Even the sometimes annoying procedure of having an NNER consultant "review" the program was useful, although seldom anticipated as an exciting opportunity! Participation also linked the college's renewal efforts to a national effort, thus gaining additional legitimacy within the institution.

Fourth, renewal fostered additional review and rethinking of core college values. Renewal is an interesting process. Simple changes in one area ripple through the system, creating stress on all parts and bringing about unanticipated consequences. Of special note were the following.

1. *Hiring of new faculty became a college-wide issue.* A teacher education program that draws from across the college and has faculty team teaching puts tremendous strain on the traditional faculty replacement philosophy. New faculty had to contribute to more than one area and have unique qualifications—an excellent teacher, a solid researcher, a commitment to educator preparation, and a graduate educator. Led by the Faculty Council, the faculty developed a new approach to selecting individuals for open positions. An essential feature was the public presentation and discussion of possible new hires. In a college where well over half the faculty have been replaced in the last ten years, this new hiring philosophy has been instrumental in sustaining the renewal process, fostering creative solutions to academic issues and enhancing communication among faculty.

2. *There was the realization that program is more than a series of courses.* Far too often an educator preparation program is merely a collection of loosely coupled courses. As a result of our intense discussions about the essential themes of the new program, it became evident that faculty needed to work more closely together, share syllabi, ensure quality assessment, and adjust their own teaching to the program's needs. Although there is always a tendency to want to slip back to individual courses taught by semi-autonomous faculty, the Division of Teacher Education faculty monitor and struggle with the problem.

3. *Attention to the preparation of teacher educators grew dramatically.* Teaching assistants are essential to the preparation programs. They assist faculty, lead reflective seminars, and engage in research activities. Through the leadership of the associate dean, significant attention has been given to preparing the next generation of teacher educators. This effort is paying dividends as we continue to place graduates who are able to provide leadership in teacher education. Feedback from new institutions is that this preparation is essential and an added advantage for our graduates. This is a unique contribution that a research institution can offer.

4. *Thinking about research, promotion, and teacher education matured.* There is a common myth that research productivity declines if faculty are involved in educator preparation programs and work in schools. What would happen at the University of Washington? The truth is that the renewal process assisted fac-

ulty in clarifying the relationship between research and the renewal of teacher education. The teacher education program
served as a platform for research and scholarship. The number
of research articles and national conference presentations directly related to teacher education increased. Data collected annually as a part of the merit review process reveal that faculty
members' productivity across both traditional categories and
more nontraditional categories such as direct involvement in
schools is steady and increasing. Some of this productivity may
be attributed to a younger faculty's activity; however, associate
and full professors are also involved in examining educator preparation issues. In addition, the college received external funding
from three multimillion dollar grants that relate, in part, to teacher
education.[11] Productive faculty are not distracted by renewal
efforts. In fact, some found it a new turf for exploration and
study.

   Another major challenge for research-oriented colleges is to overcome the power of the "you-can't-get-promoted" claim for those involved in curriculum renewal and teacher education. The literature
abounds with warnings. In fact, Goodlad notes when describing curriculum development that "the task simply is very difficult and demanding and offers few tangible rewards. Indeed, extensive involvement is dangerous to one's career."[12] Many who led the renewal effort
and worked in the schools were assistant and associate professors.
Were we dooming them to failure? The answer was "no."
   No one who has been forwarded for promotion from the college to
the president's office has been denied tenure. Nor has the faculty voted
not to recommend someone for tenure. Why? First and foremost, the
faculty recommend excellent people for the initial hires who understand the expectations. Second, within a five- to six-year period, the
college created a culture more supportive of young professors. Third,
the faculty recognize a wider interpretation of scholarship and that
there are acceptable differences across academic areas. Fourth, we
have been fortunate so far that promotions forwarded to central administration have been favorably received, due, we hope, to our continued communication regarding what we value and promote in the
college. This does not mean that moving from assistant professor to a
tenured associate is not filled with anxiety, hard work, and pressures.
It is, but no one eases into excellence.[13]

The college moved forward with renewal efforts, beginning with informal discussions in 1990 and evolving into two faculty-led curriculum teams. Assisted by a $25,000 grant from the Education Commission of the States through our contact with the Center for Educational Renewal, faculty, students, staff, and public school educators created the conceptual framework and curriculum for dramatically different elementary and secondary programs. Old programs were closed and new ones put in place by 1996. The initial shouts for joy were short-lived as we realized that renewal is like a marathon, and the race had just begun.

Conflicts and Problems of Fit

Living together in a college during a renewal process places a great deal of strain on the institution, the people, and civility. There were challenging times with heated discussions in faculty meetings, the halls, offices, and via e-mail. During one particularly difficult period, I remember listening to Mary Catherine Bateson, a speaker at an NNER annual meeting, and recalling two wonderful lines from her book, *Peripheral Visions*. She wrote:

> Ambiguity is the warp of life, not something to be eliminated. Learning to savor the vertigo of doing without answers or making shift and making do with fragmentary ones opens up the pleasures of recognizing and playing with pattern, finding coherence with complexity, sharing with multiplicity.[14]

And,

> Winning is never as simple as it seems.[15]

There were certainly times during those early days when it was somewhat difficult to find the solace in ambiguity and to savor the vertigo of doing without answers! Many of us knew winning wasn't simple; we just wanted it a little easier.[16]

Conflicts

As a college, we struggled with a number of issues. First, renewal teams became new leaders, the folks who received attention and benefits and created programs that would have an impact on resources. Why should "these" people become so influential? The changing of the leadership guard is always difficult, and we struggled with ways to provide space for dissenting or discouraged voices to be heard.[17] No matter, some faculty who were not involved in teacher preparation felt on the margins of the renewal efforts.

There were also a number of discussions about the needed resources to support the new programs. Some faculty were content if sufficient resources could be found to run the new programs but were not pleased if resources were reallocated in such a way that they were impacted— the need to teach a new class, take on additional students, or lose a teaching assistant. Others were concerned that shifting resources would detract from other graduate programs—programs that were also core to the mission of the college.

The balance between educator preparation programs (now master's level) and the other graduate programs continues to challenge faculty and resources in the college. Teacher preparation consumes an enormous amount of faculty energy and resources; however, doctoral level study is also part of the core mission of the college. While often criticized for the lack of attention to teacher preparation, research universities seldom receive the credit they deserve for preparing the next generation of education leaders for higher education and the public school. Doctoral students need to be knowledgeable and experienced in educator preparation programs. They also need preparation that goes beyond teacher education and includes required special courses, mentoring, and research experiences.

Finally, there are other very important educator preparation programs in the college: special education, school psychology, school counseling, principal preparation, superintendent preparation, and leadership in higher education. All are important to the vitality of the college. They, too, draw upon resources and must be supported by the faculty and dean. To focus solely on teacher preparation at the neglect of the others is a serious miscalculation.

Problems of Fit

Being the home institution of the Center for Educational Renewal and the leaders of the NNER sometimes created tensions. CER staff had to walk a narrow path not to show favoritism. In other cases, our unique position in a large, research university posed special problems for us as a college of education. At times, the two agendas did not match, and we occasionally acted like the cranky adolescent who didn't want to follow the rules.

Particular problems of fit centered on the NNER's agenda to link more closely with arts and sciences faculty, the goal of creating a center of pedagogy, and professional development schools. Teacher education at the University of Washington is now a five-quarter master's program with over half the students entering with degrees from other institutions. Although there are strong ties with many departments in arts and sciences, the close collaborative model proposed in *Teachers for Our Nation's Schools* and *Educational Renewal: Better Teachers, Better Schools* just doesn't fit. As one faculty member noted, "We are not Northern State University!" (a reference to the culminating chapter in *Teachers*). This problem caused us to be out of step with some NNER goals and activities.

On the positive side, a program to attract undergraduates to teaching has been created. This initiative will strengthen ties with arts and sciences colleagues. It should also enhance our recruitment efforts among undergraduates and increase the number of students of color who enter teaching. This program is a direct result of work with the NNER agenda and a strong desire by the faculty to increase the diversity of the teacher education cohort.

Establishing a center of pedagogy and professional development schools was also problematic. Faculty showed little interest in exploring the center of pedagogy model. A Division of Teacher Education was created, but it lacked many of the characteristics of a center of pedagogy. A similar problem exists with our reluctance to embrace all the concepts of the professional development school. We had learned important lessons from our involvement with the Puget Sound Educational Consortium and four model professional development schools created in the late 1980s. We learned, among other things, that these relationships are quite tenuous and unbelievably demanding. We also learned that we could not sustain our model for a professional development school with the number of students we had enrolled and the number of faculty in the college. We chose instead to create elementary partner schools and partner departments at the secondary level with the primary emphasis on teacher preparation. The models have served us well but are far from the PDS model advocated by the NNER. These variances, plus our reluctance to participate in all calls for proposals, created tensions between friends.

A Personal Note: Occasionally, colleagues from other universities would ask me what it was like having John Goodlad on the faculty. Was he a help or a hindrance to me as the dean? The simple truth was that he was (and still is) a wonderful colleague, a strong advocate for our renewal agenda, and patient with us as we find our own way. We must have driven him near distraction at times! Yet, his support for me as dean has always been there. I also had the advantage of being able to talk with John as a faculty colleague rather than always in his role as director of the CER and NNER—a wonderful advantage for me, a new dean learning on the fly.

Where Do We Go from Here?

One of the biggest challenges in any renewal process is the tendency to believe that it is over—that we did it, we have a new program, now we can do something else. The fact of the matter is that we are now revising the elementary program based on the data we collected about its effectiveness. New state standards, new NCATE standards, new calls for greater accountability, and emerging research all mean the task is far from complete. In addition, the need for massive numbers of new teachers, the growing diversity of the children entering the classroom, and the growth of technology also mean that programs must continue to evolve.

As Bridges tells us in his book, *Managing Transitions*, "beginnings involve new understandings, new values, new attitudes, and—most of all—new identities."[18] It is evident as we continue the renewal process into the coming century that the faculty have come to an understanding about the balance between the educator preparation mission and our broader graduate mission. We understand that tensions will always exist between the two and that the scarcity of resources and pressures from the outside will exacerbate these tensions. Faculty also know that if educators are to answer questions about the value of educator certification and its impact on student learning, then it will likely be the faculty at research institutions who must take the lead. To be such leaders means that we must be intimately linked with the public schools. Winning is never as simple as it seems.

Notes

1   An excellent summary of the research university and teacher education during the 1980s can be found in chapter 5, "Teachers of Teachers," in John I. Goodlad, *Teachers for Our Nation's Schools* (San Francisco: Jossey-Bass, 1990).

2   Since the 1970s, the University of Washington has been one of the top public universities in securing external funding. In 1998 external funding exceeded $550 million.

3   Ten years later, almost two hundred principals have entered the profession. The program remains an exemplary model for the preparation of school administrators. See Kenneth A. Sirotnik and Kathy Mueller, "Challenging the Wisdom of Conventional Principal Preparation Programs and Getting Away with It (So Far)," in Joseph Murphy, ed., *Preparing Tomorrow's School Leaders: Alternative Designs* (University Park, Pa.: University Council for Educational Administration, 1993).

4   Gary Wills, *Certain Trumpets: The Call of Leaders* (New York: Simon & Schuster, 1994), 11.

5   These and other ideas are discussed in John I. Goodlad, *Educational Renewal: Better Teachers, Better Schools* (San Francisco: Jossey-Bass, 1994).

6   Goodlad, *Teachers for Our Nation's Schools*, 43–44.

7   Goodlad, *Teachers for Our Nation's Schools*, 44.

8   Brochure from the College of Education, University of Washington, Student Services Office, 1997.

9   Attention to this issue paid off. The college first received temporary funding to support emerging partnerships and then received substantial permanent funding to support these efforts.

10   We eventually created a Division of Teacher Education that brings together the faculty involved in the teacher preparation program. It is headed by a director and remains a work in progress.

11   The grants include an National Science Foundation grant in mathematics, an NIH grant on reading, and an OERI grant on policies related to teacher education.

12   Goodlad, *Educational Renewal*, 154.

13   This may be an issue on which there is a broad range of opinion. Some faculty members strongly believe the current system overemphasizes research and publication. Others feel the system is fair. As dean, I fall into the latter group.

14   Mary Catherine Bateson, *Peripheral Visions* (New York: HarperCollins, 1994), 9.

15   Bateson, *Peripheral Visions*, 10.

16   Bateson, *Peripheral Visions*, 107.

17   In the fall of 1995, I wrote a long letter to the faculty and staff in which I attempted to answer questions that were circulating in the college. In the letter, I spoke candidly about some of the harsh comments being made about me (quotes from a questionnaire from the preceding spring) and about others in the renewal process. It was a painful letter to write, but it cleared the air and put in writing answers to hearsay questions.

18   William Bridges, *Managing Transitions: Making the Most of Change* (New York: Perseus Books, 1991), 50.

Chapter 16

Moving Toward Democracy: Lessons Learned

Arturo Pacheco

This small essay is about lessons learned from John Goodlad. It is written from the perspective of eight years of engagement and change in educational practice in the community of El Paso, Texas. It is from the perspective of extensive conversations about improving the schools and the life-chances of all young people in a poor, working-class community without many resources. In 1991, the community pulled its educational leaders together in the realization that only through working together toward a common good, including the sharing of resources, could El Paso have the chance of significantly improving both the individual lives of all of its young people and the collective well-being of the community as well. It did so by bringing together the mayor, the county judge, the superintendents of the three largest school districts (representing 130,000 children), the presidents of both the university and the community college, the lead organizer of the major church-based grassroots community organization, and key business leaders. These stakeholders came to the table in 1991 for an extended conversation that continues to this day. Much of the change agenda was shaped at this table, from new ways to prepare teachers, to the development of community-wide expectations and standards of excellence, to new ways to talk to, trust in, and collaborate with one another. Although there have been many notable achievements, the effort is still very much a work in progress. Many more tables have been set since then, with many new voices engaged in the ongoing conversation about the school's role in the common good of the community. John Goodlad's voice, as well as his passionate commitment to public schools in a democratic society, has been a constant presence at the table.

Choosing to Educate the Man or the Citizen

Forced to combat either nature or society, you must make your choice between the man and the citizen, you cannot train both.[1]

With these words in the opening pages of Rousseau's *Emile*, the stage is set for what is perhaps the most essential and most enduring question about education: how do we distinguish the *public* from the *private* purposes of education, and what do we do when they conflict with one another? When Rousseau wrote these lines in the middle of the eighteenth century, he was quite clear that not only did they conflict, but that it was impossible to be successful at both the public and private purposes of education. One had to choose. In *Emile*, Rousseau chose to outline for us what the education of a man would look like, *according to nature.* This was not, as is sometimes thought, a call to return to some primitive natural state, but rather what the education of an individual might look like without the interference of the state or society.

As for public education, Rousseau refers us to Plato: "If you wish to know what is meant by public education, read Plato's *Republic.* Those who merely judge books by their titles take this for a treatise on politics, but it is the finest treatise on education ever written."[2] Plato, as we know, made the other choice. He chose the citizen. In the *Republic,* he lays out for us what the education of the citizen would look like in the ideal and just state. Like Rousseau's *Emile,* Plato's *Republic* has attracted many critics, many of whom have seen it as a masterpiece of anti-democratic, even totalitarian, thinking.[3] This debate, between educating the individual and educating the citizen, between the public and private purposes of education, has not only been with us at least since the time of Plato, it remains at the core of the major educational questions of the current century. The debate in our own time is phrased in terms of the mission of the *public* school, with its massive twentieth-century growth, popularization, and bureaucratization in nations around the world. By all accounts, no one in this century denies the state's interest in the education of the young, especially as education is manifested in the schooling of the young. No longer just an option for the privileged, compulsory public schooling has been the context for vigorous debates about what the schools are for, about what should be taught, about vouchers and privatization, about freedom and authority, about the place of values in the schools, and about the school's role in a democratic society. Much of the debate and argument has been framed in terms of the public versus the private purposes of schooling, some stressing the one at the expense of the other.

Enter John Goodlad. Goodlad would seem to have it both ways. We not only can but *must* educate both the individual *and* the citizen. Although a persistent theme throughout his life's work, Goodlad's scholarly and reform work of the last two decades has been marked by a constant concern over the place of education and schooling in a democratic society. The course of this scholarship over four decades, along with a thorough review of the educational reform efforts of this century, have led Goodlad and his colleagues to the conclusion that education is a *moral* enterprise, necessarily tied to the health and well-being of a democratic society.[4] Goodlad joins a line of educational thinkers and statesmen from Jefferson to Dewey who have also thought so, and his work is at the center of the tensions in the debate over individual freedom and collective responsibility for the common good. In his work of the past twenty years, Goodlad identifies four major themes related to the mission of schools and the teachers who labor within them:

1. Enculturating the young into a political and social democracy,
2. Providing access to knowledge for all children and youths,
3. Providing pedagogical nurturing of the young, and
4. Ensuring responsible stewardship of the schools.

The first two of these themes relate to the mission of schools in a democratic society and the moral imperatives of all teachers who work within them.[5] Although none of these themes is new to the debate about the schools, grouped together they both provide and clarify an immense moral purpose for the schools, as well as lay out a direction for the reform of educational practice. There is no ambiguity here. Schooling has a clear moral purpose, and those who labor within it, as well as those who would reform it, should be aware of it. Can Goodlad have it both ways? Can education or schooling successfully address the making of both the individual and the citizen? Is there a special role for the educator in both of these endeavors? In the impulse to provide an answer, one is reminded of the opening lines of a popular essay by the Brazilian philosopher of education Paulo Freire:

All educational practice implies a theoretical stance on the educator's part. This stance in turn implies—sometimes more, sometimes less explicitly—an interpretation of man and the world. It could not be otherwise.[6]

In a provocative analysis of the relationship of schooling to work done in the 1960s by another philosopher of education, Thomas F. Green cited the following as the three major functions of American schooling: 1) socialization, 2) cultural transmission, and 3) the development of self-identity.[7] In one way or another, they are often cited in most modern discussions of the goals of schooling: as such, they constitute a good place for the start of an analysis.

We must remember that mass public schooling as we know it is a relatively new phenomenon, and until the last century, the processes of socialization, cultural transmission, and the development of self-identity took place primarily through other institutions (family, church, work guilds, etc.) in the course of daily and routine activities, both within and outside the household. In this context, one might perceive very little difference between socialization and cultural transmission; they occurred in the same context and were under the aegis of roughly the same agents, perhaps varying only in their focus on different aspects. In the United States, mass public schooling is barely a century-and-a-half old. The institutionalization of schooling seems to coincide with the development of the modern nation-state and the introduction and sophistication of the idea of citizenship. In more infant stages, we saw dramatic examples of this in the 1960s with the newly liberated or newly formed nation-states of Africa and Asia. Mass public schooling and the development of loyalty to the newly formed nation-state via the idea of citizenship seem to go hand in hand, especially in those cases where new political boundaries enclosed regions marked by tribal, ethnic, and language diversity.

It is at this point where we can begin to discern some subtle changes in the notions of socialization and cultural transmission. Both socialization and cultural transmission begin to be defined in the context of the nation-state as well as the more immediate context of family and community. New elements are introduced into the process with compulsory schooling. With the notion of socialization, the bounds of reference are extended beyond everyday social relations within immediate family and community contexts, and elements such as the development of attitudes about citizenship, occupational groups, and other reference groups, such as governmental agencies, within the nation-state are introduced. Likewise, with the notion of cultural transmission, two notions of culture begin to emerge: on the one hand, there is the culture of the community, based on a web of shared values, meanings, language, and life experiences; and, on the other hand, there is the culture (in the sense of civilization) of the nation-state, with its history, heroes, structural organization, and values—knowledge of which is perceived as necessary for the cohesiveness and maintenance of the state-society. This second sense of cultural transmission begins to approach in meaning the extended sense of socialization mentioned above.

Given these differences, we can see the very real possibility for serious dissonance to occur—a dissonance that impacts the third function of the school, the development of self-identity. The development of a healthy self-identity is to a large degree dependent on the mutual integration of the first two functions, that is, on a balanced relationship between socialization and cultural transmission. So long as there is a fairly good mesh between socialization and cultural transmission within the context of one's family and community, as well as with reference to the larger context of the state-society, one can count on the objective conditions necessary for the development of an integrated and balanced self-identity.

However, if there is a major contradiction, for example, between socialization (to a state-society) and cultural transmission (of the culture on one's family and community)—if these are separated or in conflict—the conditions for the development of alienated self-identities are created. Contradictions *do* develop because it is often precisely the objective of the state to both subvert local sources of authority, loyalty, and solidarity, and also to establish an ideology of uniformity among its citizens.[8] There would be far less likelihood for creating the social conditions for this form of cultural alienation if one could assume that there was a complete integration between the societal norms and values of the school and those cultural values traditionally transmitted by the family and community.

This development of a healthy self-identity is critical to Goodlad's sense of what education is about. In fact, it is central to his distinction between *education* on the one hand, and *schooling* on the other. It is worthwhile to quote him at length here:

> *Education* is an adventure of the self. It is natural, then, to think of education as a matter of private purpose and experience. However, adventures of the self are experienced in public contexts. The self is shaped through interpretation of social encounters; the nature of these encounters is critically impor-

tant. The private purposes of education—the cultivation and satisfaction of the self—can be pursued only in the company of public purpose. How we are with others has a great deal to do with how we are with ourselves.

Schooling, on the other hand, is a sociopolitical invention that seeks to design a context or contexts for shaping many "selfs" toward predetermined ends. Schools reflect the dominant ideology or several competing ideologies regarding what these ends should be and what should be embedded in their practices to attain them. Children can and do become educated and acquire personal identity as selfs without schools. The central idea driving schools is that part of this educating should be guided and conducted to advance not just the maturation of the self but also some public need or good. The definitions of public need and good and the prevailing balance in the satisfaction of both private and public interest vary widely from society to society.[9]

It is in this marriage of private purpose (the development of self-identity) and the public good of schooling (enculturation of the young into a political and social democracy) that Goodlad proposes the education of both the "man" and the "citizen."

In our own society, as we near the close of the twentieth century, these two "educations" have been and continue to be inextricably connected. Further, for Goodlad, it is this necessary connection in schooling that is vital to the survival of a democracy. Yet, as we examine a mature American democracy at the close of the twentieth century, there are signs of stress everywhere. There is evidence that the American public may be losing its belief in the public school as well as its vital connection to American democracy. Perhaps there is even a lessening of faith in democracy itself. Confidence in both the schools and in American democracy has moved far away from the observation made by a British educator at the beginning of the present century that "the American school is radiant with a belief in its mission, and it works among people who believe in the reality of its influence, in the necessity of its labors, and the grandeur of its task."[10]

Although all of Goodlad's work is marked by a passionate commitment to the future of public schools and to their role in making democracy work, he is very aware of two competing "stories" of public schooling. On the one hand, there is the story of universal free public education that has been the premise and the promise of the American dream. On the other hand, there is the revisionist story of differential schooling based on wealth, unfulfilled dreams, and unequal access to knowledge.[11] He laments the decline in a civic cultural consciousness and quotes an eloquent but depressing editorial from a 1990 issue of the Holistic Education Review:

Our culture does not nourish that which is best or noblest in the human spirit. It does not cultivate vision, imagination, or aesthetic or spiritual sensitivity. It does not encourage gentleness, generosity, caring, or compassion. Increasingly in the late twentieth century, the economic-technocratic-static worldview has become a monstrous destroyer of what is loving and life-affirming in the human soul.[12]

Fortunately, Goodlad does not leave us in this depressing terrain for long. In fact, there is little in his scholarship or his renewal agenda that is not filled with hope and a sense of an important future both for the public schools and for American democracy. He calls our attention again and again to a potential crisis, but he also moves us toward a potential resolution. In this, he is aided by two related and important social phenomena that push us toward collective action and resolution. The first is the re-emergence of concern over the status of democracy at the end of the twentieth century. More than 150 years after Alexis de Tocqueville's paean to American democracy, a movement led by contemporary scholars such as John Goodlad, Benjamin Barber, Linda Darling-Hammond, Roger Soder, and Jean Elshtain is raising questions about an American democracy in crisis.[13] Goodlad and his colleagues at the Center for Educational Renewal have not only raised these questions but have raised the important question about the role of the school (and the moral responsibility of teachers) in the preparation of the young for a democracy, a preparation seen as necessary for its survival. In this context, John Dewey's early twentieth-century writings on democracy and education have been rediscovered. In the beginning passages of *Democracy and Education*, Dewey, writing in 1916, poses the same dilemma that we began with, the tension between Rousseau's concern for individual freedom and liberty and Plato's focus on collective responsibility to the state. He also cites a third and possibly dangerous threat to education in a democracy, the rise of the totalitarian national state.[14]

At the same time, there is a concomitant movement of concern about the loss of community in American life and the need to get Americans thinking once again about working together toward the "common good."[15] The debate aroused by Robert Putnam's notion of too many Americans "bowling alone" in his essay of the same name has been vigorous in both scholarly journals and the popular press.[16]

This second concern for "community" and the "common good" is as equally important as the concern for democracy, and it is to the schools that many look for the appropriate preparation of young people.

Here, we find both a romantic longing for a sense of community that may have existed in some earlier settings in American society (especially rural settings), as well as the more contemporary hard-nosed realization that it is only by bringing everyone together that some communities stand a chance of successful and democratic survival.

It is to this broader sense of community that I now wish to turn my attention. Ultimately, it is in these communities that schools exist, and unless we think of them, too, as *democratic* and *educative* communities, the good work toward democracy in the schools will quickly fade in the dissonance created by communities moving in different directions. Goodlad's notion of the necessary simultaneous renewal of the public schools and the preparation programs that prepare teachers for them takes us a long way toward the educational renewal so necessary at this time. So too, his delineation of the principal instruments of that necessary change: the tripartite partnership between educators in the public schools, colleges of education, and arts and sciences faculty. This collaborative community working toward a common end enables us in preparing better teachers and thus increases the likelihood of success for all youngsters. At a minimum, there is a bridge between theory and practice and, like the clinical faculty members in teaching hospitals, the clinical faculty members in the schools could do much to ease the transition of young teachers from the university to the public school classroom. In many cases, the student about to graduate and become a teacher is faced with the challenge of integrating the seemingly disconnected experiences of visits to three alien worlds—that of the arts and sciences disciplines, the pedagogical world of colleges of education, and the world of school practice, where the children live. Bringing the caretakers of these worlds together to work with future teachers is absolutely essential if we want to create better teaching and learning environments where children will thrive.

There is, nevertheless, another equally important transition. It has to do with the communities where children live and the schools where they learn. Particularly in the case of poor urban children, there is often a radical disconnect between the cultures of the community and the culture of the school. This disconnect may be even greater now than it was in the past. For these reasons, there is an absolutely critical and necessary fourth partner in the collaboration to improve education for democracy: parents and community members. This is especially true in working-class communities where, for a variety of socioeconomic reasons, parents are even more disconnected from their children in schools. Yet, parents, with their common interests in the success and future of their children, can be crucial players in helping to make change happen. Schools and the children who inhabit them exist in communities that shape them and often determine what kinds of places they will be. Are schools the smooth extensions of the learning that goes on first in families and communities, or are they radical disjunctures in the experience of children? Are schoolhouses places where parents and community members take great pride and ownership, or are they places that are alien and unwelcoming? Are teachers comfortable and familiar with the full lives of the children in their care, or are they unaware of the daily experience of children and uncomfortable and sometimes frightened by the communities from which the children come? Do parents and teachers recognize their common purpose in the achievement and well-being of the children, or do they approach each other as antagonists working toward different ends?

Educational reform efforts have most often been "top-down" affairs, leaving out key players, most notably teachers, but also other important players such as parents and community members. With regard to parents, neither school people nor university faculty members typically have much expertise in working with parents in their communities, and it may take additional expertise in drawing parents into the life of the school in significant ways. Reform efforts are also not only top-down, but also exclusive in terms of culture and class, often leaving out of the reform conversation the voices of those who traditionally have been disenfranchised. This is particularly true in working-class or "minority" communities, where there are great differences between the culture of the school and the culture of the family and community.

Having recognized these disparities, it is impossible to think of the democracy agenda in terms of the schools alone and not in terms of communities as well. Goodlad recognizes this and, particularly in his work of the last decade, pushes us to consider the implications of a broader ecological perspective of the community for the reform of the schools.[17] How does one begin, then, with a broader renewal agenda that is inclusive of those who lives are most dependent on and affected by change in the schools, children, and their parents?

John Goodlad's insights again suggest the way to proceed toward resolution—the necessity of the "human conversation." We know that "cultures" can be very closed phenomena, and that some, especially the culture of the school, can be very closed and resistant to change. Seymour Sarason's work over the past several decades has made this amply evident, suggesting that it may be next to impossible to reform large bureaucratic cultural structures like schools.[18] To use a post-modern example from Neil Postman, the stories that people tell and the narratives that both guide our thinking and frame the questions that we ask are quite different across cultures.[19] Likewise, attempting to penetrate cultural groups from the outside, often with the perspective of a different language and history, is extremely difficult. Part of the difficulty is the insularity of discourse within the "culture" and the difficulty of communicating across cultures. No wonder that we must shift our attention to the primacy of the discourse and the human conversation.

Setting the conditions for the human conversation is the first pre-supposition of any vibrant democracy. Neither idle talk nor nonlistening argument, Goodlad's conversation is that of the purposive engagement of citizens coming together to solve their problems. It is the talk of the town hall meeting, quickly becoming an anachronism in American society:

> How do we proceed? We talk. We need to talk *across* all levels of government and all walks of life. We need to talk *within* all levels of government and walks of life: in homes, on the job, in schools, in all manner of public forums. Do we know how? Wives and husbands talk with one another and their children very little, and much of this talk is argument, not conversation. Management theory encourages talk, but managers usually do not. A major objective of schools is language development, but talk is not encouraged. The measures used to judge the educational performance of students eschew talk. Television and other technological developments render talk virtually unnecessary.[20]

We must set a larger table, then, and bring *all* of the stakeholders to it. Beyond bringing the stakeholders to sit at the table together, a long and extended conversation and dialogue will be necessary; and it will, over time, provide a common language. The diversity of the discourse is a major problem, with key actors who work within different narratives often talking right past one another, and with little understanding of each other. A common language is a necessary precondition for finding a shared vision and common values. It is this shared vision and common values that will, ultimately, give both meaning to a reform agenda and will sustain it over time. The different narratives not only determine the discourse, they frame the organizational structures of each culture, making them seem impenetrable to one another.

Although building trust, and discovering that the partners in a collaboration are embarking on a common moral enterprise (the renewal of the schools and American democracy), is probably best achieved through the development of relations with one another through extended informal conversation, the problems of governance will be significant and will likely require more formal structures. Those who are invited to a table of stakeholders to collaborate in moving a common renewal agenda forward will want to know that they have a voice and will be heard, that they bring essential ingredients to the partnership, and that they will have a significant say in the overall framing and design of the agenda. They will want some assurance that they have a vote that counts.

Ultimately, this is a democratic political process that involves giving up complete power and control over one's own turf in the name of a greater common good. Deans, superintendents, and community leaders are not traditionally socialized or trained to do this. Nor are university professors, public school teachers, or parents. A governance structure, fashioned in response to both the historical and social contexts of the specific setting, will have to be developed to guarantee these conditions.

I have argued that it is only through serious collaboration of all major stakeholders that the renewal agenda has a chance. Authentic collaboration is true democratic participation at the table. I have also argued that what will bring stakeholders to the table and keep them there is a common moral purpose. That common purpose is the well-being and success of all young people. Ultimately, it is the development of this well-being, this nurturance of the young, that is the central purpose of school. This is the public purpose of schools in a democratic society. Concomitantly, it is the same public purpose of schools that prepares the young to participate as citizens in a democracy. The ultimate purpose, then, is actually a double one: the nurturance of the young and the future of democracy.

Schools, as one of the last institutions that nearly all children share in common, are the critical vehicles for this purpose. They seem to have adequately served this purpose in the past, and perhaps do so less adequately now. Nevertheless, they remain crucial. I have also argued, with Goodlad, that the key agents of change in the schools are the teachers and administrators. Hence, the universities that prepare them, the schools that provide their workplace, and the students and communities that shape them, are all critically important partners in the overall formation of educators who will be stewards of and change the schools. These educators are actually double agents: they are *change* agents and they are *moral* agents. Moral purpose and change agency are strange bedfellows, perhaps, but on closer examination, they are natural allies.

Notes

1   Jean Jacques Rousseau, *Emile* (London: Dent Everyman's Library, 1966), 7.

2   Rousseau, *Emile*, 8.

3   See especially, Karl R. Popper, *The Open Society and Its Enemies* (New York: Harper & Row, 1962). This work, published during World War II, is especially concerned with the rise of closed totalitarian states.

4   John I. Goodlad, Roger Soder, and Kenneth A. Sirotnik, eds., *The Moral Dimensions of Teaching* (San Francisco: Jossey-Bass, 1990).

5   John I. Goodlad, *Educational Renewal: Better Teachers, Better Schools* (San Francisco: Jossey-Bass, 1994), 4.

6   Paulo Freire, *Cultural Action For Freedom,* Monograph, Series No. 1 (Cambridge: Harvard Educational Review, 1970).

7   Thomas F. Green, *Work, Leisure, and the American School* (New York: Random House, 1968), 148.

8   See, for example, Yehudi A. Cohen, "The Shaping of Men's Minds: Adaptations to the Imperatives of Culture," in Murray Wax et al., eds., *Anthropological Perspectives on Education* (New York: Basic Books, 1971), 40.

9   John I. Goodlad, "Reprise and a Look Ahead," in John I. Goodlad and Timothy J. McMannon, eds., *The Public Purpose of Education and Schooling* (San Francisco: Jossey-Bass, 1997), 155–56.

10 David Tyack and Elizabeth Hansot, *Managers of Virtue: Public School Leadership in America, 1820–1980* (New York: Basic Books, 1982), 3.

11 John I. Goodlad, *In Praise of Education* (New York: Teachers College Press, 1997), 122–23.

12 Goodlad, *In Praise of Education*, 125.

13 Benjamin R. Barber, *An Aristocracy of Everyone: The Politics of Education and the Future of America* (New York: Ballantine, 1992); Jean Bethke Elshtain, *Democracy on Trial* (New York: Basic Books, 1995); Linda Darling-Hammond, *The Right to Learn* (San Francisco: Jossey-Bass, 1997); Roger Soder, ed., *Democracy, Education, and the Schools* (San Francisco: Jossey-Bass, 1996).

14 John Dewey, *Democracy and Education* (New York: Free Press, 1966), 81–99. For a contemporary analysis, see Robert B. Westbrook, *John Dewey and American Democracy* (Ithaca, N.Y.: Cornell University Press, 1991).

15   See Robert Bellah et al., *Habits of the Heart: Individualism and Commitment in American Life* (New York: Harper and Row, 1985) and *The Good Society* (New York: Random House Vintage Books, 1991); also Amitai Etzioni, *The Spirit of Community: Rights, Responsibility, and the Communitarian Agenda* (New York: Crown, 1993).

16   Robert D. Putnam, "Bowling Alone: America's Declining Social Capital," *Journal of Democracy* 6 (January 1995): 65–78. See also his earlier, *Making Democracy Work: Civic Traditions in Modern Italy* (Princeton, NJ: Princeton University Press, 1993). For a popular response and rebuttal, see Richard Stengel, "Bowling Together," *Time*, 22 July 1996, 35–36.

17   See, for example, John I. Goodlad, "Democracy, Education, and Community," in Roger Soder, ed., *Democracy, Education, and the Schools*, 87–124. See also chapter 3 of Goodlad, *In Praise of Education*, 46–81.

18   Seymour B. Sarason, *The Culture of the School and the Problem of Change* (Boston: Allyn and Bacon, 1971, revised 1982).

19   Neil Postman, *The End of Education* (New York: Knopf, 1995).

20   Goodlad, "Democracy, Education, and Community," 105.

Chapter 17

Goodlad and Educational Policy

Calvin Frazier

A Gentle Scholar or a Cutting River?

In a treatise overviewing his seventy-year love affair with schools, Goodlad describes himself as being part of a system—as a pupil but outside the system when serving as a teacher of teachers and an inquirer—"an observer outside looking in."[1] Nowhere do you find Goodlad claiming to be a policy analyst or even one who writes with an eye to driving significant policy change. That he left for others. His personal characterization, however, seems too humble for one who has had enormous influence on American education during the latter half of this century.

Indeed, one might compare his life to that of the Colorado River as it leaves Colorado with the waters from the high country and eventually brings a richness of life to southern California and Arizona inhabitants. Along the way, it meanders through a barren land cutting steadily and deeply through the stratified sandstone and red shale to form the Grand Canyon—a place visitors come to admire the beauty of the formations and the power of the river, then turn away and move onward. It reminds one of the description of Goodlad provided by an education editor for the *Christian Science Monitor*: "This gentle scholar, long associated with calling for the best in schooling, is welcome at every educator's meeting, and his books, monographs, and shorter writings are in every teacher's room and in every teacher training institution. But few seem to hear his primary thesis."[2]

Many do hear, however, and seek to understand. Each of us has carried these beliefs into our various worlds. As one infected with the "Goodlad virus," I have drawn from his works during my career as an educator, commissioner of education, and policy specialist.

Two Educators

There is some similarity in our early experiences with schools. Goodlad began his work with children in British Columbia while I started teaching in the logging areas of southern Washington. We appear to share a common appreciation for these years. Neither area had urban resources and stimulation but both provided an understanding of children, families, and the community that became a tremendous supplement to our formal preparation as educators. There is another point in common.

In the ensuing years, Goodlad moved through higher education experiences in Illinois and Georgia before settling in the dean's position at the University of California at Los Angeles. While drawn to the challenge of leadership in one of the major American universities, there was no lessening of his commitment to the public schools. He organized and led the Southern California School-University Partnership. I, in the meantime, tried a professorship, felt the separation to be too great, and returned to the public schools. Goodlad persevered. But it was not without conflict. In more recent years, when interviewing a long-time University of Chicago professor, I asked what he remembered about John Goodlad, the professor, at the University of Chicago in the late 1950s. "He was always trying to get the faculty out into the schools. It really irritated some of the professors." My respect for Goodlad took another jump for it was this concern for elementary and secondary schools that eventually led me to become the Colorado Commissioner of Education. We were on different career paths, but in the 1970s, as I listened to his message in a University of Colorado at Boulder lecture room and talked with him for the first time, I felt I had met a kindred spirit whose ideas resonated with me as an educator, policy adviser, and human being.

The Educator and the Policy Adviser

From my vantage point, Goodlad's nationwide influence escalated from the mid-1970s on. The "observer" or the "outsider" drew attention to the importance of the early years of a child's development and spoke to the advantage of ungraded classrooms in the elementary schools. In *The Dynamics of Educational Change*,[3] well in advance of the site-based management emphasis, Goodlad argued for the importance of the school as the unit of change. Not all of Goodlad's recommendations were welcomed by educators. He once advocated for beginning school at an earlier age and paying the additional cost by dropping one year of high school. To many parents, it seemed an educationally sound proposal and was personally attractive to me for several reasons. But, after broaching the idea in a public meeting, high school coaches and the state athletic association quickly reacted, citing the adverse effect on school athletic programs. The proposal was tabled.

However, years later, in working with Colorado policymakers, the idea found life in an unexpected manner. After collaborating with legislative leaders to rewrite the school finance act, I was asked by an influential legislator what I personally might want to see added. I responded that it was time to begin a pre-school program for children in at-risk situations. Much to my surprise the amendment was drafted, passed, and signed into law. Many of Goodlad's recommendations probably have wound their way through similar mutations to find expression in state policy.

As commissioner and spokesperson for a state's educational enterprise, one regularly feels the need for good educational counsel and philosophical base to help sort out the myriad educational requests and recommendations that come to the state office. For me, Goodlad was one of a select few that I relied on to fill that role. Another was Ernest Boyer.

Goodlad and Boyer came to Colorado periodically to meet with superintendents and other Colorado leaders. The small-group seminars were designed to showcase new ideas and to inspire emerging leaders through contact with the two leaders. In many cases, the impact was significant. Years later, after retiring from the commissioner's position, I received letters from superintendents citing these visits as being some of the most meaningful contributions brought to the state by the outgoing commissioner.

Target: Public Education

By the mid-1980s, public education was blindsided by major controversies involving global education, values in the classroom, and humanism. These were not new topics for Goodlad, as he had been aligned with "humanistic" movements for several years. In fact, one of the Colorado antagonists declared Goodlad to be a prime example of a secular humanist having great influence on the schools. But for superintendents and boards of education, who were being attacked regularly, these were not familiar issues. It was not a time to retreat from the misrepresentations of a few, however, and a Commissioner's Statement on Global Education,[4] which sounded too much like Goodlad for some of the critics, appeared to bring a perspective and direction to beleaguered school leaders and drew editorial and public support.

No one in a leadership role in education in April of 1983 will forget the impact of the national commission's report, *A Nation at Risk*.[5] The release of Goodlad's *A Place Called School*[6] in 1984 proved to be particularly fortuitous. While the public was drawn to the commission report, it was possible to draw from both publications in exchanges with educators, the media, and policymakers. The commission report brought a sense of urgency to some of the Goodlad findings and moved educators and policymakers to consider how schools had evolved to some of the practices reported—and how these trends might be reversed. Why was only three-quarters of the school day being used for instruction, with routines, behavior control, and social activity taking up almost 25 percent of each school day?[7] Why was there such a range in instructional time between elementary schools spending as little as 19.6 hours a week on the various subject areas and others requiring 26 and 27 hours per week?[8] State policymakers, who may have ignored Goodlad in previous years and debates, found his material to have great relevance in unraveling some of the charges found in the commission report.

Because the concerns came from Goodlad, some educators found it easier to deal with corrective proposals that otherwise would have been stalled in professional denial. The *A Nation at Risk* report became a lightning rod for public attention; Goodlad's analysis of practices that had in some cases evolved with little rationale and intent seemed more real to school practitioners. Goodlad spoke to educators in a way few authorities did during this period. He was seen as one who understood the schools and professionals, children, families, and the system. Additionally, by combining the dean's campus responsibilities with his leadership of the Southern California Partnership, Goodlad brought a unique credibility to the educational scene that was unmatched in the 1980s. From my perspective as a commissioner of education during these years, Goodlad's research, coupled with his philosophical base, provided a badly needed grounding for the public debates.

Goodlad and Public Policy

As indicated earlier, Goodlad does not claim to be a policy analyst and has seldom written with the intent of driving significant state-level policy change. His writings might be interpreted as containing a strong disdain for state policymakers, based in part on his belief that policymakers, more often than not, botch efforts to address major educational and societal problems. The one exception to this generalization might be his opening to the Eighty-sixth Yearbook of the National Society for the Study of Education (NSSE).[9] In this work, he lays out nine assumptions that he believes can be useful in generating a state improvement agenda.[10] The statements are more like goals for state policymakers than specific recommendations to raise student achievement or improve the quality of teaching. The assumptions would make sense to most legislators and governors: "expectations set for schools by state authorities must be broad and comprehensive" or "there must be no mushiness in the state's commitment to equity."[11] But a commissioner of education is forever pushed to recommend specific strategies, and therein lies the problem. This is not to dismiss the contribution of the Goodlad recommendations, but as one educator said of similar statements, "The nation can't operate with just the Constitution and a Bill of Rights." In the dual world of educator and policy advocate, the state leader must relate to the educational enterprise, lawmakers, and the public. Though the language may at times be quite different with each audience, the message has to be consistent, professionally sound, and rooted in solidly held beliefs and values. In my case, because of Goodlad's profound influence, he indirectly influenced a wide variety of legislative acts.

The state educational leader has a fine line to walk. First, when working with state policymakers, it is important to be sensitive to public concerns—whether they appear valid or not. Inasmuch as education in the United States is "public" education, the general populace must have confidence in the schools and their leaders. Second, the state educational leader operates in a world of compromises. Agreements made in the political arena often fall short of the educational ideal, yet this is a necessary outcome if public schools are to survive.

Goodlad's sixth and seventh assumptions in the Yearbook illustrate the problem: "Sixth, the word and the concept 'accountability' must be changed to 'responsibility,' interpreted to mean responsibility for carrying out the defined functions of a given level or unit of decision making by the actors encompassed within it." And the seventh, "such level-to-level monitoring as deemed minimally necessary should focus on whether adequate mechanisms for assuring responsible performance are in place."[12] It would be very difficult to sell this approach to state

legislatures today. Twenty years ago, Goodlad would have found himself in agreement with the problems state and national leaders identified in schools across the country, but when the various task forces
and commissions concluded their studies, a very different set of solutions unfolded than those favored by Goodlad.

An example is the Education Commission of the States (ECS) Task
Force on Education for Economic Growth. When key state leaders
and nationally known leaders met in the early 1980s to consider the
status of education in America, Goodlad would have been pleased
with the opening statement provided by Governor Hunt of North Caro-
lina: "Nothing matters more—nothing. Education is the public enterprise in our country that is closest to people's hearts—and most important to their lives. And education is the enterprise that is crucial to
success in everything we attempt as a nation."[13] The ECS Task Force
concluded that among the most serious problems were the educational deficits identified throughout the system and the blurred goals
for American education. Again, Goodlad would have been pleased
with the diagnosis. However, he likely would have had trouble with the
prescription, namely, tying education to the nation's economic development instead of advancing educational principles needed for a democratic society to sustain itself. And while the strategies for change
were challenging and commendable for the most part, the tone and
focus that was to guide much of the policymaking for the next two
decades was clear: "We recommend that fair and effective programs
be established to monitor student progress through periodic testing of
general and specific skills."[14] Coupled with this was a call to "establish
firm, explicit, and demanding requirements concerning discipline, attendance, homework, grades, and other essentials of effective schooling."[15] "Measuring the effectiveness of teachers and rewarding outstanding performance" was another recommendation relative to a
quality assurance recommendation.[16]

The power of the governors and business leaders participating in
this task force increased the likelihood of attention to these recommendations by policymakers across the country. Working closely with
state leaders for the last twenty-five years, I have appreciated the
policymakers' search for excellence, but I also have tried to move state
policy leaders to consider strategies based on the broader educational
ends articulated by Goodlad. It is like good teaching. While you might
wish otherwise, you must recognize where students are in their development, help the students achieve their immediate goals, and push
them to higher levels of knowledge and aspiration.

For example, laws requiring learning standards have moved us to be more specific in terms of our expectations for students. Required testing programs have sought to ensure that some judgment be made as to the effectiveness of schools, in part to justify a rather significant educational investment by the states. The intent must be appreciated. Goals for schools in many states have been nonexistent or loosely stated and only tangentially acknowledged in terms of the school instructional program and the allocation of resources. To emphasize performance and results in state actions is, in my mind, a far superior approach—and much more appropriate—than burdening the system with procedural specifics. The shortfalls accompanying the current movement have been many, however, and are not unlike what Goodlad predicted.

The standards for students and teachers have for the most part been far too narrowly focused. Many of the debates over outcomes and standards have occurred at the state level with limited ownership and responsibility felt by school districts, schools, and institutions of higher education. The conditions needed to support higher student performance and better schools have been given too little attention. And while assessing or judging the knowledge base and performance of students and teachers is appropriate, we have devalued the judgment of the professional in evaluating growth in favor of a heavy reliance on standardized tests. Many of these concerns relate to the other assumptions outlined by Goodlad in the 1987 NSSE yearbook. It remains to be seen if the activity of the last twenty years will be a transitional period in moving to a higher level of goal setting and evaluation or if the narrow standards and testing focus will contribute to a decline in support of public education.

In many ways, policymakers and Goodlad are not far apart on basic questions about society and public education. Goodlad would, I think, feel very much at home in policymaker discussions on the purposes of schooling and education. Apart from the unfortunate proposals that often draw headlines when legislators attempt to deal with the number of hours of reading to be required or the balance in whole language and phonics instruction provided in teacher education programs, many of the legislative discussions revolve around the purposes of public education. "What should the schools be emphasizing?" "What should teachers bring to the classroom assignment?" Or one that has arisen more and more often of late: "How will we know if any of this legislation makes any real difference in the classroom or in the quality of teaching?"

The Policymaking Continuum

Eric Hoffer's book, *The True Believer*,[17] was helpful to me in conceptualizing four contributors of policymaking—each to be valued but markedly different in their behavioral, social, and psychological characteristics. At one end is the activist, radical, or mini-revolutionist who sees a wrong or an injustice and seeks change. Some activists are such "true believers" that they are not the ones to represent these beliefs to elected policymakers. Activists range in interests from Cesar Chavez and his leadership of the farm workers, to Martin Luther King and the Civil Rights Movement, to Ralph Nader who pressed industry to correct damaging pollution and eliminate safety hazards. Activists often serve as a public conscience. They seek changes that many consider radical. They are usually future oriented and believe in the human potential for change.[18]

Next on the continuum are interpreters, translators, or facilitators, who have a high sensitivity to the problem, can communicate effectively with the activists and the policymakers, and believe in the need for change. Third are the policymakers themselves, whose central role is to listen to the interpreters, identify with the problem, and have the skill and patience to work solutions through the legislative process on behalf of the public. Last, there are the implementers. These are the individuals, such as teachers and administrators, who receive and act on the legislative mandates. They contribute to the policymaking process by providing feedback on the impact of the legislation or rules and suggest changes or alternatives to achieving the public intent. This brief description of the four components suggests the importance of seeing policymaking as involving others outside the legislative halls.

I would classify Goodlad primarily as an activist although he has attributes that would fit with the other three components. I believe him to be an activist or a radical in the best sense of the word. His ideas and reports have highlighted serious problems in education. His recommendations have challenged the routine and irritated many of his colleagues who prefer to make only marginal changes—if any. Indeed, his has been in many ways, "a rather lonely undertaking," as he acknowledges in 1979 in the introduction of his book, *What Schools Are For.*[19] In this sense, while filling the role of an interpreter or facilitator over the years, I felt an affinity with Goodlad, in that neither of us served as a lobbyist representing an association or organization, but rather saw ourselves as advocates for an effective system of educa-

tion. Given this commitment, one finds himself having a loose relationship to other educators, association leaders, and policymakers at
other levels, such as the local school district or higher education governing board members. Loyalty rests with the public good, families,
and children. It is sometimes a very lonely endeavor. Beyond the stimulus of his dedication and ideas, early on I developed a great admiration
for Goodlad and the manner in which he filled this role while drawing
great respect from all groups.

Most notably in my mind were his writings in the late 1970s, when
he was deeply troubled by what he felt to be the "trivialization of the
ends and means of schooling," as schools were drawn into an increasing number of noneducational activities.[20] Boosted by Goodlad's comments, and sharing many of his concerns, I made this an issue in
various presentations in Colorado. However, we were coming off an
incredible decade of needed equity legislation, and in addition to the
federal mandates, there were many locally designed changes that added
to the duties and expectations for teachers and schools. Special interest groups, many with legitimate ends, were less than thrilled with my
message. The speeches were seen as an attempt to slow implementation of the federal and state handicapped education legislation or de-
lay attention to the 1974 Lau v. Nichols decision calling for greater
opportunity for those students limited in their English language proficiency. The most supportive group was a strong conservative element
in the Republican party that used my plea for examining the purposes
of education to raise questions about the desirability of continuing
public education. The message was right, but the Colorado messen-
ger was ill prepared for the forces that had mobilized in the 1970s.

While sharing many concerns about the well-being of public education, there have been times when Goodlad and I have not been in
sync. As a policy adviser, I have had to temper ideas and accept compromises on some proposals that fell short of the desirable, but con-
stituted the best agreement that could be achieved at that time. I'm
sure such actions disappointed and even irritated Goodlad. But beyond the many philosophical bonds that have been built over the years,
there is one belief over which there is no disagreement: the renewing
of schools, schools of education, and individuals must undergird all of
what we do as agents of change.

The Essential Goal: Renewal

Goodlad emphasizes the term "renewal" in describing his goal for
schools. Not reform, restructure, or reorganize, although each of these

terms has legitimacy. He sees renewal as the needed ingredient of any organization. A renewing unit can be counted on to be abreast of the educational problems and the needs of society, to be inquiring as to the dysfunctions and successes of the organization, and to be self-correcting. It is an ideal we both see as a goal for schools and institutions of higher education. It is a concept that has important policy implications.

In a sense, I have felt that Goodlad gave structure and direction to John Gardner's notion of self-renewal[21] and excellence[22] that I had been drawn to in the late 1960s and early 1970s. As a professor, commissioner of education, and policy consultant to state leaders, I resonated with Gardner's discussion of the need for some consensus on values—"undergirded by certain habits and attitudes which are shared by members of the society."[23] And, as though speaking directly to all educators and individuals setting policies for the educational enterprise, Gardner argues that "anyone concerned for the continuous renewal of a society must be concerned for the renewal of that society's values and beliefs. Societies are renewed—if they are renewed at all—by people who believe in something, care about something, stand for something."[24]

Years later, when I heard Goodlad articulate the simultaneous renewal concept for the National Network for Educational Renewal (NNER), I connected the Goodlad strategy to the Gardner philosophy. Both Goodlad and Gardner express an urgency over fundamental weaknesses undermining our country's well-being. Gardner, nearly forty years ago, said that "the long-run challenge to the United States is nothing less than a challenge to our sense of purpose, our vitality, and our creativity as a people."[25] He saw education as a part of "the society's larger task of abetting the individual's intellectual, emotional, and moral growth. What we must reach for is a conception of perpetual self-discovery, perpetual reshaping to realize one's best self.[26] Goodlad would use the word "renewal" to describe this process and would see it as a level of maturity to be sought by organizations as well as individuals.

The NNER, the Institute for Educational Inquiry (IEI), and the Center for Educational Renewal (CER) have wrapped themselves around these themes. No other "reform" movement or writer has given such an emphasis to renewal. The core of many change proposals in recent years has been relatively superficial in comparison.

Renewal must be a consideration in establishing state and institutional policies. Renewal recognizes the human aspect of change. It is the process by which dedicated and purposeful educational leadership has emerged. Renewal needs to be one of the criteria by which state and institutional policies are evaluated. As a policy specialist, I try to weigh proposed statutory or rule approaches in terms of their potential for enhancing or retarding individual or institutional renewal.

There is no question that educators must address the issue of accountability and the need to assure the public as to the quality of student, teacher, and school performances. Quality is a primary consideration when legislators meet to appropriate public monies. Further, it is critical that educators themselves have valid assessments for planning purposes and the personal satisfaction of knowing they have made a difference in student learning. Identifying an accountability program that achieves these diverse ends and recognizes renewal as a critical and necessary organizational component has become a personal goal.

Goodlad spoke to my professional concerns when I served as a K–12 administrator and a university faculty member. He was the unseen participant when I testified in legislative hearings. He continues to provide the research and theoretical base for me in working with state and local policymakers. But, more than anything else, Goodlad put "wheels" under the Gardner concepts that provoked my interest years ago.

And Goodlad himself? He exemplifies renewal. In rereading many of his early writings, one is struck by the enormous range of interests he has brought to education during his love affair with schooling. Throughout his work he has maintained an optimism, persevered, and inspired many of us to press—not only for reform and restructuring—but for renewal. The concept is no longer dependent on the advocacy of one individual. But Goodlad, more than any other educational leader, has made renewal a part of the educational landscape in America for three score and ten—and counting.

Notes

1 John I. Goodlad, *Romances with Schools*, unpublished draft manuscript.

2 John I. Goodlad, *What Schools Are For* (Bloomington, Ind.: Phi Delta Kappa Educational Foundation), vii.

3 John I. Goodlad, *The Dynamics of Educational Change* (San Francisco: McGraw-Hill, 1975).

4 Calvin M. Frazier, *Global Education: Analysis of the Issue and Recommendations* (Denver: Colorado Department of Education, August 1986, unpublished).

5 National Commission on Excellence in Education, *A Nation at Risk* (Washington, D.C.: U.S. Government Printing Office, 1983).

6 John I. Goodlad, *A Place Called School* (San Francisco: McGraw-Hill, 1984).

7 Goodlad, *A Place Called School*, 97.

8 Goodlad, *A Place Called School*, 133.

9 John I. Goodlad, ed., *The Ecology of School Renewal*, Eighty-sixth Yearbook of the National Society for the Study of Education, Part I (Chicago: University of Chicago, 1987).

10 Goodlad, *The Ecology of School Renewal*, 9–16.

11 Goodlad, *The Ecology of School Renewal*, 11.

12 Goodlad, *The Ecology of School Renewal*, 13.

13 Education Commission of the States, *Action for Excellence* (Denver: Education Commission of the States, 1983), 1.

14 Education Commission of the States, *Action for Excellence*, 39.

15 Education Commission of the States, *Action for Excellence*, 38.

16 Education Commission of the States, *Action for Excellence*, 39.

17 Eric Hoffer, *The True Believer* (New York: Harper & Row, 1951).

18 Hoffer, *The True Believer*, 19.

19 Goodlad, *What Schools Are For*, viii.

20 Goodlad, *What Schools Are For*, vi.

21 John W. Gardner, *Self-Renewal* (New York: Norton, 1963).

22 John W. Gardner, *Excellence* (New York: Harper & Brothers, 1961).

23   Gardner, *Self-Renewal*, 116.

24   Gardner, *Self-Renewal*, 115.

25   Gardner, *Excellence*, 146.

26   Gardner, *Excellence*, 136.

Chapter 18

Educational Renewal and the Improvement of Private Grantmaking

L. Scott Miller and Edward F. Ahnert

The November 1996 issue of the *Phi Delta Kappan* included an article by John Goodlad titled, "Sustaining and Extending Educational Renewal."[1] It described the National Network for Educational Renewal (NNER), which was founded by Goodlad, and discussed the NNER's efforts since the middle 1980s to promote the simultaneous renewal of schools and teacher education.

Readers familiar with the work of Goodlad and his colleagues were undoubtedly not surprised when the article argued that the successful pursuit of simultaneous school and teacher education renewal requires a *symbiotic* relationship between schools and universities acting in equal partnership. What may have been unexpected to many *Kappan* readers, however, was that the introductory section of the article included what was essentially a short editorial by Goodlad on the crucial role that private grantmakers have been playing in the current period of educational reform through their support of several significant, long-term school and teacher preparation reform initiatives. He suggested that private funders and grant recipients have complementary roles in serving society through their efforts to improve institutions over time.

We would like to extend the discussion that Goodlad began in his editorial by exploring the continuing societal need for private funders to strengthen their long-term grantmaking. We also will discuss how many educational reform initiatives not only offer important social investment opportunities for grantmakers, but also help funders gain a better understanding of the capabilities that the philanthropic sector needs to discharge its long-term responsibilities more effectively.

Throughout our discussion, it is important to remember the human
factor: these investment opportunities do not simply emerge, they are
the creation of very special people such as John Goodlad. In his case,
he combines a clear vision of what it means to be educated for citizenship in a democracy with an ability to work systematically in partnership with a great many colleagues in schools and universities to improve the educational capacities of these institutions on an ongoing
basis.

Philanthropy and School and Teacher Education Renewal

In his *Kappan* piece, Goodlad said:

> One feature that stands out from the stories of somewhat successful reform is
> the extent and continuity of funding by philanthropies (some of them corpo-
> rate) in order to serve the public good. . . . Philanthropic foundations seeking
> to live up to their charters with respect to public purpose inevitably struggle
> with three troublesome questions: What should we fund? Over what time
> span? And how do we capitalize on what appear to be our best choices by
> increasing their contribution to the public good? Those of us engaged in edu-
> cational improvement initiatives sustained by philanthropies over a period of
> years carry a great deal of responsibility for answering the third question. Are
> we developing a renewing capacity with respect to the common good? And,
> is this capacity extending more broadly and deeply toward advancing the pub-
> lic purpose of education? Continuing attention to these processes necessi-
> tates some introspection on our parts.[2]

It is instructive that Goodlad's statement begins with the observation that many successful initiatives in the current period of educational reform have benefited from substantial and continuous financial
support from private grantmakers. This is a telling point, since several
initiatives such as the NNER or, say, the Coalition of Essential Schools,
which was founded by Theodore Sizer, are now ten to fifteen years
old, and there is a growing body of evaluation studies and other educational research that shows that it can easily take that much or more
time to develop effective new educational strategies—and more time
still to achieve widespread use of these approaches.

Yet, for a particular initiative to garner appreciable, ongoing funding from even one foundation for a decade or more is no easy task
since a number of factors work against extended support by funders
for most projects. For example, although the pool of available philanthropic resources has tended to expand over time along with the overall growth of the economy, the societal demand for these funds always

greatly exceeds the supply. Moreover, short- or medium-term economic changes (a recession, a drop in the stock market) can quickly reduce the amount of money available to many private foundations and corporate philanthropy units for their grant programs. New issues are constantly emerging to challenge existing priorities among grantmakers as well as among professionals in education and other sectors that look to philanthropies for support. And, the inevitable turnover among foundation leaders and professionals often produces changes in decision-making perspectives and grant program objectives. Owing to these realities, Goodlad's statement that two of the most difficult questions that grantmakers continue to face are what issues or areas to invest in and how long to invest in them takes on a great deal of operational complexity.

Our experience working with Goodlad through the Exxon Education Foundation (EEF), beginning in the middle 1980s, suggests that his understanding of these realities has significantly influenced how he has approached his work since that time. Indeed, these were topics at the initial conversation that Goodlad had with EEF regarding a possible major study of teacher preparation programs in the United States. The substance of that conversation, as well as the background to it, is worth recounting here.

As many readers know, 1983 is the year often cited as the beginning of the current period of educational reform. The early 1980s had been a time of recession in the United States and of deepening concern about the international economic competitiveness of the nation. Partly for these reasons, when the National Commission on Excellence in Education (which had been appointed by then Secretary of Education, the late Terrel H. Bell) released its report, *A Nation at Risk: The Imperative for Educational Reform*, in April 1983, its bleak assessment of the educational performance of American students immediately struck a chord of concern in many political, business, and educational circles.[3] Importantly, *A Nation at Risk* was quickly followed by a series of other reports sponsored by influential organizations, such as the Education Commission of the States and the National Science Board, and by several books written by leading educators, all of which called attention to serious shortcomings in the nation's educational system. *A Place Called School: Prospects for the Future* by Goodlad, *Horace's Compromise: The Dilemma of the American High School* by Sizer, and *High School: A Report on Secondary Education in America* by Boyer were especially persuasive to many people because they reported on the findings of major studies of the characteristics of elementary and secondary schools in the United States.[4]

Very quickly, a number of foundations and corporate philanthropy units began to respond through their grantmaking to the growing calls for educational reform. After a period of review of many of the major reports and books, the Exxon Education Foundation (EEF) concluded that it could help address the need to improve the preparation of teachers. However, EEF's review of the situation suggested that grantmaking directed at overall improvement of teacher preparation would be hampered by a shortage of current empirical information on the characteristics and conditions of teacher education programs at the nation's colleges and universities. Separately, Goodlad was reaching a similar conclusion. Thus, in the spring of 1984, one of the authors (Miller) met with Goodlad at O'Hare Airport in Chicago on behalf of EEF for an initial exploratory discussion of the kind of a study of teacher education that might generate much of the empirical information needed to help justify and guide a major teacher preparation improvement effort. There also was discussion of some of the likely characteristics of successful teacher preparation reform efforts, including how long they would probably have to be pursued to promote significant changes in teacher education at a number of institutions. Finally, there was discussion of how much money would be required from philanthropic sources to underwrite a major study by Goodlad and his colleagues as well as to fund a critical mass of efforts by them and others to promote broad-based teacher education reform.

One of the most significant aspects of the conversation at O'Hare was the general agreement that it would probably take twenty to twenty-five years, or more, to promote substantive improvements in teacher preparation as well as corresponding improvements in elementary and secondary education. This assumed that, in addition to one or more major studies of teacher education programs, a number of large, long-term teacher and school reform initiatives would also be launched that made use of the best available educational research and practice. (At the time of the meeting at O'Hare, Goodlad was in his mid-sixties, yet he was planning an educational reform initiative that would span at least another generation.)

The experience of those who have been working for school and teacher education reform over the years have confirmed Goodlad's belief in the importance of mounting educational renewal initiatives with the capacity to stay the course. As previously noted, several reform efforts—the NNER, the Coalition of Essential Schools, the Accelerated Schools Program of Henry Levin, and Success for All led by Robert Slavin and his colleagues, among others—are ten to fifteen years old. Other approaches date back even further. For example, it has been three decades since James Comer and his colleagues at Yale University began the School Development Program and a quarter century since Deborah Meier and her associates launched Central Park East Elementary School in East Harlem. All of these (and several other) approaches have much to offer to those interested in improving American education, yet each one also should be viewed as a work in progress in a world in which many students need much better schooling opportunities.[5]

Given the long reform timelines discussed with Goodlad, the conversation at O'Hare in 1984 eventually turned to the question of how much support for teacher education and school reform could realistically be expected from private grantmakers, especially since neither had ever really been high priorities among large numbers of private foundations or corporate philanthropy units. Ideally, it was agreed that the proposed study of teacher education should rival in influence the famous study of medical education conducted by Abraham Flexner early in this century. Yet, Goodlad recognized that this was unlikely, because of differences in circumstances. Apart from the fact that Flexner's report was published at a time when advances in the biological sciences made a fundamental overhaul of medical education empirically persuasive (owing to these advances, some medical schools were already charting the way for reform), one important reason why his recommendations were widely embraced was that the Rockefeller family made $50 million in grants to several medical schools to act on them. Since there were only about 150 medical schools in the United States at the time, this was an enormous philanthropic commitment to reform.[6] Today, those Rockefeller grants would be the equivalent of several hundred million dollars—a sum that in 1984 seemed to Goodlad and to us at EEF to be much larger than the philanthropic community could be expected to invest in teacher education reform in the foreseeable future. So far, that judgment has proven to be accurate. And, even if that amount became available, it would have to address a set of teacher education programs that totals about 1,400.[7]

Co-evolution of Research-Influenced Institutional Change Efforts and Professional Grantmaking

The conversation that the professional staff of the Exxon Education Foundation had with John Goodlad in the mid-1980s about philanthropic support for long-term educational improvement initiatives needs to be put into historical context. One of the most extraordinary features of the twentieth century, of course, has been the rapid advance of science, from physics to biology to psychology to economics. And, one of the many dimensions of this advance has been the growth of efforts to improve the quality of key institutions, such as the school, through research-driven (or at least research-influenced) change. To people living a century ago, the current school reform movement's extensive empirical dimensions would be almost unrecognizable. Almost equally unrecognizable to them would be the heavy use of philanthropic resources provided via professionally staffed private foundations and corporate contributions units to underwrite partially or fully many of these institutional change efforts. One hundred years ago, this sector of philanthropy essentially did not exist, let alone invest heavily in initiatives concerned with improving institutions.

The importance of this institutional improvement role for the professional grantmaking sector is difficult to overestimate. Although the overall rapid advancement of science has not been dependent on the emergence of the modern private grantmaking foundation or its corporate contributions cousin, a case can be made that grantmaking philanthropies have become essential supporters of empirically driven institutional change efforts in the nonprofit and governmental sectors in the United States, and may be gaining in importance in some other societies. Earlier, we noted that research-grounded books by Goodlad, Sizer, and Boyer helped establish the course of the current period of educational reform. It is noteworthy that in all three cases, the studies on which the books were based were underwritten completely or primarily by private foundations and corporate philanthropy units. Thus, not only do many foundations play key roles in supporting specific reform initiatives, they also support much of the work that defines important educational issues. Most readers can probably get a sense of the extent of private grantmakers' contemporary role in supporting research-driven institutional improvement in education simply by perusing the acknowledgment sections of a sample of the books or monographs in their personal libraries.

Another way to assess this impact is by reading recent federal legislation designed to encourage public schools to adopt "proven, comprehensive school reform designs." Virtually all of the examples of proven reforms cited in the legislation have been developed exclusively or primarily with private foundation or corporate contributions unit support. In contrast, government has played a very limited role in the development of these strategies, despite its vast investment in public education.[8]

If those who pursue research-driven efforts to improve educational (and other) institutions in the public and nonprofit sectors have come to rely heavily on funding from grantmaking philanthropies, it can also be said that the institutional capacities and program approaches of many funders have been heavily influenced over time by those to whom they have awarded grants. One of the most obvious ways in which this influence has been felt is on the types of people employed as foundation program officers and program consultants. Grantmakers must employ program officers and/or retain consultants who have extensive knowledge in the areas in which they are seeking to support institutional improvement efforts. Otherwise, they will be unlikely to have the expertise necessary to plan or to execute their grant programs at a high level of effectiveness. The more grantmakers have directed resources to research-driven institutional change initiatives, the more they have needed such expertise.

Another way in which funders have probably been influenced by Goodlad-type grant recipients over time is by becoming more empirical in assessing the impact of their grants and programs. For example, foundations commonly fund third-party evaluations of projects that they support. And, philanthropies are now willing to invest in efforts to assess the impact of portfolios of their grants in a program area to get a better sense of the grants' collective impact using various criteria.

Yet another way in which it appears that at least some funders are being influenced by those who are working to improve educational institutions is to embrace longer time frames for achieving results with their grant programs. After all, if some of the most effective educational reformers of our era are finding that it can take ten, fifteen, twenty, or more years to achieve significant change, then it is reasonable for grantmakers to consider extending the length of time that they will work to support particular types of reform and individual reform initiatives.

Exxon Education Foundation's support for the work of Goodlad and his colleagues offers a case in point. In the spring of 1984, the Exxon Education Foundation provided a planning grant for Goodlad's proposed teacher education study and has gone on to make several multiyear commitments, first for the study and then for the work of the NNER. At the end of the current grant, EEF will have provided sixteen continuous years of support for this enterprise.

Extent of Funders' Capacities to Expand and Strengthen Their Long-Term Institutional Improvement Grantmaking

Although private foundations and corporate contributions units have collectively become an important source of funding for long-term efforts to improve schools and other institutions in the United States, the reality is that this capacity is still of modest size from a societal perspective. For example, out of the nearly $144 billion in total giving in America in 1995, private foundation grants of all kinds accounted for just $10.4 billion, or 7.3 percent, while corporations accounted for $7.4 billion, or 5.1 percent.[9] Although precise estimates are not available, it is undoubtedly true that long-term, institutional change-oriented grants to support the work of people such as John Goodlad represent only a fraction of all private foundation grants and an even smaller share of corporate contributions.

A fundamental limitation, of course, is that the subset of philanthropies that can genuinely engage in a substantial amount of this type of grantmaking is small. To have such programs requires a fairly robust grant budget and an associated professional staff large enough to specialize to some degree in a few areas. Only private foundations with fairly large endowments or contributions units of large corporations are likely to meet both of these criteria. Moreover, the largest grantmakers tend to have broad charters and, therefore, are likely to be active in several fields or subfields. Thus, only a few of the larger private foundations have as many as a half-dozen program professionals working in a field such as education. (Among the large corporate contributions units, having even one professional dedicated exclusively to a single field is relatively rare, as entire professional staffs typically number only a few people.) And in many of these cases, the professionals are likely to be working in higher as well as elementary, secondary, or early childhood education, and to be pursuing several topics of interest at each level. Under these circumstances, it can be problematic for even a relatively large foundation to invest several million dollars per year annually for a decade or more to support a portfolio of initiatives concerned with making long-term change in a particular area, such as promoting widespread use of small secondary schools, or developing and promoting broad use of more effective reading strategies for disadvantaged elementary school students, or supporting the creation of professional development schools to help prepare new teachers and to provide rigorous continuing education for experienced teachers.

One of the implications of this situation is that many people, such as Goodlad, must rely on a constantly shifting cast of grantmakers to fund their long-term work. For some costly long-term initiatives, the project leaders may need to have some of the same ability to operate under conditions of financial uncertainty that characterize entrepreneurs in the private sector; that is, they may have to launch initiatives with only partial funding and scramble in most years of the project to secure full funding for that year.

Fortunately, the grantmaking sector appears to have grown large enough to allow a fairly large number of project operators to pursue ambitious initiatives with the realistic expectation that, if their work is good, funders that drop out after a few years can be replaced by other grantmakers. As a result, the grant-program and project-support time horizons of most foundations and corporate contributions units have not had to be as long as those of institutional reformers such as Goodlad in order for much long-term work to proceed in a productive fashion.

Growing Financial Capacity of Funders to Engage in Long-Term Grantmaking

As we approach the end of this century, long-term, institutional improvement-oriented professional grantmaking is really only one long lifetime old. Arguably, its birth dates back from the establishment of the Carnegie Corporation in 1911 by Andrew Carnegie and the Rockefeller Foundation in 1913 by John D. Rockefeller Sr. Together, the creation of these foundations provided distinctive new opportunities to combine deep professional expertise, considerable financial resources, and a long institutional attention span for philanthropic purposes at a time when knowledge in the social sciences was growing rapidly.

Still, a societal capacity to engage in a significant amount of this type of grantmaking did not emerge until much later—after World War II. It was in the post-war decades that much of the accumulated resources of a number of wealthy individuals and families associated with the founding of several major corporations—and of foundations—began to reach a critical mass, aided by robust economic growth and stock market advances. For example, while the Ford Foundation, currently the nation's second largest grantmaking philanthropy, was established in 1934, it did not receive its major endowment contributions until the late 1940s, after the estates of Henry Ford Sr. and

Edsel B. Ford were settled. Its assets at that time increased to $493 million, and it became a national organization in 1950.[10]

The growth of this capacity in the private foundation sector has gained momentum in the past two decades, fueled by continued (if less rapid) economic growth, a sustained bull stock market, and the still strong willingness of founders of large companies to allocate much of their wealth to endowments of foundations that they have created. Examples of foundations that have emerged as major philanthropic actors in the past two decades are the William and Flora Hewlett Foundation, the David and Lucile Packard Foundation, and the Ewing Marian Kauffman Foundation.[11] (At his death in 1996, David Packard left much of his estate to the Packard Foundation, making it one of the very largest private philanthropies in the country.)[12]

This trend could easily continue well into the twenty-first century for several reasons. First, the number of extremely wealthy people— those with the capacity to create one or more very large grantmaking foundations—has continued to increase, and this group includes people from several nations at a time when interest in philanthropy is growing around the world.

Second, some of the wealthiest individuals in the United States have indicated publicly that they expect eventually to transfer much, if not most, of their fortunes to foundations. These include the two men who currently are regarded as the richest in the country—Bill Gates and Warren Buffett. Recently, the notion that the most wealthy citizens should give much of their money away has become a topic of conversation in the media. There are now several rankings of individuals who are giving the most money to worthy causes each year, and the giving of some wealthy individuals, such as George Soros and Ted Turner, has become news.[13]

Third, in addition to the several hundred people in the United States who measure their personal or family fortunes in the billions or hundreds of millions of dollars, there were an estimated 3.5 million people in the United States in 1995 who had a net worth of at least $1 million, and their numbers are expected to swell in the next decade to $5 million. Although $1 million is not what it used to be, this pool of individuals collectively has unprecedented giving potential, which helps explain why one foundation observer, Walter Mead of the World Policy Institute at the New School for Social Research, recently wrote that, in addition to the continuing creation of a number of highly visible billion dollar endowed foundations, "private family foundations are proliferating at a fine clip. There are about 25,000 of them and the figure is climbing by about 1,000 annually."[14]

If the stock market remains strong, Mead estimates that the parents of the Baby Boom generation alone will be able to pass on between $10 and $20 trillion. Even if only a fraction of this amount ultimately finds its way into the endowments of foundations, it could have an enormous impact on grantmaking capacities, including those concerned with promoting empirically grounded, long-term improvements in the effectiveness of educational and other institutions.

Shifting now to corporate philanthropy, the capacity of corporations to engage in at least some institutional improvement oriented philanthropy began to emerge in the decades following World War II, facilitated by a court ruling in New Jersey that provided the legal basis for a significant expansion of corporate giving. As a result, in the 1950s, a number of large corporations were able to establish organizational mechanisms to take advantage of this new philanthropic environment. (For example, General Electric established a corporate foundation in 1952, while Exxon did so in 1955.)

In the 1960s, 1970s, and into the 1980s, there was rapid growth in the overall dollar amount of corporate philanthropic contributions and a gradual emergence of a cadre of corporate contributions professionals at large companies to carry out this work. Moreover, by the 1980s, these capacities were sufficiently large and mature at several of the largest corporate philanthropy units to participate in the funding of some long-term school reform efforts. This was the first time significant amounts of corporate contributions money was made available for this purpose. It reflected a convergence of corporate giving capacity, the perception among many business leaders that fundamental improvements needed to be made in the nation's schools, and the existence of several promising reform strategies that could benefit from corporate philanthropic investment.

Over the past decade, the overall amount of corporate contributions dollars has continued to grow. However, corporate philanthropy remains very much a supporting player relative to private foundations in the long-term, institutional improvement grantmaking arena, whether one is looking at schools, colleges and universities, or other sectors of society that rely on philanthropic investments to help promote change. The Goodlads of the world can continue to look to some of the larger corporate philanthropy units for some support, but the bulk of funds they raise from philanthropic sources must come from private foundations.

In some respects, this is not surprising. For-profit companies, after all, must be primarily concerned with operating productive, economically viable businesses. Philanthropy is an adjunct responsibility for the corporate world. And, in the intensely competitive business environment of the 1980s and 1990s, most firms have found that there are limits to the number of contributions professionals that they can have on staff.

Competitive pressures may also have contributed to a greater tendency to tie corporate contributions more closely to company interests, whether by increasing the percentage of their contributions dollars to communities in which they have large numbers of employees or by linking contributions to marketing campaigns in some way.

Even such things as changes in contributions accounting may be having a negative impact on the amount of long-term corporate grantmaking. For example, companies are now required under FAS (Financial Accounting Standards) rules to charge all of a multiyear grant commitment to the year in which the commitment is made.

Looking to the Future

In the years and decades ahead, it is reasonable to believe that there will be continued growth in the number of research-influenced initiatives designed to promote long-term improvement of the nation's educational system as well as of other public and nonprofit institutions and organizations. How much growth occurs, however, will depend to a significant extent on how much expansion there will be in grantmakers' abilities to fund such efforts. Grantmakers and others concerned with the vitality of the foundation sector need to be aware of this reality and to ask themselves explicitly how much priority should be given to expanding their capacities in this area.

Assuming there is general agreement that it should be regarded as an important responsibility of the sector, they also will need to ask how experimental/empirical this work should be. If it is possible and useful to pursue research-driven improvements of schools and many other societal institutions, the same should be true for efforts to strengthen grantmaking organizations.

With regard to long-term grantmaking, there are a number of basic questions that need to be addressed. One set of questions concerns the amount of this kind of funding and its benefits: How much money from private foundations and corporate contributions units is currently being invested in educational change efforts that will take many years to produce results? What is the underlying trend in the amount of this type of funding? How important is the support of grantmakers to the launching of such initiatives and for enabling them to operate long enough to produce useful outcomes? What percentage of promising long-term efforts have difficulty garnering sufficient financing to test their approaches adequately or to promote widespread use of what has been learned?

A second set of questions focuses on attributes of funders that engage in this kind of grantmaking: Is such grantmaking heavily associated with large endowments and/or program staffs with expertise in the areas being invested in? Under what circumstances can small- or medium-size foundations undertake significant amounts of long-term work? What kinds of charters and boards do foundations that do long-term work have? How is their professional staff selected? Are there any distinctive features of the program development and program management processes at these foundations?

A third set of questions relates to whether new or modified forms of existing foundations may need to be developed, if significantly more long-term grantmaking is to be produced by funders over the next several decades: Would it be helpful to develop specialized foundations that are chartered to work on only a few issues for a specified period of time? Is it possible to raise money from several individuals to create endowments for such specialized foundations? (This would be a means of enabling many moderately wealthy individuals to help support such philanthropic work.) Should there be a deliberate effort to create many specialized foundations concerned with addressing long-term needs that are international or that are centered in countries other than the United States? (Many developing countries in the Western Hemisphere, for example, might benefit from the creation of a number of new philanthropies focused exclusively on helping them develop high quality, universal elementary, middle, and high school systems over the next several decades.)

A fourth set of questions concerns how the corporate community might organize to invest somewhat more of its resources in long-term work: What percentage of large corporations currently earmark 5 percent, 10 percent, or more of their contributions dollars to a single long-term educational or other societal issue for periods of five, ten, or more years? Should more large corporations do so? How might this case be articulated? What percentage of large corporate contributions units do not currently have a large enough professional staff to readily support long-term work on this scale? How can this staffing problem be overcome?

And a fifth set of questions concerns the societal benefit and philanthropic sector oversight case for more such grantmaking, particularly since this kind of funding is vulnerable to charges of "social engineering" and as the foundation sector has grown larger, its capacities to invest in social policy-related work are becoming more visible:[15] Is there considerable pluralism shown in the types of institutional improvement and change efforts supported by grantmakers? What major shortcomings, if any, are there in public oversight of the professionally staffed grantmaking sector?

It is instructive that *renewal* is the word John Goodlad uses to describe one of the most important capacities that he has dedicated his professional life to helping educational institutions acquire. Rather than talk primarily about promoting school *improvement* or school *reform*, for example, Goodlad talks unrelentingly about school and teacher education *renewal*. This is a much more ambitious agenda because it concerns establishing internal institutional capacity to make improvements on an ongoing basis, rather than pursuing one-time changes heavily driven from the outside. Such work has unsurprisingly involved long-term effort. For Goodlad and many other educators who pursue institutional change agendas, it has been essential to receive funding from professionally staffed private foundations and corporate contributions units. Viewed historically, not only are the Goodlads of the world engaged in a new kind of work, but their "banks" are new kinds of investment organizations. Through their work, John Goodlad and a number of other educational reformers over the past few decades have been unusually effective in setting an example for professional grantmakers about how they might productively pay much more attention to generating the capacity for renewal within the philanthropic sector. For that, grantmakers owe them a special debt.

Notes

1   John I. Goodlad, "Sustaining and Extending Educational Renewal," *Phi Delta Kappan* 78 (November 1996): 228–33.

2   Goodlad, "Sustaining and Extending Educational Renewal," 229.

3   National Commission on Excellence in Education, *A Nation at Risk: The Imperative for Educational Reform* (Washington, D.C.: U.S. Government Printing Office, 1983).

4   John I. Goodlad, *A Place Called School: Prospects for the Future* (New York: McGraw-Hill, 1984); Theodore R. Sizer, *Horace's Compromise: The Dilemma of the American High School* (New York: Houghton Mifflin, 1984); Ernest Boyer, *High School: A Report on Secondary Education in America* (New York: Harper & Row, 1983).

5   Sam Stringfield et al., *Urban and Suburban/Rural Special Strategies for Educating Disadvantaged Children* (Washington, D.C.: U.S. Department of Education, 1997); Olatokunbo S. Fashola and Robert E. Slavin, "Promising Programs for Elementary and Middle Schools: Evidence of Effectiveness and Replicability," *Journal of Education for Students Placed at Risk* 2 (1997): 251–307.

6   B. Othanel Smith, *A Design for a School of Pedagogy* (Washington, D.C.: U.S. Government Printing Office,1980), 2.

7   Smith, *A Design for a School of Pedagogy*, 11.

8   A bill sponsored by Congressmen John Porter and David Obey was passed by Congress in 1997 that authorized $145 million for grants to schools for up to three years to adopt proven reform designs. United States House of Representatives, *105th Congress Conference Report* No. 105-390 (Washington, D.C.: U.S. Congress, 1997). The fact that essentially all of the examples of proven programs cited in the legislation were developed with private funding raises questions about whether efforts should be made to improve the federal government's ability to support the creation of effective programs. For recommendations on how this might be done, borrowing in part from the approach used by the privately financed New American Schools, see, for example, Robert E. Slavin, "Design Competitions: A Proposal for a New Federal Role in Educational Research and Development," *Educational Researcher* 26 (August–September 1997): 22–28. Interestingly, similar to John Goodlad, Robert Slavin is well aware of the crucial role that private grantmakers have been playing in the development of promising educational reform strategies. Conversation between L. Scott Miller and Robert Slavin at Johns Hopkins University, 9 February 1998.

9   John Murawski, "A Banner Year for Giving," *Chronicle of Philanthropy*, 30 May 1996, 1, 27–30.

10 Francine Jones, ed., *The Foundation 1000: In-Depth Profiles of the 1000 Largest United States Foundations, 1997/1998* (New York: The Foundation Center, 1997), 887.

11 Debra E. Blum and Paul Demko, "Will 1997 Be a Boom Year for Grants?" *Chronicle of Philanthropy*, 20 February 1997, 1, 9–20.

12 Carey Goldberg, "With Fortune Built, Packard Heirs Look to Build a Legacy," *New York Times*, 6 May 1996, A1, B9.

13 "America's Most Generous," *Fortune*, 13 January 1997, 96–98.

14 Walter Russell Mead, "Outrageous Fortune," *American Benefactor* (Spring 1997): 68–71.

15 Nicholas Lemann, "Citizen 501(c)(3)," *Atlantic Monthly* (February 1997): 18, 20.

Chapter 19

Yo sé quien soy

James G. March

Not so long ago, I had the pleasure of listening to an educational administrator holding forth in praise of education and schooling. It was not a novel talk. Indeed, it was mostly a collection of familiar proclamations, distinguished not by its originality but by its spirit and its commitment to a classic litany proclaiming the value of education to American well-being. In any reasonable evaluation, it told an upbeat story, as one would expect from an upbeat leader.

The talk was filled with challenges to education and hope for educators, who made up most of the audience. It was not hard to imagine that this particular administrator would continue to struggle to make education better and would do so in a way that sustained important values. He recited a comforting list of positive contributions that education had made and continues to make to our societies and to our personal lives. It was a compelling recitation, and I felt energized by it. In short, the talk was a good one, and I was happy to find myself as a member of an enthusiastic audience.

Nevertheless, I could not help wishing for something slightly different, perhaps that the speaker had absorbed more of the writings of John Goodlad. His voice was strong and his dreams were sweet, but his justifications for education did not do justice to the claims of education on our souls. In company with many educators, as well as docents of public policy, he saw education simply as an institution serving a democratic society and a market economy, molding democratic citizens and producing valuable economic actors, as indeed it is and does.

In speaking in this way, he adopted implicitly a particular catechism of justification, a catechism in which actions and institutions are justified in terms of their good consequences, their benefits relative to their costs. This consequentialist ethic dominates modern western thinking. Jeremy Bentham is its patron saint, and economic theory is its holy scripture. The ethic is embedded in rationalism and encapsulated in the canon of decision theory and rational action. We ask: What are our alternatives? What are the possible consequences that can be anticipated for each alternative? How likely are each of those consequences? How do we value them? We act to maximize expected return, choosing the alternative with the highest return when returns are weighted by their likelihoods.

Such a theory underlies both the predictions of economics and its prescriptions for action, and it extends far beyond the narrow boundaries of the discipline of economics. It underlies much of the teaching of students of public policy and personal self-management. It is the framework for virtually all modern research on individual and collective decision making. Much of that research notes the many ways in which the human beings that we observe fail to achieve the ideal of consequential rationality. These failures are seen as deficiencies, and training in decision making is designed primarily to reduce the frequency and magnitude of human failures to achieve that ideal.

The consequentialist catechism is also a feature of ordinary discourse of justification. We expect that action will be justified by its expected consequences. Why did I do that? Because I anticipated that it would lead to consequences that I value. How do you persuade me to do what you want me to do? By persuading me that it will lead me to consequences that I will value. How can I change you? By providing incentives that change the consequences you anticipate.

Consequentialism is an elegant and noble ethic, reflecting one of the more admirable features of human character. Although the concept of human rationality was originally somewhat vaguer in tenor and broader in scope, consequentialism captures an important aspect of what it means to be rational; and rationalism captures an important aspect of what it means to be human. We respect ourselves and others when we and they find consequential reasons for our actions.

Nowhere is that ethic more honored than in the justification of education. We document the good consequences of education, in particular the demonstrable political and economic consequences. In the spirit of the talk of my educational administrator, we justify education as a whole, specific educational programs, and individual participation in them as instruments of our individual and collective desires.

And when we wish to complain about education, we complain primarily about its failure to deliver good consequences, particularly economic returns.

There is a kind of graceful elegance and seductive charm about treating education as an instrument for satisfying our practical concerns. It fits conventional expectations about justification. There is also a certain tactical advantage. Educators use a utilitarian justification for education, in part because education does rather well by most consequential calculations. Although there are occasional contrary conclusions, the vast majority of studies support a belief that informed individuals and wise societies will invest in education and educational institutions if they wish to maximize the net benefits of individual and social investments. With some important, but relatively infrequent, exceptions, investments in education have been shown to have positive individual and collective returns.

The proposition that returns to educational investment are strongly positive can be put another way: Education fails (by far) to extract from its individual and social patrons anything like the full economic value of its services. It offers substantially more in benefits from its services than it charges for them. This underpricing of education makes education a good investment, both for societies and for individuals. In standard, if somewhat inflammatory, contemporary terms, at present prices, education is a massive expropriation of intellectual property. Since it is mostly "stolen property" (neither Newton nor Tolstoy realizes anything from his contribution to it, for example), the statement is a descriptive, not a moral, one.

Claims that the economic benefits of education substantially exceed its costs are not always believed, of course. Academic studies of returns do not persuade everyone. And the studies themselves provide grounds for questioning some aspects of a too easy assumption of positive returns. There are suggestions that the studies of return obscure substantial differences in the return realized by different groups. Education appears to provide greater benefits for individuals in some groups than it does for those in other groups, thus public investment in education has distributional effects. Nor is it obvious that different components of the educational enterprise contribute equally to the benefits measured. Some education is worth more than others. Both the knowledge gained and the credentialing value of an education from some institutions is greater than that from others, and the differences are not captured entirely by differences in price.

Debates over the finer points of returns to education, like the basic observation that, in general, those returns are positive, have another—perhaps less obvious—consequence. Because such studies often portray education as offering positive individual and social returns and because such reasons seem particularly persuasive to contemporary societies, and even to ourselves, educators grow accustomed to justifying their institutions and themselves in utilitarian terms, particularly utilitarian terms linked to monetary returns and gains to economic productivity. Without always being conscious of the profundity of the acquiescence, they collaborate in making the primary terms of reference for thinking about education overwhelmingly consequentialist and economic.

It is only a short step from such an inclination to a pervasive utilitarian metaphor for education. Schools are justified by their successes in creating citizens, building community spirit, and providing childcare. But preeminently in contemporary society, education is seen as a production process with workers (teachers), managers (administrators), consumers (students or their parents), and end users (employers of students). Schools produce economic capabilities and knowledge that convert to income for the products of schooling and productivity for the employers of those products.

The problem with all of this is not that it is unequivocally wrong. Surely, schools can be seen fruitfully in consequentialist terms. Nor is the primary problem that the consequentialist terms involved have, in recent years, become largely associated with economic consequences, rather than, for example, personal, social, or political consequences. The problem (or at least the problem that is relevant here) is that utilitarian metaphors fundamentally misrepresent education, subordinating its essences to its consequences.

John Stuart Mill once described Jeremy Bentham as having the completeness of a limited man.[1] Bentham, like his modern-day disciples, saw life as choice and choice as determined by the anticipation of consequences. For Bentham, as for most modern decision analysts, choice is a matter of finding the alternative that can be expected to lead to the best outcome as evaluated from the point of view of the decision maker's preferences or social utility. Such a conception has completeness. It can accommodate a wide variety of situations and values. But it is also limited.

It is limited particularly by equating the human essence with consequential justification, by the assumption that action only achieves humanness when choices are evaluated by the outcomes they produce.

Such an assumption seems almost a truism to modern modes of thought, but it contradicts long traditions that see consequentialism as secondary to higher aspirations for human existence, and for education. The human spirit is sustained not only by a logic of consequences but also by a logic of appropriateness, the association of action with the arbitrary demands of a conception of self.

A proper human does what is appropriate to a self-conception without regard to consequences. To be human is to act in the name of one's identity. A person who embraces the identity of teacher does what teachers do, not primarily because of expectations of consequences from those actions but because that is what teachers do. Seeing action as fulfilling an identity is a vision of human dignity and character that is fundamentally different from a vision that links humanity exclusively to instrumental action.

It is, however, equally demanding of thought. Appropriate action is arbitrary with respect to consequences, but adopting and understanding an identity require deeply thoughtful engagement, as does fulfilling an identity in a particular situation. Knowing what is appropriate to one's identity is a complicated and ultimately social knowing, based on extended assessments and inferences. The pursuit of such knowledge invites conversations and contemplations directed to a set of issues somewhat different from those induced by living according to a consequential vision. We seek understanding of the nature of being a teacher or father or carpenter rather than knowledge about the uncertain future outomes produced by current actions. We evoke meanings of situations and identities and the relations among them.

The effort is demanding, but it is not unique to educators on the verge of the twenty-first century. It is central to some of our more notable traditions. Early in his wanderings around Spain, Don Quixote de la Mancha encounters a peasant from his own village who is distressed by Quixote's behavior. The peasant is a good fellow, concerned to help a man who seems to him bereft of sense, and he tries to persuade Quixote that he is confused. Quixote does not try to defend himself in terms of the good consequences he expects from his actions. Rather, he says simply: "I know who I am" ("Yo sé quien soy"). It is perhaps the most important line in the entire book, for it summarizes an idea of justification based on a code of behavior associated with an identity.

Quixote follows the dictates of his sense of himself. "I know who I am," he says. In answer to an ecclesiastic who challenges him to give up his pretenses and go home, he says, "Knight I am and Knight I will die, if it pleases almighty God."[2] It is not that Quixote is simply a bizarre, unpredictable person, unreachable by intelligent intervention. He is open to debates about what it means to be a knight. He finds it exquisitely relevant to compare his own perception of proper behavior with models of great knights of history or fiction found in books or in the encounters of others. He spends a great deal of time arguing that his actions are proper and trying to understand how they can be made more consistent with his self-conception, but he is not interested at all in discussions of what the likely outcomes of his actions will be.

He is not confused about the consequences of his actions. He is quite aware that he often appears ridiculous to others, that his exploits rarely lead to great practical achievements, and that his efforts to help others frequently hurt the objects of his aid rather than give them succor. He is not confused about the consequences of his actions, nor is he indifferent to them. However, he does not consider those consequences to be relevant to his behavior.

In one of the grander scenes of *Don Quixote*, after Quixote has—against all reason—faced a large male lion and survived, apparently miraculously, Don Diego de Miranda comments, "what could be greater rashness and folly than to strive to fight lions tooth and nail." To which Quixote replies, "No doubt, Señor Don Diego de Miranda, in your opinion you take me for a fool and a madman. It would be no wonder if you did, for my deeds bear witness to nothing else. But for all this, I would have you note that I am neither so mad nor so foolish as I must have appeared to you. . . . All knights have their special parts to play. . . . As it is my fate to be one of the knights-errant, I cannot help undertaking all that appears to me to fall within the sphere of my duties."[3]

The Quixote claim of sanity is a profound one. It is not a sanity of reality (being bound by consequences) but a sanity of identity (being bound by the obligations of self). A sanity of identity involves two things: The first is a conception of self that one embraces as essential. The second is a conception of action as a matching of one's conception of self to a situation. The identity, the situation, and the proper matching are all potentially arguable. It is important to Quixote that he correctly understands what it means to be a knight-errant, that he correctly recognizes the situation in which he finds himself from the point of view of that identity and that his action correctly matches his identity to the situation. However, neither the conception of the self,

the assessment of the situation, nor the matching of the two is deriva-
tive of calculations of consequences.

Indeed, consequential justification undermines confidence that the
fulfillment of identity is truly willful, rather than merely instrumental.
In Book I, Chapter 25 of *Don Quixote*, Sancho Panza, frustrated by
his inability to persuade Quixote to be somewhat sensible in normal
consequentialist terms, tries to suggest that being a knight may be
somewhat less useful than it once was. Sancho observes that knights
of old had reasons for their commitment to the dictates of knightly
honor and asks what justification Quixote has. Quixote replies: "For a
knight errant to make himself crazy for a reason warrants neither credit
nor thanks; the point is to be foolish without justification."[4] Our actions are of no particular human importance as moral actions if they
have utilitarian justification.

Thus, ultimately, Quixote not only claims the right to choose a different path but also claims the path he has chosen is indispensable for
a human actor. His argument is antithetical to a consequentialist ethic.
It sees consequential justification as compromising moral action, rather
than contributing to it. Extending trust to the trustworthy can be justified easily, but such trust is simply an exchange of goods, hardly a
significant human act. Only when trust is extended to the untrustwor-
thy does it become significant. Similarly, loving the lovable, whatever
consequential (exchange) value it may have, is hardly particularly human. The truly human act is to love the unlovable.

The perspective is reminiscent of Søren Kierkegaard's suggestion
that if we justify religion by its consequences, we deprive religious
faith of its fundamental character as an arbitrary act of human will.
Religion may have positive benefits, but our commitment is not based
on them, indeed is compromised by them. Education may have positive consequences, but our commitment is not based on them, indeed
is compromised by them.

Being of our age and culture, it is difficult for us to avoid the hope
that education and our own activities as educators will be blessed
with good consequences. We live much of our lives with careful attention to learning from our experiences and allowing those experiences
and our expectations about future experiences to shape the details of
what we do. It is inconceivable that we would do otherwise. However,
in Quixote's terms, we become true educators only to the extent to
which our deeper commitment is a commitment to fulfilling our identities rather than to accomplishments. The fundamentals of being a

teacher lie in a set of actions and a view of one's self that are not conditional on their consequences but on their consistency with the essential nature of being a teacher as exemplified by generations of predecessors and a thoughtful contemplation of the meaning of teaching.

To invoke the words of Quixote to describe teachers and other educators is a quixotic act, but one that I think is in the best traditions of education and educators. Perhaps Quixote overdid it, but we are in little danger of that. In the present context, it may be particularly appropriate for us to reassert the importance of having and fulfilling a meaningful identity. John Goodlad knows who he is and has for many years been trying to induce the rest of us to discover what it might mean for us to embrace education not as an instrument of individual or social well-being but as a testament, temple, and calling. And as much as anyone, he has taught us to ask whether we know who we are.

Notes

1   John Stuart Mill, *On Bentham and Coleridge* (New York: Harper & Row, 1950), 95.

2   "Caballero soy, y caballero he de morir, si place al Altísimo." Miguel de Cervantes, *El Ingenioso Hidalgo Don Quijote de la Mancha* (Madrid: Espasa-Calpe, 1940), Book II, Chapter 32, 601.

3   "¿Quien duda, señor don Diego de Miranda que vuesa merced no me tenga en su opinión por un hombre disparatado y loco? Y no sería mucho que así fuese, porque mis obras no pueden dar testimonio de otra cosa. Pues, con todo esto, quiero que vuesa merced advierta que no soy tan loco ni tan menguado como debo de haberle parecido. . . . Todos los caballeros tienen sus particulares ejercicios. . . . Como me cupo en suerte ser uno del número de la andante caballería, no puedo dejar de acometer todo aquello que á mí me paraciere que cae debajo de la juridición de mis ejercicios." Cervantes, *El Ingenioso Hidalgo Don Quijote de la Mancha*, Book II, Chapter 17, 411–12.

4   "Que volverse loco un caballero andante con causa, ni grado ni gracias: el toque está en desatinar sin ocasión." Cervantes, *El Ingenioso Hidalgo Don Quijote de la Mancha*, Book I, Chapter 25, 143.

Chapter 20

In Keeping with Character

Roger Soder

Sometime during the spring of 1998, I was talking with John about the latest spate of legislation dictating methods of teaching how to teach reading. Some of the distinguished solons in the state legislature, convinced that they knew what was what, and egged on by bands of outraged parents, were introducing bills requiring the teaching of phonics and anathematizing anything to do with what was seen as "whole language" and other evils. I mentioned to John that neither the legislatures nor the parents nor the media folks reporting the story evinced any sense of understanding the historical context. The controversy is famously old. Did people not think about, say, Rudolph Flesch and *Why Johnny Can't Read* in the 1950s? And did not he, John, find it discouraging that we were dealing with the same old issues as if nobody had ever dealt with them before?

Yes, he said, there is little understanding of context. And yes, this was old ground replowed many times. But he would not admit to discouragement. You do what has to be done, explain one more time to yet one more group of people.

The conversation was similar in many respects to what Ken Sirotnik recounts in his introductory chapter in this volume. How, Ken asked John, can he stay so "optimistic in the face of so many pendulum swings, educational fads, and a half-century of often unheeded lessons for more successful and enduring educational change?" Well, John replies, it isn't easy, "but the alternative was no more appealing than that of growing old."

Many people commonly raise the same sorts of questions in talking about Goodlad. How does he do it? In the face of such adversity, how does he keep going ahead? How does he remain so positive, so optimistic? What keeps him going? Good questions. And Goodlad's response to Ken is reasonable enough. I tell my interlocutors the same thing. As far as I know, I say, Goodlad is optimistic and positive because, well, because he is. But I'm wondering if the "what's the alternative" reason for remaining optimistic is sufficient explanation. Goodlad's optimism is not unique. But it surely is unusual, especially amongst those well into their eighth decade. More common among older people, as Aristotle reminds us, is a kind of weariness mixed with cynicism and pessimism. In *The Art of Rhetoric*, Aristotle asserts that older people think that "most things turn out badly," and that they "expect the worst," because they know that "the greater part of things that happen are bad; at least most turn out for the worse."

This view of the world hardly fits Goodlad's view. He is, indeed, an optimist. Part of optimism includes looking toward the future rather than back toward what is gone. You can't be much of an optimist without giving thought to the future. Again, Aristotle is a useful guide. Older people, he says, "live in memory more than in hope; for what is left of life is short, what is past is long, and hope is for the future, memory for what is gone."[1] (Others sound similar themes. Russian poet Osip Mandelstam spoke of being in Paris in 1923, meeting a young student who was later to take the name Ho Chi Minh. The young revolutionary was talking about what he was going to be doing in the 1940s and beyond, and in his voice, Mandelstam says, "one can hear the approach of tomorrow," he "sees and hears the agenda" some twenty five years ahead.[2]) Goodlad has a sailor's eye on the future; he is astonishingly comfortable moving decades ahead in thinking about what needs to be done now.

Surely it is not out of mere pawkiness that Goodlad goes against the grain. But we are still left with the reasons for his optimism and his future orientation. "Consider the alternative" may be all there is here, but still, perhaps there is something else going on.

Is Goodlad somehow reenacting the myth of Sisyphus? Surely not: he has not been condemned by others (or by himself) to inevitably meaningless rock rolling. And he's not just doing it because there's nothing else to do—there's plenty of joyous things to do and feel, as is obvious when you see him pilot a boat in choppy seas, or when you listen to him talk about bringing a garden along. The explanation for his optimism and a future orientation that makes sense to me lies elsewhere. In trying to understand his optimism, I'm really trying to understand what I hope is a modestly and reasonably optimistic view of the world, rather than trying to pierce Goodlad's inner psyche.

What Goodlad's perspective pushes me to do is reflect on the impermanence of change and the constantly changing circumstances. As I grow older, I am becoming less and less surprised at the transience of things. I mow the lawn. It grows. I mow it again. I can cut it shorter and mow it less often. But still it grows. It's not a policy issue I can "solve" through some application of objectives, procedures, resources, and evaluation. Grass is what it is, and I don't feel like a failure simply because the grass continues to grow after I cut it.

People in schools know quite directly what I'm getting at here. The first grade teacher isn't surprised because incoming first graders don't know how to read. It's September once again, a new batch of kids come into the classroom and, by golly, most of them don't know how to read. Of course they don't know how to read. That's what she's going to deal with. She's going to do the best job she can, and she's going to reflect on what she's doing, think about it, think about what she might do differently in the future. And most assuredly there will be a future, because there will come yet another September and another batch of kids who don't know how to read. In like manner, teachers and administrators working with parents are not shocked to find that there are new groups of parents, people with greatly varying levels of understanding of (and agreement with) what the school is trying to accomplish for children. Bryan Wilson captured this notion quite nicely in a superb analysis close to forty years ago, suggesting that the teacher's role is one of quiet normality, involving actions repeated over time, as opposed to the drama of the operating room or courtroom.[3]

The same impermanence, the same need to return again and again to the same materials and processes for new groups of people, can be seen outside of school, too. Educators can work with state legislators, hoping that progress is being made in getting those legislators to understand the complexities of schooling. But two years later, a new batch of legislators is in place (for a while) with what they think are new questions and new issues, with little sense of the past and little sense that the questions and issues are perennial. And it's likely there will be a new governor claiming to be an "education" governor (whatever that means), with new ideas for study groups, commissions, and panels all aimed at developing world class standards; it's likely, too, that the new governor out of ignorance or envy overlooks the possibility that such matters had been thought about by others. Those working with the politicians know quite well that tomorrow is indeed another day.

And as I grow older, I have come to realize more and more the wisdom of the concluding words of *The Plague*. There are no final victories, Camus tells us: There is only "what had had to be done, and what assuredly would have to be done again." True. But beyond that, I'm beginning to think, maybe there are no victories at all. There are, of course, small victories (as suggested by Samuel Freedman's *Small Victories*).[4] But in working with children or working with politicians in matters of education and schooling, it's the nature of the thing to have to do the work over and over again with an ever changing group of people.

Moreover, there's no real certainty that the doing of work in or for schools gets you closer to ultimately solving the problems of your work. There is no certainty that "progress" is being made. It might be a bit easier to accept the notion of impermanence if one had a sense of at least "two steps forward, one step back." It might be nice to think, along with the Enlightenment folks, or the Progressives, or the Beatles in Sgt. Pepper, that "things are getting better, they're getting better all the time." But, for me, what seems just as likely to occur is two steps forward, two steps back, or—quite often—two steps forward, three steps back.

Maybe all there is is the realization that without pushing for the two steps forward each time, we would always be moving back because we did not harness or create a countervailing force. Ken Sirotnik concludes his chapter in this volume by describing Goodlad in Goodlad's own words: a countervailing force, a different drummer, a drummer having *longevity*. Indeed he is. I don't know whether Goodlad would agree with what I've said about the grounding of his optimism. What I do know is that his clear perspective makes me think things through in trying to get a sense of my own grounding.

The optimism Goodlad evinces is part of something larger, something we might, in an untrendy and old-fashioned way, call "character." I said earlier that people ask lots of questions about him and what it means to work with him. They don't ask much about his fame, finances, research methodology, time management. They ask, as already said, about his optimism. They ask what it's like to work with him. They ask, in effect, about character. They want to know about ethos. They have some real sense that you simply can't do what Sir Peter claims in *The School for Scandal*: "I'm called away by particular business. But I leave my character behind me" (II, ii). Character and work go hand in hand, and I don't think you can make good and virtuous leaders out of bad characters any more than you can secure democracy through undemocratic means.

I have some comments to make here about character and some aspects of Goodlad's character that are of particular importance to me. It is difficult to talk about character in general or someone's character in particular. I do not want to engage in hagiography. Goodlad is not perfect. But at the same time I don't see the necessity of sharing instances of imperfection—something so popular these days (e.g., *Intellectuals*, wherein Paul Johnson takes endless delight in showing that Tolstoy, Rousseau, and a host of others were just awful people, no matter what they wrote).[5] What I want to talk about are four aspects of Goodlad's character that are especially important to me. In what follows, I am not going to try to prove that Goodlad manifests these aspects of character in ways superlative to others. What I do want to say is that these aspects or traits of character are important to me, and to the extent I see them in Goodlad, I want to think about them and find ways of manifesting them in myself in some modest way.

One part of Goodlad's character of particular concern for me has been noted by others in this volume. Gary Fenstermacher suggests that Goodlad has pushed him to reconsider some things. Jim March sounds a similar note, in suggesting that one of the things Goodlad ultimately does is ask us to consider who we are. The push to reflect on ourselves is an ethical matter, a matter of ethos, a matter of character. In the opening scene of Plato's *Gorgias*, Socrates and his young friend, Chaerephon, are on their way to talk with Gorgias. They are informed that the great sophist will respond to all questions. Wonderful, says Socrates, and bids his friend to "ask him." "Ask him what," says Chaerephon. "Who he is," replies Socrates. As James Boyd White—a most perceptive critic of these matters—notes, the question is innocuous but deeply threatening.[6] Elsewhere, White rephrases the question to help us see its implications, by creating an imagined conversation between Socrates and two lawyers. Socrates begins, "What I really what to know is who you are and what you do. I know you are called a 'lawyer,' but what I want to know is this: what do you do in the world that makes you what you are."[7]

Here I am reminded of Liszt's approach to piano technique and fingering, as related in Alan Walker's superb biography. Liszt believed that "each hand is different, that the only 'correct' solutions are the ones that each individual player finds most comfortable—and discovers for himself through trial and error. And what is comfortable at one time of life may be uncomfortable at another. This is why Liszt refused to teach technique. . . . Liszt held his chief duty to be to place before his students a clear and correct 'sonic image' of each piece to be studied. Only picture the image, he seemed to say, and the body will find its own way to project it."[8] Not by his directives, but by his being, Goodlad does indeed push us to think further about who we are. There are no givens here, no fixed path.

The second aspect bearing on character has to do with the distinction between being guided by a categorical idea, an *idée fixe*, as it were, and something quite different—principles. The basic distinction was noted by Prince Metternich in, naturally, military language. "A categorical idea . . . is like a fixed gun. . . . It is dangerous for those who stand or move along the line of its trajectory. Principles, on the other hand, may be compared to a gun that can turn around and fire at untruth in every direction."[9] People with categorical or fixed ideas tend to have little flexibility and tend to let principles go this way and that in order to keep to their idea. On the other hand, people guided by principles can and do change ideas while maintaining course. Again, Alan Walker: "Liszt was particularly sensitive to acoustics, recognizing that the very hall in which he conducted was an instrument whose reverberations could make or break the performance, and he would modify his interpretation accordingly."[10] The principles of action do not change, but the actions do.

Once more skirting and dodging hagiography, I want to turn to the third aspect of character: patience. It takes, I believe, a certain kind of patience or forbearance to write with such insight and understanding (as, say, Dick Williams alludes to in his discussion of *The Dynamics of Educational Change* or Gary Fenstermacher in his discussion of *Behind the Classroom Door* or Bob Anderson in discussion of *The Nongraded Elementary School*) some decades earlier only to have to write the same thing again and again for new (and often old) audiences. It must take, I should think, a certain kind of patience to refrain from saying, in effect, "I believe you'll find I've said the same thing—several times over, actually—back in the 1960s." It is humbling and a bit disconcerting to advance, in a staff meeting, a grand plan or idea and have Goodlad invite serious consideration, only to discover later on (as I have in revisiting some of his writings) that he had put forth the same grand plan or idea not once but several times over the decades; he had been there before, but he wouldn't say so in response to a staff suggestion.

✓ Magnanimity encompasses the fourth aspect of character that is of great importance to me. As with most critical variables, it has its negative side. C. P. Snow observed of Churchill that magnanimity can provoke envy rather than reduce it.[11] And, similarly, Tacitus in the *Annals*: "Services are welcome as it seems possible to repay them, but when they greatly exceed that point they produce not gratitude but hatred" (iv, 17). You have to have magnanimity in order to be magnanimous. I am not toying with words here. Because of the negative side inherent in this aspect of character, it's difficult to manifest it without having to exercise it many times over. Again I go back to Alan Walker on Liszt:

> When Liszt settled in Weiner, he took it to be his primary mission to continue to help musical talent, wherever he found it. . . . It is strange, therefore, that so many of the prominent musicians he supported turned against him. Most of the great musicians whom Liszt observed struggling for recognition—Chopin, Schumann, Wagner, and Berlioz among them—took the thoroughly mundane view that they had to vie with everyone else for a place in the sun. At various times and in various places Liszt helped them all, thinking only to improve the general conditions of music. But even as he did so, the others, lacking his detachment, saw him helping a rival, and this was never truer than when he diverted financial and material aid towards artistic goals of which they disapproved. As long as Liszt was throwing the full weight of his resources behind Wagner, Wagner was hardly in a position to complain. But what comfort could this bring to Berlioz? By the same token, when Liszt helped Berlioz, the cause of Wagner was temporarily held in abeyance. Largesse for others always appears to be less just than largesse for oneself. The conclusion may seem bizarre, but it will withstand scrutiny. So many of Liszt's contemporaries turned against his universal beneficence precisely because it *was* universal, and not reserved for their exclusive use.[12]

As with the other traits considered here, I am not going to argue that Goodlad always evinces magnanimity—I've only known him since 1985—but I have observed enough situations that suggest Walker is correct: magnanimity is a noble trait, but when extended to all, there is sometimes a reaction of ingratitude specifically because all have shared.

Optimism. Knowing (by inquiring) who we are. Principles. Patience. Magnanimity. My seeing these in John reinforces their importance for me. Sometime during the years to come, maybe I'll ask him more about these things. Probably he'll just smile.

Notes

1 In Aristotle, *The Art of Rhetoric*, Book 2, Chapter 13 (1390a). This chapter ("The Character of the Old") and chapters 12 ("The Character of the Young") and 14 ("The Character of Those in the Prime of Life") are often anthologized and with good reason.

2 Osip Mandelstam, "An Interview With Ho Chi Minh–1923," *Commentary* 44 (August 1967): 80–81.

3 Bryan Wilson, "The Teacher's Role: A Sociological Analysis," *British Journal of Sociology* 13 (March 1962): 15–32.

4 Samuel Freedman, *Small Victories: The Real World of a Teacher, Her Students, and Their High School* (New York: Harper & Row, 1990).

5 Paul Johnson, *Intellectuals* (New York: Harper & Row, 1988).

6 James Boyd White, *When Words Lose Their Meaning: Constitutions and Reconstitutions of Language, Character, and Community* (Chicago: University of Chicago Press, 1984). Of immediate relevance here is chapter 4, "The Reconstitution of Language and Self in a Community of Two: Plato's Gorgias," but the entire volume demands detailed and sustained study.

7 James Boyd White, *Heracles' Bow: Essays on the Rhetoric and the Poetics of the Law* (Madison: University of Wisconsin Press, 1985), 216.

8 Alan Walker, *Franz Liszt: Volume Three, The Final Years: 1861–1886* (New York: Knopf, 1996), 232.

9 As quoted in John Lukacs, *The Duel: 10 May–31 July 1940: The Eighty-Day Struggle Between Churchill and Hitler* (New York: Ticknor & Fields, 1991), 50.

10 Alan Walker, *Franz Liszt: Volume Two, The Weimar Years, 1848–1861* (New York: Knopf, 1989), 278.

11 C. P. Snow, "Churchill," in *Variety of Men* (New York: Scribner's, 1966). In addition to the discussion of Churchill, Snow gives us extraordinarily insightful portraits of Rutherford, Hardy, Wells, Einstein, Lloyd George, Frost, Hammarskjold, and Stalin. Out of print, but worth seeking out.

12 Alan Walker, *Franz Liszt: Volume Two, The Weimar Years, 1848–1861*, 12–13.

Appendix

A Selected and Annotated Bibliography of John I. Goodlad's Publications

Jianping Shen

This annotated bibliography is arranged according to the following substantive categories—nongrading, curriculum inquiry, schooling, teacher education, strategies for educational renewal, and strategies for and reflections on educational research. Although a chronological approach to organizing this bibliography could have been taken, a substantive approach was selected in order to represent both the breadth of Goodlad's research and writings, and the thematic interconnections throughout. Under each category, the entries are further divided into two subcategories—articles and books.

Nongrading

Articles

John I. Goodlad, "Some Effects of Promotion and Nonpromotion upon the Social and Personal Adjustment of Children," *Journal of Experimental Education* 22 (June 1954): 301–28.

Experimental results are reported pertaining to the impact of promotion and retention upon the social and personal adjustment of the children in two groups. Based on the conclusion that repeating a grade is detrimental to the social and personal development of boys and girls, it is recommended that schools adopt policies of regular progress and appropriate instructional techniques that meet the individual children where they are and guide them forward according to their own potentialities and capabilities.

John I. Goodlad and Robert H. Anderson, "Educational Practices in Nongraded Schools: A Survey of Perceptions," *Elementary School Journal* 63 (October 1962): 33-40.

> Results are reported of the 1960 survey pertaining to reasons for introducing the nongraded plan, changes in the program as a result of introducing the nongraded plan, current modifications in school practices related to the nongrading, long-term plans for the future, and the practice of reporting the nongrading process to the parents. It is argued that organizational reform is a beginning and not an end in itself, and that nongrading should simultaneously or subsequently give attention to fundamental questions of school function, curriculum design, teaching, and evaluation.

John I. Goodlad, "The Nongraded School in the United States," *Prospects in Education* 1 (1969): 31–36.

> A comprehensive theoretical framework is developed to support the idea of nongrading by discussing individual difference as well as the nature of knowledge, learning, and mankind. Also, the theory and practice of nongrading in the United States is reviewed and suggestions are offered for how to start a nongraded school.

Books
John I. Goodlad and Robert H. Anderson, *The Nongraded Elementary School* (New York: Teachers College Press, 1987, reissued edition).

> The book begins with a criticism of the graded practices in elementary schools by discussing intraindividual and interindividual differences and the negative effects of retention. Discussion then proceeds to the status of nongraded schools and the issues involved in developing and operating a nongraded elementary school (such as establishing curriculum, reporting pupil progress, and setting realistic standards).

Curriculum Inquiry

Articles
John I. Goodlad, "Curriculum: The State of the Field," *Review of Educational Research* 30 (June 1960): 185–98.

The article summarizes the curriculum research and practice on the societal, institutional, and instructional levels and concludes that "curriculum theorizing to date is best described as abstract speculation; curriculum research as 'dust-bowl' empiricism." Two major recommendations are made: First, conceptual systems need to be formulated that identify the major questions to be answered in developing a curriculum. Second, theoretical constructs are needed from which hypotheses might be derived and empirically tested. Research studies would then be derived to determine how values and expectations of individuals and groups end up influencing curriculum.

John I. Goodlad, "Curriculum: State of the Field," *Review of Educational Research* 39 (June 1969): 367–75.

Following the 1960 review, this 1969 review identifies the progress in defining curricular objectives, analyzing ends/means relationship, ordering stimuli for learning, and evaluation. Goodlad concludes, however, that in the realm of explaining curricular realities, people appeared to know little more in 1969 than they did in 1960, and that curriculum theory with exploratory and predictive power was virtually nonexistent.

John I. Goodlad, "A New Look at an Old Idea: Core Curriculum," *Educational Leadership* 44 (November 1986/January 1987): 8–16.

Goodlad analyzes how the meaning of core curriculum has shifted with societal pressures and educational trends. He contends that we educators should affirm the American ideal of equal and excellent schooling by defining what is central to the education of all students, and ensure for all of our elementary and secondary students common encounters with the most significant domains of human experience.

Books

John I. Goodlad, *School, Curriculum, and the Individual* (Waltham, Mass.: Blaisdell, 1966).

This book consists of a collection of previously published articles on school, curriculum, and promotion policy. Discussion centers on issues related to how to organize the school, classroom, and curriculum so that each student can benefit substantially from his or her school experience.

John I. Goodlad and Associates, *Curriculum Inquiry: The Study of Curriculum Practice* (New York: McGraw-Hill, 1979).

    The authors argue for the importance of conceptualizing curriculum as a field of practice. A framework is developed for guiding curriculum practice and inquiry, which includes the societal domain (social, political, and economic contexts), institutional domain (school, college, university), instructional domain (teachers), and personal experiential domain (students), and the factors influencing these domains.

Gary D Fenstermacher and John I. Goodlad, eds., *Individual Differences and the Common Curriculum*, the Eighty-second Yearbook of the National Society for the Study of Education, Part I (Chicago: University of Chicago Press, 1983).

    Authors discuss the psychological, sociological, legal, and biological bases for individual differences. Inquiries follow into what all learners can and should learn in mathematics, natural sciences, language and literature, aesthetics and fine arts, and social studies. The volume concludes with a discussion of school practices that need to be changed and how to translate the proposal of common curriculum into functional policies.

Schooling: Its Aims, Goals, and Functions

Articles

John I. Goodlad, "The Schools vs. Education," *Saturday Review*, 19 April 1969, 59–61, 80–82.

    Goodlad argues that although during the education decade (1957–1967) the school years were extended upward and downward, the educational function of schooling was diminishing. He proposes that the *educational* role of the school, rather than its various ancillary functions (such as babysitting, social stratification, and economic investment), should be revitalized.

John I. Goodlad, "Schools Can Make a Difference," *Educational Leadership* 33 (November 1975): 108–17.

    It is argued here that under the proper conditions, schools *can* make a difference—a constructive, positive difference in the lives of those associated with them and, in turn, to the society of which schools are a part. Moreover, the single school is the most likely unit for significant educational change.

John I. Goodlad, "Educational Leadership: Toward the Third Era,"
Educational Leadership 35 (January 1978): 322–24, 326–27,
329–31.

It is contended that the first era of educational leadership relied on experience while the second relied on the scientific approach. Goodlad then argues and predicts that the third era of
leadership will be to do the right thing—ensuring comprehensive, quality educational programs in each and every school in
just and equitable ways.

John I. Goodlad, "On the Cultivation and Corruption of Education,"
Educational Forum 42 (March 1978): 267–78.

Distinctions are drawn between the aims of education and the
goals of schooling. Goodlad contends that the direction for improving the school is not doing better what we now do; rather,
we must begin by asking whether much of what we now do should
be done at all.

John I. Goodlad, "An Ecological Version of Accountability," *Theory
into Practice* 18 (December 1979): 308–15.

This is a critique of the linear, ends-means system with a narrow focus on standardized achievement scores. Proposed instead
is an ecological model that has goals coming from both the inside and outside of the educational system, which focuses on
qualitative data and conducts contextual appraisal for improvement.

John I. Goodlad, "The Great American Schooling Experiment," *Phi
Delta Kappan* 67 (December 1985): 266–71.

Goodlad describes the expansion of secondary education and,
to a lesser degree, higher education, discussing the issues involved in the expansion such as core curriculum and equal access to knowledge. It is argued that the American experiment in
schooling is not yet finished.

Kenneth A. Sirotnik and John I. Goodlad, "The Quest for Reason
Amidst the Rhetoric of Reform: Improving Instead of Testing
Our Schools," in William J. Johnston, ed., *Education on Trial*
(San Francisco: Institute for Contemporary Studies Press, 1985),
277–98.

The authors discuss such issues as morality vs. normality, constructive evaluation vs. ritualistic testing, accountability vs. re-

sponsibility, and argue that instead of ritualistic testing, educators at all levels of schooling should be provided more professional working environments where a wealth of information including but not limited to good achievement measures is used constructively to promote understanding of what they do and how they might do it better.

Books

John I. Goodlad, M. Frances Klein, and Associates, *Looking Behind the Classroom Door: A Useful Guide to Observing Schools in Action* (Worthington, Ohio: Charles A. Jones Publishing Company, 1974).

   This book provides (1) useful and practical information about innovations, expectations, and problems of reconstructing schooling; (2) detailed descriptions of what actually goes on in schools and classrooms; and (3) an extensive instrument for the systematic observation of schools in action to look behind school and classroom doors.

John I. Goodlad, M. Frances Klein, Jerrold M. Novotney, and Associates, *Early Schooling in the United States* (New York: McGraw-Hill, 1973).

   These authors report the results of a survey of nursery schools in nine major American cities with a focus on what actually goes on in nursery schools. They conclude that the activities in most nursery schools remain basically unchanged from what they were two decades previously.

John I. Goodlad, M. Frances Klein, Jerrold M. Novotney, Kenneth A. Tye, and Associates, *Toward a Mankind School: An Adventure in Humanistic Education* (New York: McGraw-Hill, 1974).

   The book reports a project that involves (1) identifying the basic ideas related to the concept of mankind and their possible meaning for education and schooling; (2) translating these ideas into a curriculum and pedagogical procedures, and (3) conducting an experimental summer program for school children at the University Elementary School at the University of California at Los Angeles. The authors contend that education is the long-term answer to critical issues and problems plaguing the human condition.

John I. Goodlad, *What Schools Are For* (Bloomington, Ind.: Phi Delta Kappa Educational Foundation, 1979).

Goodlad defines three aspects of the question "What schools are for"—goals (what schools are asked, expected, or called upon to do), functions (what schools do or are used for), and aims (what schools should do)—and discusses the tension among these three aspects. A comprehensive list of educational aims and school goals is provided.

John I. Goodlad, *A Place Called School* (New York: McGraw-Hill, 1984).

Based on detailed empirical data collected from trained observers, parents, teachers, and students in thirty-eight schools during A Study of Schooling, Goodlad depicts and analyzes what transpires in the schools by using such commonplaces as educational goals and teaching practices. Extensive discussions of the inequities in schooling due to tracking are included. The book concludes with two plans for school improvement: "Improving the Schools We Have" (chapter 9) and "Beyond the Schools We Have" (chapter 10).

John I. Goodlad, *In Praise of Education* (New York: Teachers College Press, 1997).

This is a thought-provoking reflection on issues such as "education and democracy," "education and community," "education and schooling," and "education and the self." Goodlad argues, for example, that "there must be continuous, deliberate attention to all of the contextual contingencies to ensure cultivation of individual and collective democratic character" and that "schools must serve a common public purpose that, above all private purposes, justifies their support as part of our democratic infrastructure."

Teacher Education

Articles

John I. Goodlad, "The Reconstruction of Teacher Education," *Teachers College Record* 72 (September 1970): 61–72.

This paper begins with the identification of problems pertaining to educational change, with special reference to teacher education. It is then argued that nothing short of a simultaneous reconstruction of preservice teacher education, in-service teacher education, and schooling will suffice if the change process is to be adequate. The article concludes with a set of recommendations for reconstructing teacher education and schooling.

John I. Goodlad, "The Occupation of Teaching in Schools," in John I. Goodlad, Roger Soder, and Kenneth A. Sirotnik, eds., *The Moral Dimensions of Teaching* (San Francisco: Jossey-Bass, 1990), 3–34.

This first chapter describes the historical and political context in which we might view teaching as a moral matter and the efforts to professionalize teaching. Goodlad argues that the professional status of teaching in schools must arise out of the special layered context of the work, the complexity of this context, and the special knowledge, skills, and personal characteristics required for the burden of judgment entailed.

John I. Goodlad, "The Moral Dimensions of Schooling and Teacher Education," *Journal of Moral Education* 21 (1992): 87–97.

Based on his Kohlberg Memorial Lecture, Goodlad argues that we should go beyond the individual as the focus when we discuss moral education. Instead we should discuss whether educational institutions and educational programs are moral. Moral dimensions of both schooling and teacher education are discussed.

Books

John I. Goodlad, *Teachers for Our Nation's Schools* (San Francisco: Jossey-Bass, 1990).

The book is based on the Study of Education of Educators, a nationwide, five-year inquiry into the conduct of teacher education. It centers on issues such as the history, institutional and regulatory context, curriculum, and the relationship between schools and universities. A comprehensive agenda is proposed for renewing the education of educators based on nineteen comprehensive postulates.

John I. Goodlad, Roger Soder, and Kenneth A. Sirotnik, eds., *The Moral Dimensions of Teaching* (San Francisco: Jossey-Bass, 1990).

The book consists of a series of papers that advance the argument that teaching is essentially a moral enterprise. The discussions include the rhetoric of the professional status of teaching; teaching as a public profession; the moral basis for claiming teaching as a profession; moral responsibility of the public school; legal and moral responsibilities of teachers; the tension between the need for public control and the need for professional autonomy; the relation between the teacher and the taught; and ethical roots underlying society, schooling, teaching, and preparing to teach.

John I. Goodlad, Roger Soder, and Kenneth A. Sirotnik, eds., *Places Where Teachers Are Taught* (San Francisco: Jossey-Bass, 1990).

After setting the contemporary context for the discussion of the evolution of teacher education, the volume explores the evolution of teacher education (1) from institutional perspectives by reporting case studies in liberal arts colleges, normal schools, private universities, and major universities; and (2) from the state perspectives by reporting case studies of Georgia and Pennsylvania. The following enduring themes in the evolution of teacher education are discussed in a concluding chapter: research orientation and the loss of identity, search for higher status, intrusion of external forces, and competition for resources both within and outside the institution.

Strategies for Educational Renewal

Articles

John I. Goodlad, "The Individual School and Its Principal: Key Setting and Key Person in Educational Leadership," *Educational Leadership* 13 (October 1955): 2–6.

This article first presents an argument to support the thesis that individual schools, over any other organizational units, are the natural settings for initiating educational change, and then goes on to identify the concerns that must be encompassed by the principals in assuming leadership roles.

John I. Goodlad, "Can Our Schools Get Better?" *Phi Delta Kappan* 60 (January 1979): 342–47.

Goodlad suggests that we can, indeed, improve our schools, but improvement will require not only new visions of accountability, schooling, and the educative society, but also a huge cooperative effort by enlightened citizens and professionals. The proposition that the school is the unit of change is justified from four different perspectives.

John I. Goodlad, "A Study of Schooling: Some Implications for School Improvement," *Phi Delta Kappan* 64 (April 1983): 552–58.

Based on an initial analysis of the data from A Study of Schooling, Goodlad indicates that even the most successful schools appear not to place the central business of educating students at the top of their agendas for school improvement. It is argued that the necessary renewal of the system of schooling must ultimately take place from within. Recommendations for improving schools—such as clear goals at the state, district, and school level, reconfiguring the schooling system, and developing new staff patterns for schools—are discussed.

John I. Goodlad, "School-University Partnerships for Educational Renewal: Rationale and Concepts," in Kenneth A. Sirotnik and John I. Goodlad, eds., *School-University Partnerships in Action: Concepts, Cases, and Concerns* (New York: Teachers College Press, 1988), 3–31.

This chapter constructs the argument for school-university partnership by reviewing the growth of schooling and the largely unsuccessful efforts to intervene significantly into the regularities of schools or those of universities. Goodlad describes his personal and intellectual experiences in renewal-oriented projects such as the Atlanta Area Teacher Education Service, the Englewood Project, the League of Cooperating Schools, and the National Network for Educational Renewal. He also discusses the possible purpose, agenda, and structure of school-university partnerships.

John I. Goodlad, "School-University Partnerships and Partner Schools," *Educational Policy* 7 (March 1993): 24–39.

It is proposed here that school-university partnerships can have positive effects on both institutions. At the core of this symbiosis is the concept of partner schools where school-based and university-based educators come together for the simultaneous renewal of both schooling and the education of educators. It describes the genesis and nature of the concept of partner schools and the developmental efforts and major problems confronted in the National Network for Educational Renewal.

Books

John I. Goodlad, *The Dynamics of Educational Change: Toward Responsive Schools* (New York: McGraw-Hill, 1975).

Goodlad reports the findings of the Study of Educational Change and School Improvement based on the ideas and activities of the League of Cooperating Schools (a consortium of eighteen school districts in southern California, the University of California at Los Angeles, and the Research Division of the Institution for Development of Educational Activities). A critique of the RDDE (research, development, dissemination, and evaluation) model is offered and an argument is developed for the DDAE (dialogue, decision, action, and evaluation) model. Guidelines for school improvement are summarized in chapter 7.

John I. Goodlad, ed., *The Ecology of School Renewal*, the Eighty-sixth Yearbook of the National Society for the Study of Education, Part I (Chicago: University of Chicago Press, 1987).

This collection of papers, with focus on the culture and function of the public schools in the context of federal, state, and local responsibilities for public schools, argues for an ecological perspective on educational change and school renewal. The ultimate criterion for judging the health of the ecosystem beyond each school is how well it functions to support individual schools. A healthy school ecology is one that is critically attuned to the development and maintenance of sound educational practices. Specific issues addressed include authority and responsibility, evaluation, school culture, school improvement, school-community connections, connections of research and practice, and networking, among others.

Kenneth A. Sirotnik and John I. Goodlad, eds., *School-University Partnerships in Action: Concepts, Cases, and Concerns* (New York: Teachers College Press, 1988).

Corresponding to the subtitle, the book is divided into three parts: the first part inquires into what a genuine, collaborative relationship is between the school and the university; the second part reports and analyzes five different cases of school-university partnership across the country; and the third part discusses a design for inquiry into school-university partnerships and the future of school-university partnerships.

John I. Goodlad, *Educational Renewal: Better Teachers, Better Schools* (San Francisco: Jossey-Bass, 1994).

Following *Teachers for Our Nation's Schools*, this book unpacks the nineteen postulates for a sound teacher education program and offers suggestions for simultaneous renewal of both schooling and the education of educators by discussing issues such as school-university partnerships, partner schools, teacher education programs, and centers of pedagogy. Examples of simultaneous renewal from the National Network for Educational Renewal are reported and analyzed.

Strategies for and Reflections on Educational Research

Articles

John I. Goodlad, "Thought, Invention, and Research in the Advancement of Education," *Educational Forum* (November 1968): 7–18.

Based on his presidential address for the 1968 American Educational Research Association meeting, Goodlad discusses the conditions and strategies for advancing education as a field of study. He argues for the interplay of the theoretical-deductive and empirical-inductive modes of thought, the importance of studying innovative educational practice, the close collaboration between conceptually oriented researchers and forward-looking practitioners, and the ultimate purpose of research to improve educational practice.

John I. Goodlad, "Perspectives on Theory, Research and Practice," in Daniel L. Duke, ed., *Classroom Management*, the Seventy-eighth Yearbook of the National Society for the Study of Education, Part II (Chicago: the University of Chicago Press, 1979), 391–412.

Goodlad maintains that the function of educational research is dual—both to understand and improve education. It is wrong, however, to view understanding as the domain of researchers and implementation the domain of practitioners—understanding and improvement must go hand in hand. The production or factory model for educational understanding and renewal is eschewed, and instead, an ecological perspective is advanced for understanding and studying the commonplaces of schools and their ongoing interactions.

John I. Goodlad, "Reflections on Schools: Tidying the Mind in an Untidy World," in Derek L. Burleson, ed., *Reflections: Personal Essays by 33 Distinguished Educators* (Bloomington, Ind.: Phi Delta Kappa Educational Foundation, 1991), 188–99.

  Reflecting on his experiences in teaching in Canadian schools, the Atlanta Area Teacher Education Service, the Englewood Project, and the Study of Educational Change and School Improvement, Goodlad emphasizes the importance of "messing around" in schools in order to understand and improve them. The development of the working hypothesis that the "individual school is the unit for change" is illustrated through the experience of "messing around in schools."

Index

Note: 'i' following page number indicates an illustration